SERIES 99
EXAM STUDY GUIDE 2025
+ TEST BANK

SECURITIES INSTITUTE
SECURITIES LICENSING SERIES

The Securities Institute of America proudly publishes world class textbooks, test banks and video training classes for the following Financial Services exams:

Securities Industry Essentials exam / SIE exam
Series 3 exam
Series 4 exam
Series 6 exam
Series 7 exam
Series 9 exam
Series 10 exam
Series 22 exam
Series 24 exam
Series 26 exam
Series 39 exam
Series 57 exam
Series 63 exam
Series 65 exam
Series 66 exam
Series 79 exam
Series 99 exam

For more information, visit the website at www.securitiesCE.com.

SERIES 99
EXAM STUDY GUIDE 2025
+ TEST BANK

The Operations Professional Examination

The Securities Institute of America, Inc.

Copyright © by The Securities Institute of America, Inc. All rights reserved.

Published by The Securities Institute of America, Inc.

No part of this publication may be reproduced, stored in a retrieval system, or transmitted in any form or by any means, electronic, mechanical, photocopying, recording, scanning, or otherwise, except as permitted under Section 107 or 108 of the 1976 United States Copyright Act, without either the prior written permission of The Securities Institute of America, Inc.

Limit of Liability/Disclaimer of Warranty: While the publisher and author have used their best efforts in preparing this book, they make no representations or warranties with respect to the accuracy or completeness of the contents of this book and specifically disclaim any implied warranties of merchantability or fitness for a particular purpose. No warranty may be created or extended by sales representatives or written sales materials. The advice and strategies contained herein may not be suitable for your situation. You should consult with a professional where appropriate. Neither the publisher nor author shall be liable for any loss of profit or any other commercial damages, including but not limited to special, incidental, consequential, or other damages.

ISBN 978-1-937841-76-8 (Paperback)

Printed in the United States of America.

10 9 8 7 6 5 4 3 2 1

Contents

ABOUT THE SERIES 99 EXAM IX

ABOUT THIS BOOK XIII

ABOUT THE TEST BANK XV

ABOUT THE GREENLIGHT GUARANTEE XVII

ABOUT THE SECURITIES INSTITUTE OF AMERICA XIX

CHAPTER 1
EQUITY AND DEBT SECURITIES 1

What Is a Security? 1
Capitalization 2
Common Stock 3
Preferred Stock 9
Types of Dividends 12
Rights 13
Warrants 14
Options 16
American Depositary Receipts (ADRs)/American Depositary Shares (ADSs) 20
Debt Securities/Bonds 22
The Money Market 37
Limited Partnerships 39
Pretest 47

CHAPTER 2
BROKERAGE OFFICE PROCEDURES AND BACK-OFFICE OPERATIONS — 51

Hiring New Employees	51
Resignation of a Registered Representative	53
Registration Exemptions	54
Persons Ineligible to Register	54
Disciplinary Actions Against a Registered Representative	55
Termination for Cause	57
Outside Employment	57
Private Securities Transactions	57
Gift Rule	58
Sharing in a Customer's Account	59
Borrowing and Lending Money	59
Order Tickets	60
Executing an Order	60
Becoming a Stockholder	62
Clearly Erroneous Reports	64
Execution Errors	64
Unconfirmed Trades	65
Securities Settlement Options	66
When-Issued Securities	68
Accrued Interest	68
Close Outs	69
Customer Confirmations	70
Rules for Good Delivery	71
Rejection of Delivery	73
Reclamation	73
Marking to the Market	74
Customer Account Statements	74
Dividend Distribution	75
Proxies	77
Operations Professionals Covered Persons	78
Operational Red Flags	79
Pretest	81

Contentsiii

CHAPTER 3
RECORD KEEPING, FINANCIAL REQUIREMENTS, AND CLEARING85

Blotters	85
General Ledger	86
Customer Accounts	86
Suspense Account	86
Subsidiary (Secondary) Records	86
Securities Position Book (Ledger) Stock Record	87
Order Tickets	87
Confirmations and Notices	87
Monthly Trial Balances and Net Capital Computations	87
Employment Applications	87
Records Required to Be Maintained for 3 Years	88
Records Required to Be Maintained for 6 Years	88
Records Required to Be Maintained for the Life of the Firm	88
Requirement to Prepare and Maintain Records Under SEC 17a-3 and 17a-4	90
Financial Requirements	91
Box Counts	93
Missing and Lost Securities	94
The Customer Protection Rule	95
FINRA Financial Requirements	98
Fidelity Bonds	99
Carrying of Customer Accounts	100
The Depository Trust & Clearing Corporation (DTCC)	101
The Fixed Income Clearing Corporation (FICC)	103
The Option Clearing Corporation (OCC)	103
American vs. European Exercise	103
Expiration and Exercise	104
Pretest	105

CHAPTER 4
ISSUING CORPORATE SECURITIES109

The Prospectus	110

The Final Prospectus	110
Prospectus to Be Provided to Aftermarket Purchasers	111
SEC Disclaimer	112
Misrepresentations	112
Tombstone Ads	112
Free Riding and Withholding/FINRA Rule 5130	113
Underwriting Corporate Securities	114
Types of Underwriting Commitments	115
Types of Offerings	117
Exempt Securities	119
Exempt Transactions	120
Rule 137 Nonparticipants	127
Rule 138 Nonequivalent Securities	128
Rule 139 Issuing Research Reports	128
Rule 415 Shelf Registration	129
Securities Offering Reform Rules	129
Sec Rule 405	130
Additional Communication Rules	131
Crowdfunding	132
Pretest	133

CHAPTER 5
TRADING SECURITIES — 137

Types of Orders	137
The Exchanges	141
The Role of the Designated Market Maker	142
Crossing Stock	145
Do Not Reduce (DNR)	145
Adjustments for Stock Splits	146
Super Display Book (SDBK)	146
Short Sales	147
Threshold Securities	151
Over the Counter/Nasdaq	152

Non-Nasdaq OTC MKT	156
SEC Rule 15C2-11	157
Third Market	158
Fourth Market	159
The Consolidated Audit Trail system (CATS)	159
Broker vs. Dealer	160
FINRA's 5% Markup Policy	161
Markups/Markdowns When Acting as a Principal	161
Riskless Principal Transactions	162
Net Transactions with Customers	163
Proceeds Transactions	163
Firm Quote Rule	163
Pretest	165

CHAPTER 6
GENERAL SUPERVISION — 169

The Role of the Principal	169
Continuing Education	171
Maintaining Qualifications Program	172
Tape Recording Employees	173
Heightened Supervisory Requirements	174
Information Obtained from an Issuer	174
Customer Complaints	174
Investor Information	175
Member Offices	175
Annual Compliance Review	177
Business Continuity Plan	178
Currency Transactions	179
The Patriot Act	179
Identity Theft	181
Information Security	181
FINRA Rule 3241	182
Pretest	185

CHAPTER 7
CUSTOMER ACCOUNTS — 189

- Opening a New Customer Account — 189
- Holding Securities — 192
- Mailing Instructions — 193
- Types of Ownership — 193
- Death of a Customer — 195
- Partnership Accounts — 195
- Trusts — 196
- Corporate Accounts — 196
- Trading Authorization — 196
- Accounts for Employees of Other Broker Dealers — 202
- Numbered Accounts — 203
- Prime Brokerage Accounts — 203
- Account Transfers — 203
- Bulk Account Transfers — 205
- Margin Accounts — 207
- Guaranteeing a Customer's Account — 208
- Day Trading Accounts — 208
- Commingling Customer's Pledged Securities — 209
- Wrap Account — 209
- Regulation S-P — 209
- Pretest — 215

CHAPTER 8
MARGIN ACCOUNTS — 219

- Regulation of Credit — 219
- House Rules — 222
- Establishing a Long Position in a Margin Account — 222
- Establishing a Short Position in a Margin Account — 228
- Margin Requirements for Day Trading — 232
- Combined Margin Accounts — 233
- Portfolio Margin Accounts — 234
- Securities Backed Lines of Credit — 235

| Minimum Margin for Leveraged ETFs | 235 |
| Pretest | 237 |

CHAPTER 9
INVESTMENT COMPANIES — 241

Investment Company Philosophy	241
Types of Investment Companies	242
Investment Company Registration	244
Investment Company Components	246
Mutual Fund Distribution	249
Distribution of Mutual Fund Shares	250
Mutual Fund Prospectus	250
Additional Disclosures by a Mutual Fund	252
Anti-Reciprocal Rule	252
Money Market Funds	253
Valuing Mutual Fund Shares	253
Mutual Fund Sales Charges	253
Sales Charge Reductions	255
Voting Rights	259
Portfolio Turnover	260
Recommending Mutual Funds	260
Exchange Traded Funds/ETFs	261
Exchange Traded Notes/ETNs	261
ETFs That Track Alternatively Weighted IndEXES	262
Alternative Funds	262
Floating Rate Bank Loan Funds	263
Structured Retail Products/SRPs	263
Pretest	265

CHAPTER 10
VARIABLE ANNUITIES AND RETIREMENT PLANS — 269

Annuities	269
Recommending Variable Annuities	273
Retirement Plans	279

ERISA 404C SAFE HARBOR	294
Department of Labor Fiduciary Rules	294
Department of Labor Prohibited Transactions	295
Health Savings Accounts	297
Pretest	299

CHAPTER 11
SECURITIES INDUSTRY RULES AND REGULATIONS — 303

The Securities Exchange Act of 1934	303
Becoming a Member of FINRA	307
Registration of Agents/Associated Persons	308
State Registration	309
Retail Communications/Communications with the Public	309
Securities Investor Protection Corporation Act of 1970	315
The Securities Acts Amendments of 1975	316
The Insider Trading and Securities Fraud Enforcement Act of 1988	316
Firewalls	317
Telemarketing Rules	317
The Penny Stock Cold Call Rule	318
Violations and Complaints	319
Political Contributions	323
Investment Adviser Registration	325
Investment Adviser Representatives	327
Investment Adviser Advertising and Sales Literature	327
Soft Dollars	329
The Uniform Securities Act	331

PRETEST — 333

ANSWER KEYS — 337

GLOSSARY OF EXAM TERMS — 345

About the Series 99 Exam

Congratulations! You are on your way to becoming a registered operations professional, licensed to perform a variety of covered operational functions for a broker dealer. The Series 99 exam will be presented in a 50-question multiple-choice format. Each candidate will have 1 hour and 30 minutes to complete the exam. A score of 68% or higher is required to pass. Your textbook and exam prep software from The Securities Institute will make sure that you have the required knowledge to pass the Series 99 and that you are confident in the application of that knowledge during the exam.

> **IMPORTANT EXAM NOTE**
>
> Candidates who wish to take the Series 99 exam must also successfully complete the SIE exam to become fully registered.

TAKING THE SERIES 99 EXAM

The Series 99 exam is presented in multiple-choice format on a touch-screen computer known as the PROCTOR system. No computer skills are required, and candidates will find that the test screen works in the same way as an ordinary ATM. Each test is made up of 50 questions that are randomly chosen from a test bank of several thousand questions. The test has a time limit of 1 hour and 30 minutes, which is designed to provide enough time for all candidates to complete the exam. Each Series 99 exam will comprise questions that focus on the following areas:

Knowledge Associated with the Securities Industry and Broker-Dealer Operations	35	70%
Professional Conduct and Ethical Considerations	15	30%
TOTAL	**50 questions**	**100%**

HOW TO PREPARE FOR THE SERIES 99 EXAM

For most candidates, the combination of reading the textbook, watching the video class lectures and taking practice questions proves to be sufficient to successfully complete the exam. It is recommended that candidates spend at least 50 to 60 hours preparing for the exam by reading the textbook, underlining key points, and answering as many practice questions as possible. We recommend that candidates schedule their exam no more than 1 week after finishing their Series 99 preparation.

Test-Taking Tips

- Read the full question before answering.
- Identify what the question is asking.
- Identify key words and phrases.
- Watch out for hedge clauses, such as *except* and *not*.
- Eliminate wrong answers.
- Identify synonymous terms.
- Be wary of changing answers.

WHAT TYPE OF POSITIONS MAY A SERIES 99 REGISTERED OPERATIONS PROFESSIONAL HOLD?

A Series 99 registered operations professional may act in the capacity of a covered person and may perform a variety of covered operation functions for a broker dealer.

WHAT SCORE IS NEEDED TO PASS THE EXAM?

A score of 68% or higher is needed to pass the Series 99 exam.

ARE THERE ANY PREREQUISITES FOR THE SERIES 99?

Candidates who wish to take the Series 99 exam must also successfully complete the SIE exam to become fully registered.

HOW DO I SCHEDULE AN EXAM?

Ask your firm's compliance department to schedule the exam for you or to provide a list of test centers in your area. You must be sponsored by a FINRA member firm prior to making an appointment. The Series 99 exam may be taken any day that the exam center is open.

WHAT MUST I TAKE TO THE EXAM CENTER?

A picture ID is required. All other materials will be provided, including a calculator and scratch paper.

HOW SOON WILL I RECEIVE RESULTS OF THE EXAM?

The exam will be graded as soon as you answer your final question and hit the Submit for Grading button. It will take only a few minutes to get your results. Your grade will appear on the computer screen, and you will be given a paper copy at the exam center.

If you do not pass the test, you will need to wait 30 days before taking it again. If you do not pass on the second try, you will need to wait another 30 days. If you do not pass on the third try, you must wait 6 months to take the test again.

About This Book

The writers and instructors at The Securities Institute have developed the Series 99 textbook, exam prep software, and videos to ensure that you have the knowledge required to pass the test and that you are confident in the application of that knowledge during the exam. The writers and instructors at The Securities Institute are subject-matter experts as well as Series 99 test experts. We understand how the test is written, and our proven test-taking techniques can dramatically improve your results.

Each chapter includes notes, tips, examples, and case studies with key information, hints for taking the exam, and additional insight into the topics. Each chapter ends with a practice test to ensure that you have mastered the concepts before moving on to the next topic.

Some of the material contained in this book is designed to cover the information tested on the SIE exam. This material has been included intentionally to ensure candidates who have already passed the SIE exam have maintained their knowledge of that material. Many concepts tested on the SIE may also be tested on the Series 99 exam. Those concepts also provide the foundation for your understanding of the material tested on the Series 99 exam.

About the Test Bank

This book is accompanied by a test bank of hundreds of questions to further reinforce the concepts and information presented here. The test bank is provided to help students who have purchased our book from a traditional bookstore or from an online retailer such as Amazon. This test bank is only available to the original purchaser. If you have purchased this textbook as part of a package from our website containing the full version of the software, you are all set. Simply use the login instructions that were emailed to you at the time of purchase. Otherwise, if you are the original purchaser, please email your purchase receipt to sales@securitiesce.com. We will activate your account and email you your login instructions. This test bank provides a small sample of the questions and features that are contained in the full version of the exam prep software.

If you have not purchased the full version of the exam prep software with this book, we highly recommend it to ensure that you have mastered the knowledge required for your exam. To purchase the exam prep software for this exam, visit The Securities Institute of America online at: www.securitiesce.com or call 877-218-1776.

ONLINE TRAINING PACKAGES

If you have purchased this textbook as part of a training package from our website you were sent your login information instantly at the time you placed your order. If you have purchased this book as part of a training package and need access to your videos and test banks, please send your purchase receipt to sales@securitiesce.com. We will send you your login information to access your additional training tools. Online training resources are only available to original purchasers.

If you have not purchased our online video training classes we highly recommend them. Our video training follows this book chapter by chapter providing more details and examples of how the topics are being tested. To purchase the video training class for this exam, visit The Securities Institute of America online at: www.securitiesce.com or call 877-218-1776.

ONLINE ACCOUNT SETUP

We set up online access during normal business hours. Our hours are 9AM - 5PM EST. Students who request account activation during normal business hours will receive their login instructions the same day. Students who email requests outside of normal business hours will receive their login information during the next business day.

About The Greenlight Guarantee

Quite simply the Greenlight guarantee is as follows:
Pass our Greenlight exam within 5 days of your actual exam, and if you do not pass we will refund the money you paid to The Securities Institute. If you only have access to the Limited Test Bank through the purchase of this textbook, you may upgrade your online account for a small fee to include the Greenlight exam and receive the full benefits of our greenlight money back pass guarantee.

About The Securities Institute of America

The Securities Institute of America, Inc. Helps thousands of securities and insurance professionals build successful careers in the financial services industry every year. In more than 25 years we have helped students pass more than 400,000 exams. Our securities training options include:

- Classroom training

- Private tutoring

- Interactive online video training classes

- State-of-the-art exam prep test banks

- Printed textbooks

- ebooks

- Real-time tracking and reporting for managers and training directors

As a result, you can choose a securities training solution that matches your skill level, learning style, and schedule. Regardless of the format you choose, you can be sure that our securities training courses are relevant, tested, and designed to help you succeed. It is the experience of our instructors and the quality of our materials that make our courses requested by name at some of the largest financial services firms in the world.

To contact The Securities Institute of America, visit us on the Web at: www.securitiesce.com or call 877-218-1776.

CHAPTER 1

Equity and Debt Securities

> **INTRODUCTION**
>
> The first chapter will lay the foundation on which the rest of the text is built. A thorough understanding of this material will be necessary in order to successfully complete the Series 99 exam. Because a Series 99 operations professional provides the operational support for the firm's transactions in equity, debt, and derivative securities, it is an important starting point.

WHAT IS A SECURITY?

A security is any investment product that can be exchanged for value and involves risk. In order for an investment to be considered a security, it must be readily transferable between two parties and the owner must be subject to the loss of some or all of their invested principal. If the product is not transferable or does not contain risk, then it is not a security.

Types of Securities	Types of Nonsecurities
Common and preferred stock	Whole life insurance
Bonds	Term life insurance
Mutual funds	Retirement plans
Variable annuities	Fixed annuities

(Continued)

Types of Securities	Types of Nonsecurities
Variable life insurance	Prospectus
Exchange traded funds/ETS	
Echange traded notes/ETNs	

Securities are broken up into two major categories for the Series 99: equity and debt. Let's begin by comparing the two different types of securities:

EQUITY = STOCK

The term *equity* is synonymous with the term *stock*. Throughout your preparation for this exam, as well as on the exam itself, you will find many terms that are used interchangeably. Equity or stock creates an ownership relationship with the issuing company. Once an investor has purchased stock in a corporation, he or she becomes an owner of that corporation. The corporation sells off pieces of itself to investors in the form of shares in an effort to raise working capital. Equity is perpetual, meaning there is no maturity date for the shares and investors may own the shares until they decide to sell them. Most corporations use the sale of equity as their main source of business capital.

DEBT = BONDS

A bond, or any other debt instrument, is actually a loan to the issuer. By purchasing a bond, the investor has made a loan to the corporation and becomes a creditor of the issuing company.

Debt instruments, unlike their equity counterparts, have a time frame or maturity date associated with them. Whether it is 1 year, 5 years, or 30 years, at some point the issue will mature, and the investor will receive his or her principal back and will cease to be a creditor of the corporation. We will examine how investors may purchase stocks and bonds, but first we must look at how the corporation uses the sale of these securities to meet its organizational goals.

CAPITALIZATION

The term *capitalization* refers to the sources and makeup of the company's financial picture. To determine a company's capital composition, an investor must look at the corporation's balance sheet. The balance sheet is like a snapshot of the corporation's finances at the time it was produced. It shows a list of the company's assets and liabilities as well as the company's net worth, or stockholders' equity. Most publicly traded companies have to disclose or report their performance at least quarterly.

THE BALANCE SHEET EQUATION

$$\text{assets} - \text{liabilities} = \text{net worth}$$

ASSETS
Assets are everything that a company owns, including cash, securities, investments, inventory, property, and accounts receivable.

LIABILITIES
Liabilities are everything that a company owes, including accounts payable and both long- and short-term debt, as well as any other obligations.

NET WORTH
The company's net worth is equal to the value of all assets after all liabilities have been paid. This corporation's net worth is the stockholders' equity. Remember that the stockholders own the company.

COMMON STOCK

There are thousands of companies whose stock trades publicly and that have used the sale of equity as a source of raising business capital. All publicly traded companies must issue common stock before they may issue any other type of equity security. The two types of equity securities are common stock and preferred stock. Although all publicly traded companies must have sold or issued common stock, not all companies may want to issue or sell preferred stock. Let's take a look at the creation of a company and how common stock is created.

CORPORATE TIMELINE

AUTHORIZED STOCK
Authorized stock is the maximum number of shares that a company may sell to the investing public in an effort to raise cash to meet the organization's goals. The number of authorized shares is determined arbitrarily and is set at

the time of incorporation. A corporation may sell all or part of its authorized stock. If the corporation wants to sell more shares than it is authorized to sell, the shareholders must approve an increase in the number of authorized shares.

ISSUED STOCK

Issued stock is stock that has been authorized for sale and has actually been sold to the investing public. The total number of authorized shares typically exceeds the total number of issued shares so that the corporation may sell additional shares in the future to meet its needs. Once shares have been sold to the investing public, they will always be counted as issued shares regardless of their ownership or subsequent repurchase by the corporation. It is important to note that the total number of issued shares may never exceed the total number of authorized shares.

Additional authorized shares may be issued in the future to:

- Pay a stock dividend.
- Expand current operations.
- Exchange common shares for convertible preferred or convertible bonds.
- Satisfy obligations under employee stock options or purchase plans.

OUTSTANDING STOCK

Outstanding stock is stock that has been sold or issued to the investing public and that actually remains in the hands of the investing public.

TREASURY STOCK

Treasury stock is stock that has been sold to the investing public and that has subsequently been repurchased by the corporation. The corporation may elect to reissue the shares or it may retire the shares that it holds in treasury stock. Treasury stock does not receive dividends nor does it vote.

A corporation may elect to repurchase its own shares to:

- Maintain control of the company.
- Increase earnings per share.
- Fund employee stock purchase plans.
- Use shares to pay for a merger or acquisition.

To determine the amount of treasury stock, use the following formula:

issued stock − outstanding stock = treasury stock

VALUES OF COMMON STOCK

The market value of a common stock is determined by supply and demand and may or may not have any real relationship to what the shares are actually worth. The market value of common stock is affected by the current and future expectations for the company.

BOOK VALUE

The book value of a corporation is the theoretical liquidation value of the company. It is calculated by taking all of the company's tangible assets and subtracting all of its liabilities. To determine the book value per share, divide the total book value by the total number of outstanding common shares.

PAR VALUE

Par value, in a discussion regarding common stock, is only important if you are an accountant looking at the balance sheet. For investors, it has no relationship to any measure of value that may otherwise be employed.

RIGHTS OF COMMON STOCKHOLDERS

As an owner of common stock, investors are owners of the corporation. As such, investors have certain rights that are granted to all common stockholders.

PREEMPTIVE RIGHTS

As a stockholder, an investor has the right to maintain a percentage interest in the company. This is known as a preemptive right. Should the company wish to sell additional shares to raise new capital, it must first offer the new shares to existing shareholders. If the existing shareholders decide not to purchase the new shares, they may be offered to the general public.

A shareholder's preemptive right is ensured through a rights offering. The existing shareholders will have the right to purchase the new shares at a discount to the current market value for 45 days. This is known as the subscription price. Once the subscription price is set, it remains constant for 45 days, while the price of the stock is moving up and down in the marketplace. The three possible outcomes for a right are that it is exercised or sold or that it expires.

>  **TESTFOCUS!**
>
> | Number of Existing Shares | Number of New Shares | Total Shares After Offering |
> |---|---|---|
> | 100,000 | 100,000 | 200,000 |
> | 10,000 | 10,000 | 20,000 |
> | 10% ownership | 10% of offering | 10% ownership |
>
> In this example, the company has 100,000 shares of stock outstanding and an investor has purchased 10,000 of those original shares. As a result, the investor owns 10% of the corporation. The company wishing to sell 100,000 new shares to raise new capital must first offer 10% of the new shares to the current investor (10,000 shares) before the shares may be offered to the general public. So if the investor decides to purchase the additional shares, as is the case in the example, the investor will have maintained a 10% interest in the company.

EXERCISED

The investor decides to purchase the additional shares and sends in the money as well as the rights to receive the additional shares.

SOLD

The rights have value, and if the investor does not want to purchase the additional shares they may be sold to another investor who would like to purchase the shares.

EXPIRE

The rights will expire if no one wants to purchase the stock. This will only occur when the market price of the share has fallen below the subscription price of the right and the 45 days have elapsed.

VOTING

A common stockholder has the right to vote on major issues facing the corporation. Common stockholders are part owners of the company and, as a result, have the right to say how the company is run. The biggest emphasis is placed on the election of the board of directors.

Common stockholders may also vote on:

- The issuance of bonds or additional common shares.
- Stock splits.

CHAPTER 1 Equity and Debt Securities

- Mergers and acquisitions.
- Major changes in corporate policy.

METHODS OF VOTING

There are two methods by which the voting process may be conducted: the statutory and cumulative methods. A stockholder may cast one vote for each share of stock owned, and the statutory or cumulative method will determine how those votes are cast. The test focuses on the election of the board of directors, so we will use that in our example.

EXAMPLE

An investor owns 200 shares of XYZ. There are two board members to be elected and there are four people running in the election. Under both the statutory and cumulative methods of voting, the number of votes the shareholder has is decided by multiplying the number of shares owned by the number of people to be elected. In this case, 200 shares × 2 = 400 votes. The cumulative or statutory methods dictate how those votes may be cast.

Candidate	Statutory	Cumulative
1	200 votes	400 votes
2		
3		
4	200 votes	

The statutory method requires that the votes be distributed evenly among the candidates the investor wishes to vote for.

The cumulative method allows the shareholder to cast all of their votes in favor of one candidate if they so choose. The cumulative method is said to favor smaller investors for this reason.

LIMITED LIABILITY

Stockholders' liability is limited to the amount of money they have invested in the stock. They cannot be held liable for any amount that exceeds their invested capital.

INSPECTION OF BOOKS AND RECORDS

All stockholders have the right to inspect the company's books and records. For most shareholders, this right is ensured through the company's filing of quarterly and annual reports. Stockholders also have the right to obtain a list of shareholders, but they do not have the right to review other corporate financial data that the corporation may deem confidential.

RESIDUAL CLAIM TO ASSETS

In the event of a company's bankruptcy or liquidation, common stockholders have the right to receive their proportional interest in residual assets. After all other security holders, as well as all creditors of the corporation, have been paid, common stockholders may claim the residual assets. For this reason, common stock is the most junior security.

WHY DO PEOPLE BUY COMMON STOCK?

CAPITAL APPRECIATION/GROWTH

The main reason people invest in common stock is for capital appreciation. They want their money to grow in value over time. An investor in common stock hopes to buy the stock at a low price and sell it at a higher price at some point in the future.

EXAMPLE An investor purchases 100 shares of XYZ at $20 per share on March 15, 2011. On April 30, 2012, the investor sells 100 shares of XYZ for $30 per share, realizing a profit of $10 per share, or $1,000 on the 100 shares.

INCOME

Many corporations distribute a portion of their earnings to their investors in the form of dividends. This distribution of earnings creates income for the investor. Investors in common stock generally receive dividends quarterly.

EXAMPLE ABC pays a $.50 quarterly dividend to its shareholders. The stock is currently trading at $20 per share. What is its current yield (also known as the dividend yield)?

annual income/current market price = current yield

$.50 × 4 **quarters** = $2.00

$2/$20 = 10%

The investor in this example is receiving 10% of the purchase price of the stock each year in the form of dividends.

CHAPTER 1 Equity and Debt Securities

WHAT ARE THE RISKS OF OWNING COMMON STOCK?

The major risk in owning common stock is that the stock may fall in value. There are no sure things in the stock market, and even if a company seems great, an investor may end up losing money.

DIVIDENDS MAY BE STOPPED OR REDUCED

Common stockholders are not entitled to receive dividends just because they own part of the company. It is up to the company to elect to pay a dividend. The corporation is in no way obligated to pay common shareholders a dividend.

JUNIOR CLAIM ON CORPORATE ASSETS

A common stockholder is the last person to get paid if the company is liquidated. It is very possible that after all creditors and other investors are paid there will be little or no money left for the common stockholder.

PREFERRED STOCK

Preferred stock is an equity security with a fixed-income component. Like a common stockholder, the preferred stockholder is an owner of the company. However, the preferred stockholder is investing in the stock for the fixed income that the preferred shares generate through their semiannual dividends. Preferred stock has a stated dividend rate, or a fixed rate, that the corporation must pay to its preferred shareholders. Growth is generally not achieved through investing in preferred shares.

FEATURES OF PREFERRED STOCK

PAR VALUE

Par value on preferred stock is very important because it is what the dividend is based on. Par value for preferred shares is $100. Companies generally express the dividend as a percentage of par value for preferred stock.

EXAMPLE

An investor buys 100 shares of TWT 9% preferred. How much would the investor receive in annual income from the investment?

$$\$100 \times .09 = \$9 \text{ per share} \times 100 = \$900$$

PAYMENT OF DIVIDENDS

The dividend on preferred shares must be paid before any dividends are paid to common shareholders. This gives the preferred shareholder a priority claim on the corporation's distribution of earnings.

DISTRIBUTION OF ASSETS

If a corporation liquidates or declares bankruptcy, the preferred shareholders are paid prior to any common shareholder, giving the preferred shareholders a higher claim on the corporation's assets.

PERPETUAL

Preferred stock, unlike bonds, is perpetual, with no maturity date. Investors may hold shares for as long as they wish or until they are called in by the company under a call feature.

NONVOTING

Most preferred stock is nonvoting. Occasionally, if the company has been in financial difficulty and has missed preferred dividend payments for an extended period of time, preferred shareholders may receive the right to vote.

INTEREST RATE SENSITIVE

Because of the fixed income generated by preferred shares, their price will be more sensitive to a change in interest rates than the price of their common stock counterparts. As interest rates decline, the value of preferred shares tends to increase. When interest rates rise, the value of the preferred shares tends to fall. This is known as an inverse relationship.

TYPES OF PREFERRED STOCK

Preferred stock has more features associated with it than common stock. Most of the features are designed to make the issue more attractive to investors.

STRAIGHT/NONCUMULATIVE PREFERRED

Straight, or noncumulative, preferred stock has no additional features. The holder is entitled to the stated dividend rate and nothing else. If the corporation is unable to pay the dividend, it is not owed to the investor.

CUMULATIVE PREFERRED

A cumulative feature protects the investor in cases when a corporation is having financial difficulties and cannot pay the dividend. Dividends on cumulative preferred stock accumulate in arrears until the corporation is able to pay them. If the dividend on a cumulative preferred stock is missed, it is still owed to the holder. Dividends in arrears on cumulative issues are always the first dividends to be paid. If the company wants to pay a dividend to common shareholders, it must first pay the dividends in arrears as well as the stated preferred dividend before common shareholders receive anything.

> **TESTFOCUS!**
>
> GNR has an 8% cumulative preferred stock outstanding. It has not paid the dividend this year or for the prior 3 years. How much must the holders of GNR cumulative preferred be paid per share before the common stockholders are paid a dividend?
>
> The dividend has not been paid this year nor for the previous 3 years, so the holders are owed 4 years worth of dividends or
>
> 4 × $8 = $32 per share

PARTICIPATING PREFERRED

Holders of participating preferred stock are entitled to receive the stated preferred rate as well as additional common dividends. The holder of participating preferred stock receives the dividend payable to the common stockholders over and above the stated preferred dividend.

CONVERTIBLE PREFERRED

A convertible feature allows the preferred stockholder to convert or exchange their preferred shares for common shares at a fixed price known as the conversion price.

EXAMPLE TRW has issued a 4% convertible preferred stock, which may be converted into TRW common stock at $20 per share. How many shares may the preferred stockholder receive upon conversion?

par value/conversion price = number of shares

$100/$20 = $5

The investor may receive five common shares for every preferred share.

CALLABLE PREFERRED

A call feature is the only feature that benefits the company and not the investor. A call feature allows the corporation to call in or redeem the preferred shares at its discretion or after some period of time has expired. Most preferred stock that is callable cannot be called in the first few years after its issuance. This is known as call protection. Many callable preferred shares will be called at a premium price above par. For example, a $100 par preferred stock may be called at $103. The main reasons a company would call in its preferred shares would be to eliminate the fixed dividend payment or to sell a new preferred stock with a lower dividend rate when interest rates decline. Preferred stock is more likely to be called by the corporation during a decline in interest rates.

TYPES OF DIVIDENDS

CASH

A cash dividend is the most common form of dividend, and it is one that the test focuses on. With a cash dividend, a corporation will send out a cash payment in the form of a check directly to the stockholders. For those stockholders who have their stock held in the name of the brokerage firm, a check will be sent to the brokerage firm, and the money will be credited to the investor's account. Securities held in the name of the brokerage firm are said to be held in street name. To determine the amount that an investor will receive, simply multiply the amount of the dividend to be paid by the number of shares.

EXAMPLE

JPF pays a $.10 dividend to shareholders. An investor who owns 1,000 shares of JPF will receive $100:

1,000 shares × $.10 = $100

STOCK

A corporation that wants to reward its shareholders, but also wants to conserve cash for other business purposes may elect to pay a stock dividend to its shareholders. With a stock dividend, investors will receive an additional number of shares based on the number of shares that they own. The market price of the stock will decline after the stock dividend has been distributed to reflect that there are now more shares outstanding, but the total market value of the company will remain the same.

> **EXAMPLE**
>
> If HRT pays a 5% stock dividend to its shareholders, an investor with 500 shares will receive an additional 25 shares. This is determined by multiplying the number of shares owned by the amount of the dividend to be paid:
>
> $500 \times 5\% = 25$

PROPERTY/PRODUCT

A corporation may send out to its shareholders samples of its products or portions of its property. This is the least likely way in which a corporation would pay a dividend, but it is a permissible dividend distribution.

RIGHTS

A right is issued to existing shareholders by a corporation that wants to sell additional common shares to raise new capital. All common stockholders have a preemptive right to maintain the proportional ownership in the company. If the corporation were allowed to sell additional shares to the general public, the existing shareholders' interest in the company would be diluted. As a result, any new offering of additional common shares first must be made to the existing shareholders. Common shareholders will receive a notice of their right to purchase the new shares. They will be offered the opportunity to purchase the new shares at a price that is below the current market value of the stock. This is known as the subscription price. The shareholder will have the right to purchase the new shares for 45 days.

POSSIBLE OUTCOMES FOR A RIGHT

EXERCISED

The shareholder may elect to purchase the additional shares. This is known as exercising the right. The investor sends in the rights as well as a check for the total purchase price to the rights agent, and the additional shares are issued to the investor.

SOLD

The investor may not want to purchase the additional shares and may elect to sell the rights to another investor. The investor who purchases the right will then have the opportunity to purchase the stock at the subscription price for the duration of the original 45-day period.

EXPIRE

The right to purchase the additional shares will expire at the end of the 45-day period if no one has elected to purchase the shares. A right will only expire if the stock's market price has fallen below the subscription price of the right. While market price of the stock is fluctuating during the 45-day period, the subscription price of the right remains fixed.

TERMS

The particular terms of the rights will be printed on the right certificate, and each share of outstanding stock will be issued one right. The terms will include the subscription price, the final date for exercising the right, the number of rights required to purchase additional shares, and the date that the new shares will be issued.

STANDBY UNDERWRITING

A corporation may retain a brokerage firm to purchase any shares that existing shareholders do not purchase. This is known as a standby underwriter. The brokerage firm will purchase the shares that were not bought by the existing shareholders and resell them to the investing public.

WARRANTS

A warrant is a security that gives the holder the opportunity to purchase common stock. Like a right, the warrant has a subscription price; however, the subscription price is always above the current market value of the common stock when the warrant is originally issued. A warrant has a much longer life than a right—the holder of a warrant may have up to 10 years to purchase the stock at the subscription price. The long life is what makes the warrant valuable, even though the subscription price is higher than the market price of the common stock when the warrant is issued.

CHAPTER 1 Equity and Debt Securities

HOW DO PEOPLE GET WARRANTS?

UNITS
Oftentimes companies will issue warrants to people who purchased their common stock during its initial public offering (IPO). A common share, which comes with a warrant attached to purchase an additional common share, is known as a unit.

ATTACHED TO BONDS
Many times companies will attach warrants to their bond offerings as a "sweetener" to help market the bond offering. The warrant to purchase the common stock makes the bond more attractive to the investor and may allow the company to issue the bonds with a lower coupon rate.

SECONDARY MARKET
Warrants will often trade in the secondary market just like the common stock. An investor who wishes to participate in the potential price appreciation of the common stock may elect to purchase the corporation's warrant instead of its common shares.

POSSIBLE OUTCOMES OF A WARRANT

A warrant, like a right, may be exercised or sold by the investor. A warrant also may expire if the stock price is below the warrant's subscription price at its expiration.

RIGHTS VS. WARRANTS

Rights		Warrants
Up to 45 days	**Term**	Up to 10 years
Below the market	**Subscription price**	Above the market
May trade with or without common stock	**Trading**	May trade with or without common stock or bonds
Issued to existing shareholders to ensure preemptive rights	**Who**	Offered as a sweetener to make securities more attractive

OPTIONS

An option is a contract between two parties, the buyer and the seller, that determines the time and price at which a security may be bought or sold. The buyer of the option pays money, known as the option's premium, to the seller. For this premium, the buyer obtains a right to buy or sell the security, depending on what type of option is involved in the transaction. The seller, because he or she received the premium from the buyer, now has an obligation to perform under that contract. Depending on the type of option involved, the seller may have an obligation to buy or sell the security.

CALLS

A call option gives the buyer the right to buy, or to "call," the security from the option seller at a specific price for a certain period of time. The sale of a call option obligates the seller to deliver or sell that security to the buyer at that specific price for a certain period of time.

PUTS

A put option gives the buyer the right to sell, or to "put," the security to the seller at a specific price for a certain period of time. The sale of a put option obligates the seller to buy the security from the buyer at that specific price for a certain period of time.

BULLISH VS. BEARISH

BULLISH

Investors who believe that a security's price will increase over time are said to be bullish. Investors who buy calls are bullish on the underlying security. That is, they believe that the security's price will rise, and they have paid for the right to purchase the security at a specific price, known as the exercise price. An investor who has sold puts is also considered bullish on the security. The seller of a put has an obligation to buy the security, and therefore believes that the security's price will rise.

CHAPTER 1 Equity and Debt Securities

BEARISH

Investors who believe that a security's price will decline are said to be bearish. The seller of a call has an obligation to sell the security to the purchaser at a specified price and believes that the security's price will fall and is therefore bearish. Buyers of a put want the price to drop so that they may sell the security at a higher price to the seller of the put contract. They are also considered bearish on the security.

	Calls	**Puts**
Buyers	Bullish	Bearish
	Have right to buy stock; want stock price to rise	Have right to sell stock; want stock price to fall
Sellers	Bearish	Bullish
	Have obligation to sell stock; want stock price to fall	Have obligation to buy stock; want stock price to rise

CHARACTERISTICS OF ALL OPTIONS

The Options Clearing Corporation (OCC) issues all option contracts and guarantees their performance. Standardized options trade on the exchanges, such as the Chicago Board Options Exchange and the American Stock Exchange.

All option contracts are for one round lot of the underlying security, or 100 shares. To determine the amount that an investor either paid or received for the contract, take the premium and multiply it by 100. If an investor paid $4 for 1 KLM August 70 call, then the investor paid $400 for the right to buy 100 shares of KLM at $70 per share until August.

EXERCISE PRICE

The exercise price is the price at which an option buyer may buy or sell the underlying security, depending on the type of option involved in the transaction.

BUYER VS. SELLER

Buyer		**Seller**
Owner	**Known as**	Writer
Long	**Known as**	Short
Rights	**Has**	Obligations
Maximum speculative profit	**Objective**	Premium income
Exercise	**Wants the option to**	Expire

POSSIBLE OUTCOMES FOR AN OPTION

EXERCISED
If the option is exercised, the buyer has elected to exercise its rights to buy or sell the security depending on the type of option involved. Exercising an option obligates the seller to perform under the contract.

SOLD
Most individual investors will elect to sell their rights to another investor rather than exercise their rights. The investor who buys the option from them will acquire all the rights of the original purchaser.

EXPIRE
If the option expires, the buyer has elected not to exercise its right, and the seller of the option is not required to perform.

OPTION PREMIUMS

The price of an option is known as its premium. Factors that determine the value of an option and, as a result, its premium, are:

- The relationship of the underlying stock price to the option's strike price.
- The amount of time to expiration.
- The volatility of the underlying stock.
- Supply and demand.
- Interest rates.

An option can be:

- In the money.
- At the money.
- Out of the money.

These terms describe the relationship of the underlying stock to the option's strike price. These terms do not describe how profitable the position is.

IN-THE-MONEY OPTIONS
A call is in the money when the underlying stock price is greater than the call's strike price.

EXAMPLE An XYZ June 40 call is $2 in the money when XYZ is at $42 per share.

A put is in the money when the underlying stock price is lower than the put's strike price.

EXAMPLE An ABC October 70 put is $4 in the money when ABC is at $66 per share.

It would only make sense to exercise an option if it was in the money.

AT-THE-MONEY OPTIONS

Both puts and calls are at the money when the underlying stock price equals the option's exercise price.

EXAMPLE If FDR is trading at $60 per share, all of the FDR 60 calls and all of the FDR 60 puts will be at the money.

OUT-OF-THE-MONEY OPTIONS

A call is out of the money when the underlying stock price is lower than the option's strike price.

EXAMPLE An ABC November 25 call is out of the money when ABC is trading at $22 per share.

A put option is out of the money when the underlying stock price is above the option's strike price.

EXAMPLE A KDC December 50 put is out of the money when KDC is trading at $54 per share.

It would not make sense to exercise an out-of-the-money option.

	Calls	Puts
In the money	stock price > strike price	stock price < strike price
At the money	stock price = strike price	stock price = strike price
Out of the money	stock price < strike price	stock price > strike price

INTRINSIC VALUE AND TIME VALUE

An option's total premium is composed of intrinsic value and time value. An option's intrinsic value is equal to the amount the option is in the money. Time value is the amount by which an option's premium exceeds its intrinsic value. In effect, the time value is the price an investor pays for the opportunity to exercise the option. An option that is out of the money has no intrinsic value; therefore, the entire premium consists of time value.

EXAMPLE An XYZ June 40 call is trading at $2 when XYZ is trading at $37 per share. The June 40 call is out of the money and has no intrinsic value; therefore, the entire $2 premium consists of time value. If an XYZ June 40 put is trading at $3 when XYZ is at $44 dollars per share, the entire $3 is time value.

If, in the above example, the options were in the money and the premium exceeded the intrinsic value of the option, the remaining premium would be time value.

EXAMPLE An XYZ June 40 call is trading at $5 when XYZ is trading at $42 per share. The June 40 call is in the money and has $2 in intrinsic value; therefore, the rest of the premium consists of the time value of $3. If an XYZ June 40 put is trading at $4 when XYZ is at $39, the put is in the money by $1 and the rest of the premium, or $3, is time value.

AMERICAN DEPOSITARY RECEIPTS (ADRs)/ AMERICAN DEPOSITARY SHARES (ADSs)

American depositary receipts (ADRs) facilitate the trading of foreign securities in the U.S. markets. An ADR is a receipt that represents the ownership of the foreign shares that are being held abroad in a branch of a United States bank. Each ADR represents ownership of between 1 and 10 shares of the foreign stock, and the holder of the ADR may request the delivery of the foreign shares. Holders of ADRs also have the right to vote and the right to receive dividends that the foreign corporation declares for payment to shareholders.

CURRENCY RISKS

The owner of an ADR has currency risk along with the normal risks associated with the ownership of the stock. Should the currency of the country decline relative to the U.S. dollar, the holder of the ADR will receive fewer U.S. dollars when a dividend is paid and fewer U.S. dollars when the security is sold. It is important to note that the dividend on the ADR is paid by the corporation in the foreign currency and is converted so that the dividend is received by the holder of the ADR in U.S. dollars.

REAL ESTATE INVESTMENT TRUSTS (REITs)

A real estate investment trust, or REIT, is a special type of equity security. REITs are organized for the specific purpose of buying, developing, or managing a portfolio of real estate. REITs are organized as a corporation or as a trust, and publicly traded REITs will trade on the exchanges or in the over-the-counter market just like other stocks. A REIT is organized as a conduit for the investment income generated by the portfolio of real estate. REITs are entitled to special tax treatment under Internal Revenue Code subchapter M. A REIT will not pay taxes at the corporate level so long as:

- It receives 75% of its income from real estate.
- It distributes at least 90% of its taxable income to shareholders.

So long as the REIT meets the above requirements, the income will be allowed to flow through to the shareholders and will be taxed at their rate. Eighty percent of the dividends received by REIT shareholders will continue to be taxed as ordinary income.

NON-TRADED REITs

Non-traded real estate investment trust or REITs lack liquidity, have high fees, and can be difficult to value. The fees for investing in a non-traded REIT may be as much as 15% of the per shares price. These fees include commissions and expenses which cannot exceed 10% of the offering price. Investors are often attracted to the high yields offered by these investments. Firms who conduct business in these products must conduct ongoing suitability determination on the REITs they recommend. Firms must react to red flags in the financial statements and from the REIT's management and adjust the recommendation process accordingly or stop recommending if material changes take place that would make the REIT unsuitable. Holding periods can be 8 years or more and the opportunities to liquidate the investments may be very limited. Furthermore the distributions from the REITs themselves may be based on the use of borrowed funds and may include a return of principal which may be adversely impacted and cause the distributions to be vulnerable to being significantly reduced or stopped altogether. Distributions may exceed cash flow and the amount of the distributions in any are at the discretion of the Board of Directors Non-traded REITs like exchange-traded REITs must distribute 90% of the income to shareholders and must file 10-Ks and 10-Qs with the SEC. Broker dealers who sell non-traded REITs must provide investors with a valuation of the REIT within 18 months of the closing of the offering of shares.

DEBT SECURITIES/BONDS

Many different types of entities issue bonds in an effort to raise working capital. Corporations and municipalities as well as the U.S. government and U.S. government agencies issue bonds in order to meet their capital needs. A bond represents a loan to the issuer in exchange for a promise to repay the face amount of the bond, known as the principal amount at maturity. On most bonds, the investor receives semiannual interest payments, during the bond's term. These semiannual interest payments, as well as any capital appreciation or depreciation at maturity, represent the investor's return. A bondholder invests primarily for the interest income that will be generated during the bond's term.

CORPORATE BONDS

Corporations will issue bonds in an effort to raise working capital to build and expand their business. Corporate bondholders are not owners of the corporation; they are creditors of the company. Corporate debt financing is known as leverage financing because the company pays interest only on the loan until maturity. Bondholders do not have voting rights as long as the company pays the interest and principal payments in a timely fashion. If the company defaults, the bondholders may be able to use their position as creditors to gain a voice in the company's management. Bondholders will always be paid before preferred and common stockholders in the event of liquidation. Interest income received by investors on corporate bonds is taxable at all levels: federal, state, and local.

THE U.S. GOVERNMENT

The U.S. government is the largest issuer of debt. It is also the issuer with the least amount of default risk. Default risk is also known as credit risk, which is the risk that the issuer will not be able to meet its obligations under the terms of the bond in a timely fashion. The U.S. government issues debt securities with maturities ranging from 3 months to 30 years. The Treasury Department issues the securities on behalf of the federal government, and they are a legally binding obligation of the federal government. Interest earned by the investors from U.S. government securities is only taxed at the federal level. State and local governments do not tax the interest income.

U.S. GOVERNMENT AGENCIES

The U.S. government has many agencies that operate to provide financial and other assistance to American businesses and families. These agencies also must raise capital to operate, and much of the money is raised through the sale of agency securities. These debt instruments have only a slightly higher risk of default than the direct government obligations. As a result of the small increase in risk, the interest rate earned by investors will, in most cases, only be slightly higher than those on Treasury securities. Interest income earned by investors on agency securities is taxable at all levels: federal, state, and local.

MUNICIPAL BONDS

Both state and local governments will issue debt securities to meet their goals. Municipal bonds are issued to meet a variety of needs, from working capital to bridge and tunnel projects. Once bonds have been issued, they become a legally binding obligation of the state or municipality. Interest earned by investors will be free from federal taxes and may be free from state and local taxes if the investor purchases a municipal bond issued by the state in which he or she resides.

TYPES OF BOND ISSUANCE

BEARER BONDS

Bonds that are issued in coupon or bearer form do not record the owner's information with the issuer, and the bond certificate does not have the legal owner's name printed on it. As a result, anyone who possesses the bond is entitled to receive the interest payment by clipping the coupons attached to the bond and depositing them in a bank or trust company for payment. Additionally, the bearer is entitled to receive the principal payment at the bond's maturity. Bearer bonds are no longer issued within the United States; however, they are still issued outside the United States.

REGISTERED BONDS

Most bonds are now issued in registered form. Bonds that have been issued in registered form have the owner's name recorded in the books of the issuer, and the buyer's name will appear on the bond certificate.

PRINCIPAL-ONLY REGISTRATION

Bonds that have been registered as principal only have the owner's name printed on the bond certificate. The issuer knows who owns the bond and who is entitled to receive the principal payment at maturity. However, the bondholder will still be required to clip the coupons to receive the semiannual interest payments.

FULLY REGISTERED

Bonds that have been issued in fully registered form have the owner's name recorded for both the interest and principal payments. The owner is not required to clip coupons, and the issuer will send out the interest payments directly to the holder on a semiannual basis. The issuer also will send the principal payment as well as the last semiannual interest payment directly to the owner at maturity. Most bonds in the United States are issued in fully registered form.

BOOK ENTRY/JOURNAL ENTRY

Bonds that have been issued in book entry or journal entry form have no physical certificate issued to the holder as evidence of ownership. The bonds are fully registered, and the issuer knows who is entitled to receive the semiannual interest payments and the principal payment at maturity. The investor's only evidence of ownership is the trade confirmation, which is generated by the brokerage firm when the purchase order has been executed.

BOND CERTIFICATE

If a bond certificate is issued, it must include:

- Name of issuer.
- Principal amount.
- Issuing date.
- Maturity date.
- Interest payment dates.

CHAPTER 1 Equity and Debt Securities

- Place where interest is payable (paying agent).
- Type of bond.
- Interest rate.
- Call feature (if any or noncallable).
- Reference to the trust indenture.

BOND PRICING

Once issued, bonds trade in the secondary market between investors similar to the way equity securities do. The price of bonds in the secondary market depends on the following:

- Rating
- Interest rates
- Term
- Coupon rate
- Type of bond
- Issuer
- Supply and demand
- Other features (e.g., callable, convertible)

Bonds are always priced as a percentage of par. Par value for all bonds is $1,000.

PAR VALUE
The par value of a bond is equal to the amount that the investor has loaned to the issuer. The terms par value, face value, and principal amount are all synonymous and always equal $1,000. The principal amount is the amount that will be received by the investor at maturity, regardless of the price the investor paid for the bond. An investor who purchases a bond in the secondary market for $1,000 is said to have paid par for the bond.

DISCOUNT
In the secondary market, many different factors affect the price of the bond. It is not unusual for an investor to purchase a bond at a price that is below the bond's par value. Anytime an investor buys a bond at a price that is below the par value, they are said to be buying the bond at a discount.

PREMIUM

Oftentimes market conditions will cause the price of existing bonds to rise, making it attractive for investors to purchase a bond at a price that is greater than its par value. When an investor buys a bond at a price that exceeds its par value, the investor is said to have paid a premium.

CORPORATE BOND PRICING

All corporate bonds are priced as a percentage of par in fractions of a percent. For example, a quote for a corporate bond reading 95 actually translates into:

95% × $1,000 = $950

A quote for a corporate bond of 97.25 translates into:

97.25% × $1,000 = $972.50

TREASURY BOND AND NOTE PRICING

Treasury notes and bonds are also quoted as a percentage of par. However, unlike their corporate counterparts, Treasury notes and bonds are quoted as a percentage of par down to 32nds of 1%. For example, a bond quote of 92.02 translates into:

92-2/32% × $1,000 = $920.625

A quote of 98.04 translates into:

98.125% × $1,000 = $981.25

It is important to remember that the number after the decimal points represents 32nds of a percent.

TREASURY BILL PRICING

Treasury bills do not pay semiannual interest and are issued at a discount from par. The bill's appreciation up to par at maturity represents the investor's interest. Treasury bills are quoted on a discounted yield basis. Series 99 candidates are unlikely to see a Treasury bill quote on the exam.

MUNICIPAL BOND PRICING

Most municipal bonds are also quoted on a yield basis; however, they are quoted on a yield-to-maturity basis. Some municipal bonds are quoted as a percentage of par, just like corporate bonds, and they are known as dollar bonds.

BOND YIELDS

A bond's yield is the investor's return for holding the bond. Many factors affect the yield an investor will receive from a bond, such as:

- Current interest rates
- Term of the bond
- Credit quality of the issuer
- Type of collateral
- Convertible or callable
- Purchase price

An investor who is considering investing in a bond needs to be familiar with the bond's nominal yield, current yield, and yield to maturity.

NOMINAL YIELD

A bond's nominal yield is the interest rate that is printed, or named, on the bond. The nominal yield is always stated as a percentage of par. It is fixed at the time of the bond's issuance and never changes. The nominal yield may also be called the coupon rate. For example, a corporate bond with a coupon rate of 8% will pay the holder $80 per year in interest:

$8\% \times \$1,000 = \$80$

Thus, the nominal yield is 8%.

CURRENT YIELD

The current yield is a relationship between the annual interest generated by the bond and the bond's current market price. To find any investment's current yield use the following formula:

annual income/current market price

For example, let's take the same 8% corporate bond we used in the previous example on nominal yield and see what its current yield would be if we paid $1,100 for the bond:

annual income = $8\% \times \$1,000 = \$80$

current market price = $110\% \times \$1,000 = \$1,100$

current yield = $\$80/\$1,100 = 7.27\%$

In this example we have purchased the bond at a premium or a price that is higher than par, and we see that the current yield on the bond is lower than the nominal yield.

Let's take a look at the current yield on the same bond if we were to purchase the bond at a discount, or a price that is lower than par. Let's see what the current yield for the bond would be if we paid $900 for the bond:

annual income = 8% × $1,000 = $80

current market price = 90% × $1,000 = $900

current yield = $80/$900 = 8.89%

In this example, the current yield is higher than the nominal yield. By showing examples calculating the current yield for the same bond purchased at a premium and at a discount, we have demonstrated the inverse relationship between prices and yields. That is to say that prices and yields on income-producing investments move in the opposite direction. As the price of an investment rises, the investment's yield will fall. Conversely, as the price of the investment falls, the investment's yield will rise.

YIELD TO MATURITY

The yield to maturity of a bond is the investor's total annualized return for investing in the bond. A bond's yield to maturity takes into consideration the annual income received by the investor as well as any difference between the price the investor paid for the bond and the par value that will be received at maturity. The yield to maturity is the most important yield for an investor who purchases the bond.

YIELD TO MATURITY: PREMIUM BOND

The yield to maturity for a bond purchased at a premium will be the lowest of all the investor's yields. Although an investor may purchase a bond at a price that exceeds the par value of the bond, the issuer is only obligated to pay the bondholder the par value upon maturity. For example: An investor, who purchases a bond at 110, or for $1,100, will receive only $1,000 at maturity and therefore will lose $100. This loss is what causes the yield to maturity to be the lowest of the three yields for an investor who purchases a bond at a premium.

YIELD TO MATURITY: DISCOUNT BOND

The yield to maturity for a bond purchased at a discount will be the highest of the investor's yields. In this case, the investor has purchased the bond at a price that is less than the par value of the bond. In this example, even though the investor paid less than the par value for the bond, the issuer is still obligated to pay the full par value of the bond at maturity, or the full $1,000. For example: An investor who purchases a bond at 90, or for $900, will still be entitled to receive the full par amount of $1,000 at maturity, therefore gaining $100. This gain is what causes the yield to maturity to be the highest of the three yields for an investor who purchases a bond at a discount.

The following illustration demonstrates the inverse relationship between prices and yields.

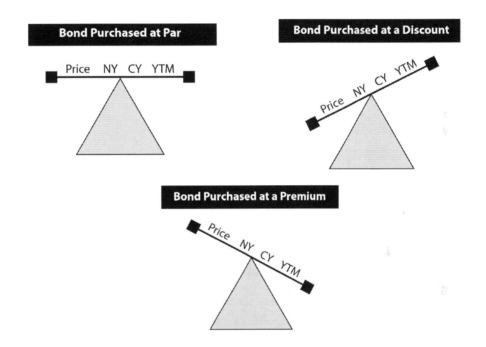

A corporation will issue or sell bonds as a means to borrow money to help the organization meet its goals. Corporate bonds are divided into two main categories: secured and unsecured.

SECURED BONDS

A secured bond is one that is backed by a specific pledge of assets. The assets that have been pledged become known as collateral for the bond issue or the loan. A trustee will hold the title to the collateral, and in the event of default the bondholders may claim the assets that have been pledged.

The trustee will then attempt to sell off the assets in an effort to pay off the bondholders.

MORTGAGE BONDS

A mortgage bond is a bond that has been backed by a pledge of real property. The corporation will issue bonds to investors and will pledge real estate owned by the company as collateral. A mortgage bond works in a similar fashion to a residential mortgage. In the event of default, the bondholders take the property.

EQUIPMENT TRUST CERTIFICATES

An equipment trust certificate is backed by a pledge of large equipment that the corporation owns. Airlines, railroads, and large shipping companies will often borrow money to purchase the equipment that they need through the sale of equipment trust certificates. Airplanes, railroad cars, and ships are all good examples of the types of assets that might be pledged as collateral. In the event of default, the equipment will be liquidated by the trustee in an effort to pay off the bondholders.

COLLATERAL TRUST CERTIFICATES

A collateral trust certificate is a bond that has been backed by a pledge of securities that the issuer has purchased for investment purposes or by shares of a wholly owned subsidiary. Both stocks and bonds are acceptable forms of collateral as long as they have been issued by another issuer. Securities that have been pledged as collateral are generally required to be held by the trustee for safekeeping. In the event of a default, the trustee will attempt to liquidate the securities that have been pledged as collateral and divide the proceeds among the bondholders.

It is important to note that while having a specific claim against an asset that has been pledged as collateral benefits the bondholder, bondholders do not want to take title to the collateral. Bondholders invest for the semiannual interest payments and the return of their principal at maturity.

UNSECURED BONDS

Unsecured bonds are known as debentures and have no specific asset pledged as collateral for the loan. Debentures are only backed by the good faith and credit of the issuer. In the event of a default, the holder of a debenture is treated like a general creditor.

SUBORDINATED DEBENTURES

A subordinated debenture is an unsecured loan to the issuer that has a junior claim on the issuer in the event of default relative to the straight debenture. Should the issuer default, the holders of the debentures and other general creditors will be paid before the holders of the subordinate debentures.

INCOME/ADJUSTMENT BONDS

Corporations, usually those in severe financial difficulty, issue income or adjustment bonds. The bond is unsecured, and the investor is only promised to be paid interest if the corporation has enough income to do so. As a result of the large risk that the investor is taking, the interest rate is very high, and the bonds are issued at a deep discount to par. An income bond is never an appropriate recommendation for an investor seeking income or safety of principal.

ZERO-COUPON BONDS

A zero-coupon bond is a bond that pays no semiannual interest. It is issued at a deep discount from the par value and appreciates up to par at maturity. This appreciation represents the investor's interest for purchasing the bond. Corporations, the U.S. government, and municipalities will all issue zero-coupon bonds in an effort to finance their activities. An investor might be able to purchase the $1,000 principal payment in 20 years for as little as $300 today. Because the zero-coupon bonds pay no semiannual interest and the price is so deeply discounted from par, the price of the bond will be the most sensitive to a change in the interest rates. Both corporate and U.S. government zero-coupon bonds subject the investor to federal income taxes on the annual appreciation of the bond. This is known as phantom income.

CONVERTIBLE BONDS

A convertible bond is a corporate bond that may be converted or exchanged for common shares of the corporation at a predetermined price, known as the conversion price. Convertible bonds have benefits to both the issuer and the investor. Because the bond is convertible, it usually will pay a lower rate of interest than nonconvertible bonds. This lower interest rate can save the corporation an enormous amount of money in interest expense over the life of the issue. The convertible feature will also benefit the investor if the common stock does well. If the shares of the underlying common stock appreciate, the investor could realize significant capital appreciation in the price of the bond and may also elect to convert the bond into common stock in the hopes of realizing additional appreciation. As an investor in the bond, the investor maintains a senior position as a creditor while enjoying the potential for capital appreciation.

CONVERTING BONDS INTO COMMON STOCK

All Series 99 candidates must be able to perform the conversion calculations for both convertible bonds and preferred stock. It is essential that prospective representatives are able to determine the following:

Number of shares: To determine the number of shares that can be received upon conversion use the following formula:

par value/conversion price

EXAMPLE XYZ has a 7% subordinated debenture trading in the marketplace at 120. The bonds are convertible into XYZ common stock at $25 per share. How many shares can the investor receive upon conversion?

$1,000/$25 = 40 shares

The investor is entitled to receive 40 shares of XYZ common stock for each bond owned.

PARITY PRICE

A stock's parity price determines the value at which the stock must be priced in order for the value of the common stock to be equal to the value of the bond that the investor already owns. The value of the stock that can be received by the investor upon conversion must be equal to or at parity with the value of the bond, otherwise converting the bonds into common stock would not make economic sense. Determining the parity price is a two-step process. First, the number of shares that can be received must be determined by using the formula: par value/conversion price. Then it is necessary to calculate the price of each share at the parity price. To determine the parity price, use the following formula:

$$\frac{\text{current market value of the convertible}}{\text{number of shares to be received}}$$

In the above example, the convertible bond was quoted at 120, which equals a dollar price of $1,200. We determined that the investor could receive 40 shares of stock for each bond, so the parity price equals:

$1,200/40 = $30

If the question is looking for the number of shares or the parity price for a convertible preferred stock, the formulas are the same; the only thing that changes is the par value. Par value for all preferred stocks is $100, instead of $1,000 par value for bonds.

THE TRUST INDENTURE ACT OF 1939

The Trust Indenture Act of 1939 requires that corporate bond issues in excess of $10,000,000 dollars that are to be repaid during a term in excess of 1 year issue a trust indenture for the issue. The trust indenture is a contract between the issuer and the trustee. The trustee acts on behalf of the bondholders and ensures that the issuer is in compliance with the promises and covenants made to the bondholders. The trustee is appointed by the corporation and is usually a bank or a trust company. The Trust Indenture Act of 1939 only applies to corporate issuers. Federal and municipal issuers are exempt.

TREASURY BILLS, NOTES, AND BONDS

Treasury Security	Type of Interest	Term	Priced
Bill	None	4, 13, 26, 52 weeks 1, 3, 6, 12 months	At a discount from par
Note	Semiannual	1–10 years	As a percentage of par to 32nds of 1%
Bond	Semiannual	10–30 years	As a percentage of par to 32nds of 1%

The minimum denomination for purchasing a Treasury bill, note, or bond through TreasuryDirect.gov is $100.

 TAKENOTE!

The Treasury does not currently sell 1-year bills. However this is a policy decision; the Treasury may at any time elect to issue 1-year bills, just as it recently decided to reissue 30-year bonds.

PURCHASING TREASURY BILLS

Treasury bills range in maturity from 4 to 52 weeks and are auctioned off by the Treasury Department through a weekly competitive auction. Large banks and broker dealers, known as primary dealers, submit competitive bids or tenders for the bills being sold. The Treasury awards the bills to the bidders who submitted the highest bid and work their way down to lower bids until all of the bills are sold. Treasury bills pay no semiannual interest and are issued at a discount from par. The bill appreciates up to par at maturity and the appreciation represents the investor's interest. Because bills are priced at a discount from par, a higher dollar price represents a lower interest rate for the purchaser. All noncompetitive tenders are filled before any competitive tenders are filled. A bidder who submits a noncompetitive tender agrees to accept the average of all the yields accepted by the Treasury and does not try to get the best yield. All competitive tenders are limited to a maximum amount of $500,000. All bids that are accepted and filled by the Treasury are settled in fed funds. Treasury bills range in denominations from $100 up to $1,000,000.

> **TAKENOTE!**
>
> A quote for a Treasury bill has a bid that appears to be higher than the offer. But remember that the bills are quoted on a discounted yield basis. The higher bid actually represents a lower dollar price than the offer.

EXAMPLE

Bid	Ask
1.91	2.75

TREASURY STRIPS

The term Treasury "STRIPS" stands for Separate Trading of Registered Interest and Principal Securities. The Treasury securities are separated into two parts: a principal payment and semiannual interest payments. A Treasury STRIP is a zero-coupon bond that is backed by U.S. government securities. An investor may purchase the principal payment component of $1,000, due on a future date, at a discount. An investor seeking some current income may wish to purchase the semiannual coupon payments, due over the term of the Treasury securities.

TREASURY RECEIPTS

Treasury receipts are similar to Treasury STRIPS except that broker dealers and banks create them. Broker dealers and banks will purchase large amounts of Treasury securities, place them in a trust, and sell off the interest and principal payments to investors.

CHAPTER 1 Equity and Debt Securities

AGENCY ISSUES

The federal government has authorized certain agencies and quasi-agencies to issue debt securities that are collectively referred to as agency issues. These agency securities are secured by revenues generated through taxes, fees, and interest income. Investors who purchase agency securities are offered interest rates that generally fall between the rates offered by similar-term Treasury and corporate securities. Investors who purchase agency issues in the secondary market will be quoted prices for the agency issues that are based on a percentage of par, just like corporate issue.

GOVERNMENT NATIONAL MORTGAGE ASSOCIATION (GNMA)

The Government National Mortgage Association (GNMA), often referred to as Ginnie Mae, is a wholly owned government corporation and is the only agency whose securities are backed by the full faith and credit of the U.S. government. The purpose of Ginnie Mae is to provide liquidity to the mortgage markets. Ginnie Mae buys up pools of mortgages, which have been insured by the Federal Housing Administration and the Department of Veteran Affairs. The ownership in these pools of mortgages is then sold off to private investors in the form of pass-through certificates. Investors in Ginnie Mae pass-through certificates receive monthly interest and principal payments based on their investment. As people pay down their mortgages, part of each payment is interest and part is principal, and both portions flow through to the investor on a monthly basis. The only real risk in owning a Ginnie Mae is the risk of early refinancing. As the interest rates in the marketplace fall, people are more likely to refinance their homes, and, as a result, the investor will not receive the higher interest rates for as long as they had hoped. Ginnie Mae pass-through certificates are issued with a minimum denomination of $1,000, and the interest earned by investors is taxable at all levels: federal, state, and local.

FEDERAL NATIONAL MORTGAGE ASSOCIATION (FNMA)

The Federal National Mortgage Association (FNMA), also known as Fannie Mae, is a public for-profit corporation. Fannie Mae's stock trades in the market and earns a profit by providing mortgage capital. It is called an *agency security* because Fannie Mae has a credit facility with the government and receives certain favorable tax considerations. Fannie Mae purchases mortgages and, in turn, packages them to create mortgage-backed securities. These mortgage-backed notes are issued in denominations from $5,000 to $1,000,000 and pay interest semiannually. Interest earned by investors from Fannie Mae securities is taxable at all levels: federal, state, and local. Fannie Mae has been placed in conservatorship, and its debt is guaranteed by the federal government.

FEDERAL HOME LOAN MORTGAGE CORPORATION (FHLMC)

The Federal Home Loan Mortgage Corporation (FHLMC), also known as Freddie Mac, is also a publicly traded corporation whose stock trades in the market. Freddie Mac purchases residential mortgages from lenders, packages them into pools, and sells off interest in those pools to investors. Interest earned by investors from FHLMC-issued securities is taxable at all levels: federal, state, and local. Freddie Mac has been placed in conservatorship, and its debt is guaranteed by the federal government.

COLLATERALIZED MORTGAGE OBLIGATION (CMO)

A collateralized mortgage obligation (CMO) is a mortgage-backed security issued by private finance companies as well as by FHLMC and FNMA. The securities are structured much like a pass-through certificate, and their term is set into different maturity schedules, known as tranches. Pools of mortgages on one- to four-family homes collateralize CMOs. Because CMOs are backed by mortgages on real estate, they are considered relatively safe investments. The only real risk that the owner of a CMO faces is the risk of early refinance. CMOs pay interest and principal monthly. However, they pay the principal to only one tranche at a time in $1,000 payments.

CMOs AND INTEREST RATES

CMOs, like other interest-bearing investments, will be affected by a change in the interest rate environment. CMOs may experience the following if interest rates change:

- If interest rates fall, homeowners will refinance more quickly and the holders of CMOs will be paid off more quickly than they had hoped.
- The rate of principal payments may vary.
- If interest rates rise, refinancing may slow down and the investors will be paid off more slowly than they had hoped.

Most CMOs have an active secondary market and are considered relatively liquid securities. However, the more complex CMOs may not have an active secondary market and may be considered illiquid. Interest earned by investors from CMOs is taxable at all levels: federal, state, and local.

MUNICIPAL BONDS

State and local governments will issue municipal bonds in order to help the local governments meet their financial needs. Most municipal bonds are considered almost as safe as Treasury securities issued by the federal government. However, unlike the federal government, from time to time an issuer of municipal securities does default. The degree of safety varies from state to state and from municipality to municipality.

THE MONEY MARKET

The money market is a place where issuers go to obtain short-term financing. An issuer who needs funds for a short term, typically less than 1 year, will sell short-term instruments, known as money market instruments, to obtain the necessary funds. Corporations, municipalities, and the U.S. government all use the money market to obtain short-term financing.

MONEY MARKET INSTRUMENTS

Money market instruments are highly liquid fixed-income securities issued by governments and corporations with high credit ratings. Because of the high quality of the issuers and the short-term maturities, money market instruments are considered very safe.

CORPORATE MONEY MARKET INSTRUMENTS

Both corporations and banks sell money market instruments to obtain short-term financing. These money market instruments include:

- Bankers' acceptances
- Negotiable certificates of deposits
- Commercial paper
- Federal funds
- Repurchase agreements

BANKERS' ACCEPTANCES

Corporations, in order to facilitate foreign trade (import/export), use bankers' acceptances (BAs). The BA acts like a line of credit or a postdated check. The BA is a time draft that will be cleared by the issuing bank on the day it becomes due to whoever presents it for payment. The maturity dates on BAs range from as little as one day to a maximum of 270 days (9 months).

NEGOTIABLE CERTIFICATES OF DEPOSIT

A negotiable certificate of deposit (CD) is a time deposit with a fixed interest rate and a set maturity ranging from 30 days to 10 years or more. A negotiable CD, unlike the traditional CD, may be exchanged or traded between investors. The minimum denomination for a negotiable CD is $100,000. Many negotiable CDs are issued in denominations exceeding $1,000,000, but the Federal Deposit Insurance Corporation (FDIC) only insures the first $250,000.

COMMERCIAL PAPER

Commercial paper is used by the largest and most creditworthy corporations as a way to obtain short-term funds. Commercial paper is an unsecured promissory note, or an IOU, issued by the corporation. Corporations will sell commercial paper to finance such things as short-term working capital or to meet their cash needs due to seasonal business cycles. Commercial paper maturities range from 1 day to a maximum of 270 days. Commercial paper is issued at a discount of its face value and has an interest rate that is below what a commercial bank would typically charge for the funds. Corporate debt securities with less than 1 year to maturity, regardless of their original maturity, may be traded in the money market as long as their credit rating qualifies.

FEDERAL FUND LOANS

Federal fund loans are loans between two banks that are typically made for short periods of time. These loans may be exchanged in the money market between investors.

REPURCHASE AGREEMENTS

A repurchase agreement is a fully collateralized loan made between large financial institutions. These loans are collateralized with U.S. government securities that have been sold to the lender. The borrower agrees to repurchase the securities from the lender at a slightly higher price. The slightly higher price represents the lender's interest.

CHAPTER 1   Equity and Debt Securities

GOVERNMENT MONEY MARKET INSTRUMENTS

The U.S. government and many of its agencies will go to the money market to obtain short-term funds. Some of the government money market instruments include:

- Treasury bills
- Treasury and agency securities with less than 1 year remaining
- Short-term discount notes issued by government agencies

Government issues with less than 1 year to maturity, regardless of the original maturity, may be traded in the money market.

LIMITED PARTNERSHIPS

A limited partnership (LP) is an entity that allows all of the economic events of the partnership to flow through to the partners. These economic events are:

- Income.
- Gains.
- Losses.
- Tax credits.
- Deductions.

The two types of partners in a limited partnership are the limited partners and the general partner. The limited partners:

- Put up the investment capital.
- Losses are limited to their investment.
- Receive the benefits from the operation.
- May not exercise management over the operation.
- May vote to change the objective of the partnership.
- May vote to switch or remove the general partner.
- May sue the general partner, if the general partner does not act in the best interest of the partnership.

A limited partner may never exercise any management or control over the limited partnership. Doing so would jeopardize the limited partner's limited status, such that he or she may be considered a general partner.

The general partner is the person or corporation that manages the business and has unlimited liability for the obligations of the partnership business. The general partner may also:

- Buy and sell property for the partnership.
- Receive compensation for managing the partnership.
- Enter into legally binding contracts for the partnership.

The general partner also must maintain a financial interest in the partnership of at least 1%. The general partner may not:

- Commingle funds of the general partner with the funds of the partnership.
- Compete against the partnership.
- Borrow from the partnership.

It is important to note that there are no tax consequences at the partnership level. In order to qualify for the preferential tax treatment, a direct participation program (DPP) or LP must avoid at least two of the six characteristics of a corporation. These characteristics are:

- Continuity of life.
- Profit motive.
- Central management.
- Limited liability.
- Associates.
- Freely transferable interest.

Several of the characteristics cannot be avoided, such as associates and a profit motive. The easiest two characteristics of a corporation to avoid are continuity of life and freely transferable interest. The LP can put a termination date on the partnership, and substitute limited partners may not be accepted or may only be accepted once the general partner has agreed.

STRUCTURING AND OFFERING LIMITED PARTNERSHIPS

The foundation of every limited partnership is the partnership agreement. All limited partners must be given a copy of the partnership agreement. The partnership agreement will spell out all of the terms and conditions, as well as the business purpose for the partnership. The powers and limitations of the general partner's authority will be one of the main points detailed in the partnership agreement. Prior to forming a limited partnership, the general partner will have to file a certificate of limited partnership in the state in which the partnership is formed. The certificate will include:

- Name and address of the partnership.
- A description of the partnership's business.
- The life of the partnership.
- Size of limited partner's investments (if any).
- Conditions for assignment of interest by limited partners.
- Conditions for dissolving the partnership.
- Conditions for admitting new limited partners.
- The projected date for the return of capital, if one is set.

A material change to any of these conditions must be updated on the certificate within 30 days.

Most limited partnerships will be offered to investors through a private placement. All investors who purchase a limited partnership through a private placement must receive a private placement memorandum. Private placements, with very limited exceptions, may only be offered to accredited investors. However, a few limited partnerships will be offered to the public through a standard public offering. All investors who purchase a limited partnership though a public offering must receive a prospectus. If the partnership is sold through a syndicator, the syndicator is responsible for filing the partnership documents. The maximum fee that may be received by the syndicator is limited to 10% of the offering. If a secondary market develops for a partnership, the partnership will be known as a master limited partnership, or MLP. All investors wishing to become a limited partner must complete the partnership's subscription agreement. The subscription agreement will include:

- A power of attorney appointing the general partner.
- A statement of the prospective limited partner's net worth.
- A statement regarding the prospective limited partner's income.
- A statement from the prospective limited partner that he or she understands and can afford the risks related to the partnership.

TYPES OF LIMITED PARTNERSHIPS

A limited partnership may be organized for any lawful purpose. Limited partnerships are most commonly set up to:

- Invest in real estate.
- Invest in oil and gas wells.
- Engage in equipment leasing.

There are several types of real estate partnerships. They are:

- Existing property.
- New construction.
- Raw land.
- Government assisted housing.
- Historic rehabilitation.

Type of LP	Risk	Advantages	Disadvantages	Tax Benefits
Existing Property Purchase income property	Low	Immediate predictable cash flow	Rental problems and repairs	Deductions for mortgage interest and depreciation
New Construction Build units for appreciation or rental	Higher	Potential capital gains low maintenance	No deduction for current expenses and no promise of rental or sale	Deduction of expenses and depreciation only after completion
Raw Land Purchase land for appreciation	Highest	Only appreciation potential	No tax deductions or income	No tax benefits

CHAPTER 1 Equity and Debt Securities

Type of LP	Risk	Advantages	Disadvantages	Tax Benefits
Government-Assisted Housing Low-income housing	Low	Government rent, subsidies, and tax credits	High maintenance costs; risk of a change in government programs	Tax credits and any losses on the property
Historic Rehabilitation Restore sites for use	Higher	Tax credits	Financing trouble; no rental history	Tax credits, deductions, and depreciation

An investor can participate in several types of oil and gas partnerships. They are:

- Income programs.
- Developmental programs.
- Exploratory or wildcatting.

Intangible drilling costs are usually 100% deductible in the year they are incurred. Intangible drilling costs (IDC) include:

- Geological surveys
- Wages
- Supplies
- Well casings

Investors in oil and gas programs will be given a depletion allowance for the decreasing reserves.

Type of LP	Risk	Advantages	Disadvantages	Tax Benefits
Income Buys existing wells	Low	Immediate predictable cash flow	Reserves run out or prices fall	Depletion allowance
Developmental Drills near proven reserves	Higher	Higher probability to find reserves than wildcatting	Not many fields ever produce	Immediate deductions for IDCs
Exploratory/Wildcatting Drills to find new reserves	Highest	Huge payoff if significant reserves are found	Not many fields ever produce	Immediate deductions for a high level of IDCs

EQUIPMENT LEASING PROGRAMS

Equipment leasing programs are formed to purchase equipment with the intention of leasing it to a corporation. The program generates income from the lease payments received from the corporation. Investors will receive tax benefits from operating expenses, depreciation of equipment, and any interest expenses paid by the program.

TAX REPORTING FOR DIRECT PARTICIPATION PROGRAMS

Direct participation programs (DPP) are organized as either limited partnerships or as subchapter S corporations. These entities allow for the flow through of income and losses, and the DPP has no tax consequences. The DPP will only report the results of its operation to the IRS. The responsibility for paying any taxes due rests with the partners or shareholders. DPPs allow the losses to flow through to the investors. Losses from DPPs can only be used to offset the investor's passive income. Investors may not use the losses to shelter or offset the ordinary income. Investors should not purchase DPPs simply for the tax benefits; they should purchase them to earn a return. Any DPP that is found to have been formed simply to create tax benefits may subject the investors to strict penalties. Investors could owe back taxes, fines, or be prosecuted for fraud.

LIMITED PARTNERSHIP ANALYSIS

Before investing in a limited partnership, the investor should analyze the key features of the partnership to ensure that the partnership's objectives meet their investment objectives. The investor should review:

- The economic viability of the program.
- Tax considerations.
- Management's ability.
- Lack of liquidity.
- Time horizon.
- Whether it is a blind pool or a specified program.
- Internal rate of return.

A blind pool is a partnership where less than 75% of the assets that the partnership is going to acquire have been identified. In a specified program, more than 75% of the assets that the partnership is going to acquire have been identified.

A partnership's internal rate of return is the discounted present value of its projected future cash flow.

TAX DEDUCTIONS VS. TAX CREDITS

Tax deductions that are generated by partnerships are used to lower the investor's taxable income. A tax credit results in a dollar-for-dollar reduction in the amount of taxes due from the investor.

OTHER TAX CONSIDERATIONS

If a limited partnership has used up all of its deductions and has a gain on the sale of a depreciated asset, the sale above the asset's depreciated cost basis may subject the limited partners to a taxable recapture. There are two types of loans that a partnership may take out: a nonrecourse loan and a recourse loan. With a nonrecourse loan, if the partnership defaults, the lender has no recourse to the limited partners. With a recourse loan, in the event of the partnership's default, the lender can go after the limited partners for payment. A recourse loan can increase the investor's cost base. Partners must monitor their cost base and adjust it for:

- Cash or property contributions to the partnership.
- Recourse loans.
- Any cash or property received from the partnership.

Investors are responsible for any gain on the sale of their partnership interest in excess of their cost basis.

DISSOLVING A PARTNERSHIP

A partnership will terminate on the date set forth in the partnership agreement, unless earlier terminated. A partnership may dissolve if a majority of the limited partners vote for its dissolution. If the partnership terminates its activities, the general partner must cancel the certificate of limited partnership and liquidate the partnership assets. The priority of payment will be as follows:

- Secured lenders
- General creditors

- Limited partners' profits first, then return of investment
- General partner for fees first, then profits, then return of capital

CHAPTER 1

Pretest

EQUITY AND DEBT SECURITIES

1. Which of the following is NOT a right of common stockholders?
   a. Right to elect the board of directors
   b. Right to vote for executive compensation
   c. Right to vote for a stock split
   d. Right to maintain their percentage of ownership in the company

2. Which of the following is NOT true regarding ADRs?
   a. They are receipts of ownership of foreign shares being held abroad in a U.S. bank.
   b. Each ADR represents 100 shares of foreign stock, and the ADR holder may request delivery of the foreign shares.
   c. ADR holders have the right to vote and receive dividends that the foreign corporation declares for shareholders.
   d. The foreign country may issue restrictions on the foreign ownership of stock.

3. Which of the following is NOT true of authorized stock?
   a. It is the maximum number of shares a company may sell.
   b. It is arbitrarily determined at the time of incorporation and may not be changed.
   c. It may be sold in total or in part when the company goes public.
   d. It may be sold to investors to raise operating capital for the company.

4. Which of the following issues standardized options?
   a. The exchanges
   b. The OCC
   c. The company
   d. Nasdaq

5. Common stockholders do not have the right to vote on which of the following issues?
   a. Election of the board of directors
   b. Stock splits
   c. Issuance of additional common shares
   d. Bankruptcy

6. Which type of bond requires the investor to deposit coupons to receive interest payments but have the owner's name recorded on the books of the issuer?
   a. Registered bonds
   b. Bearer bonds
   c. Book entry/journal entry bonds
   d. Principal-only bonds

7. Which bonds are issued as a physical certificate without the owner's name on them and require whoever possesses these bonds to clip the coupons to receive their interest payments and to surrender the bond at maturity in order to receive the principal payment?
   a. Registered bonds
   b. Book entry/journal entry bonds
   c. Principal-only registered bonds
   d. Bearer bonds

8. In a DPP all of the following may be depreciated, EXCEPT:
   a. buildings.
   b. machinery.
   c. equipment.
   d. raw land.

9. Which of the following are true about an option?
    I. It is a contract between two parties that determines the time and place at which a security may be bought or sold.
    II. The two parties are known as the buyer and the seller. The money paid by the buyer of the option is known as the option's premium.
    III. The buyer has bought the right to buy or sell the security depending on the type of option.
    IV. The seller has an obligation to perform under the contract, possibly to buy or sell the stock depending on the option involved.
    a. II, III, and IV
    b. I, II, III, and IV
    c. I, II, and III
    d. III and IV

10. Which of the following are bearish?
    I. Call seller
    II. Put seller
    III. Call buyer
    IV. Put buyer
    a. II and III
    b. II and IV
    c. I and IV
    d. I and II

CHAPTER 2

Brokerage Office Procedures and Back-Office Operations

> **INTRODUCTION**
>
> Guidelines for the practices that a brokerage firm uses to conduct the operation of its daily business are regulated by industry, state, and federal regulators. These guidelines are the foundation for the way that the firm handles all business, from hiring a new agent to executing a customer's order. All Series 99 candidates must have a full understanding of a brokerage firm's operations and procedures to successfully complete the exam.

HIRING NEW EMPLOYEES

A registered principal of a firm will be the individual who interviews and screens potential new employees. The principal will be required to make a thorough investigation into the candidate's professional and personal backgrounds. With few exceptions, other than clerical personnel, all new employees will be required to become registered as an associated person with the firm. The new employee will begin the registration process by filling out and submitting a Uniform Application for Securities Industry Registration, also known as Form U4. Form U4 is used to collect the applicant's personal and professional history, including:

- 10-year employment history
- Five-year resident history

- Legal name and any aliases used
- Any legal or regulatory actions

The principal of the firm is required to verify the employment information for the last three years and must attest to the character of the applicant by signing Form U4 prior to its submission to FINRA. All U4 forms will be sent to the Central Registration Depository (CRD) along with a fingerprint card for processing and recording. The employing firm must maintain written procedures to verify the accuracy of the information on the new hire's U4 form. A comprehensive review of the information must take place within 30 days of the form being submitted to FINRA. Fingerprint cards may be submitted in hard copy or electronically. The candidate's fingerprints will be submitted to the FBI for review. If after three good faith attempts to submit fingerprints the FBI determines that the fingerprints are ineligible or cannot be read the candidate will not be asked to submit a fourth set of fingerprints and the FBI will conduct a name check to search the candidate's history. Any applicant who has answered yes to any of the questions on the form regarding his or her background must give a detailed explanation in the DRP pages attached to the form. The applicant is not required to provide information regarding:

- Marital status
- Educational background
- Income or net worth

Information regarding the employee's finances will be disclosed on Form U4 if the associated person has ever declared bankruptcy, if the employee has any unsatisfied judgements or liens, or entered into a compromise with creditors. For example, if a registered person entered into a short sale in a real estate transaction, and the bank forgave any portion of the loan, this must be reported on the employee's form U4. Interestingly, if the representative is in the process of being foreclosed upon for their primary residence, this action need not be reported by the employee. Any development that would cause an answer on the associated person's U4 to change requires that the member update the U4 within 30 days of when the member becomes informed of the event. In the case of an event that could cause the individual to become statutorily disqualified, such as a felony conviction or misdemeanor involving cash or securities, the member must update the associated person's U4 within 10 business days of learning of the event. Additionally, broker dealers are required to perform independent background checks on its employees every

5 years to ensure that no judgements, liens or disclosable events have gone unreported by the registered person. Registered persons who fail to disclose any unsatisfied judgements or liens are subject to significant regulatory action that could result in the person being barred from the industry in extreme cases. If a member firm conducts employee drug testing, and a registered person fails the drug test, this is neither reportable on form u4 nor a reason for statutory disqualification.

RESIGNATION OF A REGISTERED REPRESENTATIVE

If a registered representative voluntarily resigns or has his or her association with a member firm terminated for any reason, the member must fill out and submit a Uniform Termination Notice for Securities Industry Registration, which is known as Form U5. The member must submit the U5 to FINRA within 30 days of the termination. The member firm is required to give a copy of the U5 to the representative upon termination. The member must also state the reason for the termination, either voluntary or for cause. An associated person's registration is nontransferable. A representative may not simply move his or her registration from one firm to another. The employing firm that the representative is leaving must fill out and submit a U5 to FINRA, which terminates the representative's registration. The new employing firm must fill out and submit a new U4 to begin a new registration for the associated person with the new employer. The new employer is required to obtain a copy of the U5 form filed by the old employing member either from the employee or directly from FINRA within 60 days of submitting the new U4. The previous employer is not required to provide a copy to the new member firm. If the new employing member asks the associated person for a copy of the U5, it must be provided within two business days. If the member requests a copy of the U5 from an agent who has not received a copy of the U5 from the old employer, the agent must promptly request it from the old employer and provide it to the new employer within two business days of receipt. A representative who leaves the industry for more than 24 months is required to requalify by exam. During a period of absence from the industry of 2 years or less FINRA retains jurisdiction over the representative in cases involving customer complaints and violations. Agents who volunteer or who are called to active duty with the military have their registrations and continuing education requirements "tolled," and their registrations are placed in special inactive status. During this time, the 24-month requirement is not in effect. The agent may continue to receive compensation from transactions but may not contact customers during the period of active military duty.

REGISTRATION EXEMPTIONS

The following individuals are exempt from registration:

- Clerical personnel
- Nonsupervising officers and managers not dealing with customers
- Non-U.S. citizens working abroad
- Floor personnel

PERSONS INELIGIBLE TO REGISTER

Individuals applying for registration must meet the association's requirements in the following areas:

- Training
- Competence
- Experience
- Character

Anyone who fails to meet the association's requirements in any of the previously listed areas may not become registered. An individual may also be disqualified by statute or through rules for any of the following:

- Expulsion, suspension, or disciplinary actions by the Securities and Exchange Commission (SEC) or any foreign or domestic self-regulatory organization (SRO).
- The individual caused the expulsion or suspension of a broker dealer or principal.
- The individual made false or misleading statements on the application for registration on Form U4 or Form B-D.

- Felony conviction or misdemeanor involving securities, bribery, falsification of reports, perjury, or any other felony within the last 10 years.
- Court injunction or order barring the individual.

A member firm may seek to maintain the employment of or to initially hire a person who has been statutorily disqualified by filing an appeal to FINRA's registration and disclosure (RAD) department. The appeal may be decided by the department or referred to the National Adjudicatory Counsel (NAC). A hearing may be held by the Statutory Disqualification Committee and appealed to the NAC. The position being applied for under the appeal may only be clerical in nature and may not entail duties of a registered agent. A person who has been convicted of a felony that occurred less than 10 years ago may apply for a waiver to FINRA or the broker dealer's self-regulatory organization. If a waiver is granted the SRO must notify the SEC of the granting of such waiver. The SEC may overturn or object to the waiver being granted. If the waiver is granted, the person covered by the waiver will be subject to heightened supervisory procedures.

 TAKENOTE!

A person who was convicted of a felony more than 10 years ago is always required to disclose it on form U4.

DISCIPLINARY ACTIONS AGAINST A REGISTERED REPRESENTATIVE

If another industry regulator takes disciplinary action against a representative, the employing member firm must notify FINRA. Actions by any of the following should be immediately disclosed to the association:

- The SEC
- An exchange or association
- A state regulator
- A clearing firm
- A commodity regulatory body

Also immediately reportable to FINRA are any of the following:

- A customer compliant alleging theft, forgery, or misappropriation of customer assets
- Indictment, conviction, or plea of guilty or no contest to a criminal matter
- If the agent becomes a respondent or a defendant in a matter in excess of $15,000 or if the firm becomes a respondent or defendant in a matter in excess of $25,000
- An agent is disciplined by the employing member firm or commissions are withheld from an agent or the agent is fined in either case in amounts in excess of $2,500

FINRA defines immediate notification for the above-listed matters as being within 10 days. All disclosures must include the type of action brought as well as the name of the party bringing the actions and the name of the representative involved. The firm will make the disclosure on Form U4. FINRA will submit disciplinary actions that are taken by FINRA on Form U6 and they will be recorded on the employee's record. All disciplinary actions, along with a record of the agent's registrations and employment history, are available through FINRA's BrokerCheck program. FINRA members are required to regulate the activities of its associated people and must disclose to the association any action that the member takes against a registered representative. Should a registered representative feel that the information disclosed through the BrokerCheck program is inaccurate the representative may request an amendment to the disclosure by filling out and submitting a BrokerCheck comment form. Additionally, should the CRD contain information that is deemed to be inaccurate, factually impossible or otherwise false that information may be expunged and permanently removed from the agent's record.

TERMINATION FOR CAUSE

A member may terminate a registered representative for cause if the representative has:

- Violated firm policy.
- Violated the rules of the New York Stock Exchange (NYSE), FINRA, the SEC, or any other industry regulator.
- Violated state or federal securities laws.

A firm may not terminate a representative who is the subject of investigation by any securities industry regulator until the investigation is completed.

OUTSIDE EMPLOYMENT

If a registered representative wants to obtain employment outside of his or her position with a member firm, the registered representative must first provide written notification to the employing member firm. The member firm may reject or limit the representative's outside employment. Exceptions to this rule are if the registered representative is a passive investor in a business, is a board member of a nonprofit organization or if the representative owns rental property. Neither the rental property nor the income received is required to be reported. However, if a registered representative obtains a real estate license or acts as a property manager for a large rental property, these would qualify as outside business activities and must be disclosed to the employer as well as on Form U4. Note that the representative need not inform his/her employer regarding outside employment of a spouse or other family members.

PRIVATE SECURITIES TRANSACTIONS

A registered representative may not engage in any private securities transactions without first obtaining the broker dealer's prior written approval. The registered representative must provide the employing firm with all documentation regarding the investment and the proposed transaction. An example of a private securities transaction would be if a representative helped a startup business raise money through a private placement. If the representative is going to receive compensation, the employing member firm must supervise the transaction as if the firm itself executed the transaction. If a representative sells investment products that the employing member does not conduct business in without the member's knowledge, then the representative has committed a violation known as selling away. An exception to this is if the representative is helping an immediate family member raise money and the representative receives no compensation for his or her role in the private transaction. In this case, the notification and permission of the member is not required.

GIFT RULE

Broker dealers may not pay compensation to employees of other broker dealers. If a broker dealer wants to give a gift to an employee of another broker dealer, it must:

- Be valued at less than $100 per person per year.
- Be given directly to the employing member firm for distribution to the employee.
- Have the employing member's prior approval for the gift.

The employing member must obtain a record of the gift, including the name of the giver, the name of the recipient, and the nature of the gift. These rules have been established to ensure that broker dealers do not try to influence the employees of other broker dealers. An exception to this rule would be in cases where an employee of one broker dealer performs services for another broker dealer under an employment contract. The following are also excluded from the $100 limit:

- Occasional meals
- Business-related travel
- Lucite prospectus and awards
- Occasional tickets to sporting events

A key to determine if tickets are a gift or entertainment is if the person providing the tickets attends the event. If the person attends it is considered entertainment. Records of gifts and employment contracts must be retained for 3 years. Prior FINRA approval is not required for employment contracts between members. The gift rule also applies to gifts given to or received from customers of the firm or agent. In the case of a mutual fund holding a seminar, the mutual fund may pay for a registered representative's travel-related expenses and the seminar must be held at a "reasonable" location. Spouses of agents are allowed to attend; however, the mutual fund may only pay for the travel expenses of the agent. The agent's expenses may not be paid for by the fund in exchange for past sales or the promise of sales in the future. Virtual entertainment has evolved as a result of the covid 19 pandemic and has become a popular way to entertain. Member firms often host private virtual events and send food and beverages to attendees. The hosting firm will often hire celebrities and other prominent individuals to entertain or speak to the guests. FINRA deems this to be a form of entertainment and the value of the food and the fees paid to the speakers do not constitute a violation of the gift rule, even if the value exceeds $100 per person.

> Firms and agents also may not give a gift to influence any report or dissemination of information designed to influence the price of a security.

SHARING IN A CUSTOMER'S ACCOUNT

It is permissible for a representative to maintain a joint account with a customer as long as the firm approves it in advance. The representative may share in the profit and loss of the account only in direct relation to the representative's contribution to the account. A registered representative is precluded from sharing in the profit and loss of an account without making any financial contribution to the account. The one exception to this rule is when a registered representative establishes a joint account with an immediate family member. A registered representative may share disproportionately in the profits and losses of an account when the joint account is established with an immediate family member.

BORROWING AND LENDING MONEY

Borrowing and lending of money between registered persons and customers is strictly regulated. If the member firm allows borrowing and lending between representatives and customers the firm must have policies in place that will allow for the loans to be made. Loans may be made between an agent and a customer if the customer is a bank or other lending institution, where there is a personal or outside business relationship and that relationship is the basis for the loan, or between two agents registered with the same firm. The firm must provide the agent with written preapproval for the loan unless the loan is being made between the agent and an immediate family member or a bank. The approval documentation must be maintained for 3 years from the date when the loan was repaid or 3 years from the rep's termination from the firm.

ORDER TICKETS

Prior to executing a customer's order the representative must fill out the appropriate order ticket and present it to the trading department or wire room for execution. All order tickets will include:

- Buy or sell
- Name of security
- Number of shares or bonds
- Account name and number
- Account type (i.e., cash or margin)
- Price and time limits, if any
- Solicited or unsolicited
- Discretionary authority exercised or discretionary authority not exercised, if applicable
- Time stamp when entered, executed, changed, or canceled

EXECUTING AN ORDER

An important part of executing a customer's order lies in the operational procedures that route the order to the markets and handle trade input functions for the order once it has been executed. The brokerage firm assigns specific departments to handle all of the important functions of trade execution and input. The departments are:

- Sales department.
- Order room/wire room.
- Purchase and sales department.

- Margin department.
- Cashiering department.
- Custody department.
- Corporate action department

SALES DEPARTMENT

The sales department is where registered representatives interact with the investing public. Representatives work with individual and institutional investors, manage portfolios, make recommendations, and accept orders.

ORDER ROOM/WIRE ROOM

Once a representative has received an order from a client, the representative must present the order for execution to the order room. The order room will promptly route the order to the appropriate market for execution. Once the order has been executed, the order room will forward a confirmation of the execution to the registered representative and to the purchase and sales department.

PURCHASE AND SALES DEPARTMENT

Once the order has been executed, the purchase and sales department inputs the transaction to the customer's account. The purchase and sales department, sometimes called P&S, is also responsible for mailing confirmations to the customer and for all billing.

MARGIN DEPARTMENT

All transactions, regardless of the type of account, are sent through the margin department. The margin or credit department calculates the amount of money owed by the customer and the date when the money is due. The margin department will also calculate any amount due to a customer.

CASHIERING DEPARTMENT

The cashiering department handles all receipts and distributions of cash and securities. All securities and payments delivered from clients to the firm are processed by the cashiering department. The cashiering department will also issue checks to customers and, at the request of the margin department, forward certificates to the transfer agent.

CUSTODY DEPARTMENT

The custody department maintains physical control of customer and firm assets. The custody department, sometimes referred as the "cage," safeguards the physical securities in the firm's possession. Employees in the custody department will create stock records for each security in the firm's control and will record which securities belong to the firm and which securities belong to customers. The box count of physical securities will take place in the custody department, and any long or short differences in securities positions will be investigated by members of the custody department.

CORPORATE ACTION DEPARTMENT

The corporate action department handles communications between the investors and the issuers of securities. The corporate action department will mail proxies and prospectuses to beneficial owners of securities and handles mergers, reorganizations, and name changes relating to issuers. The corporate action department also manages the collection of interest and dividend payments.

BECOMING A STOCKHOLDER

Although some people purchase the shares directly from the corporation when the stock is offered to the public directly, most investors purchase the shares from other investors. These investor-to-investor transactions take place in the secondary market on the exchange or in the over-the-counter (OTC) market. Although the transaction in many cases only takes seconds to execute, trades actually take several days to fully complete. We will now review the important dates regarding transactions which are done for a regular-way settlement.

TRADE DATE

The trade date is the day when the order is actually executed. Although an order has been placed with a broker, it may not be executed on the same day. Certain types of orders may take several days or even longer to execute. A market order, however, will be executed as soon as it is presented to the market, making the trade date the same day the order was entered.

CHAPTER 2 Brokerage Office Procedures and Back-Office Operations

SETTLEMENT DATE

The buyer of a security actually becomes the owner of record on the settlement date. When an investor buys a security from another investor, the selling investor's name is removed from the security and the buyer's name is recorded as the new owner. Settlement date for regular way transactions is one business day after the trade date. This is known as T+1. All transactions in common stock, preferred stock, ETFs, corporate bonds, municipal bonds, government bonds and options settle the next business day following the trade date. Any trade done on a cash basis settles on the same day, regardless of the security involved in the transaction. Settlement dates are set by the Uniform Practice Code.

PAYMENT DATE

The payment date is the day when the buyer of the security has to have the money to the brokerage firm to pay for the purchase. Under industry rules, the payment dates for securities purchases are regulated by the Federal Reserve Board. Regulation T of The Securities Exchange Act of 1934 requires investors to pay for transactions within 2 business days after the settlement date. Looking at this based on the trade date, investors must pay for purchases by the third business day. This is known as T+3. Although many brokerage firms require their customers to have their money in to pay for their purchases sooner than the rules state, the customer has up to three business days to pay for the trade.

VIOLATION

If the customer fails to pay for the purchase within the three business days allowed, the customer is in violation of Regulation T. As a result, the brokerage firm will "sell out" and freeze the customer's account. On the fourth business day following the trade date, the brokerage firm will sell out the securities for which the customer failed to pay. The customer is responsible for any loss that may occur as a result of the sell out and the brokerage firm may sell out shares of another security in the investor's account in order to cover the loss. The brokerage firm then will freeze the customer's account, which means that the customer must deposit money up front for any purchases they want to make in the next 90 days. After the 90 days have expired, the customer is considered to have reestablished good credit and then may conduct business in the regular way and take up to three business days to pay for their trades. If a customer has a valid reason, a broker dealer may request an extension of time to pay for the trade. The broker dealer must submit the request to FINRA or the NYSE before the expiration of the third business day. A broker dealer may ignore a call for cash of $1,000 or less.

CLEARLY ERRONEOUS REPORTS

If a registered representative reports the execution of a trade to a customer and that report is clearly an error, then that report is not binding on the agent or the firm. The customer must accept the trade as it actually occurred, not as it was erroneously reported, so long as the transaction was in line with the terms of the order. A reporting error usually occurs verbally. However, occasionally the terms of the trade may be printed incorrectly on the customer's confirmation. If the terms of the trade are reported incorrectly on the customer's confirmation, the firm will send the customer a corrected confirmation with the terms of the trade as it actually occurred by mail or e-mail, depending on how the customer elects to receive confirmations. If a trade is executed and the trade is posted to the wrong account, the posting error will be corrected through the cancel and rebill process. Posting the trade to the wrong customer account or wrong account type, such as cash or margin, are typical errors. The cancel and rebill of the trade will generate confirmations for both accounts, and all corrections must be approved by a principal.

EXECUTION ERRORS

If a transaction is executed away from a customer's limit price or is executed for too many shares of stock, the customer in not obligated to accept the transaction. A registered representative who is informed of an execution error should immediately inform the principal of the error.

If the firm has executed an order at the wrong price, size, or side of the market or in the wrong security, the trade should promptly be moved into the firm's error account and offset as soon as possible. If the error involved a customer order, the order as it was executed will be journaled into the error account and subsequently posted to the customer's account in line with the customer's instructions. Execution errors for too many shares or away from a customer's limit price are examples of trades that will be moved to the error account. The representative or trader may move the trade to the error account and must notify the supervisor promptly; traders or representatives who move trades to the error account must fully document the error for review by the principal.

Once a security has been moved to the error account, neither the firm nor the agent may solicit trades to resolve the error and remove it from the error account. However, should the firm receive an unsolicited customer order during the time the trade is in the error account, the firm may use those shares to satisfy the unsolicited order.

> **EXAMPLE** A customer who maintains an account with a broker dealer enjoys working with his agent when making investment decisions. Virtually all of the customer's orders are executed by his registered rep once a trading decision has been made. The customer has owned 500 shares ABC Microchips for some time and his rep is on vacation in the week just prior to ABC releasing its earnings. Concerned about how the report will be received, the customer logs onto his account to sell his 500 shares of ABC. Not being familiar with the online trading platform, the customer enters the order to buy 500 shares of ABC instead of entering an order to sell 500 shares. The customer, who is now long 1,000 shares of ABC, should be advised to enter an offsetting order to sell 1,000 shares of ABC. Any losses as a result of the customer's error will be absorbed by the customer and are not the responsibility of the firm.

UNCONFIRMED TRADES

Although most transactions are automatically confirmed between the buying and selling firms through the Depository Trust & Clearing Corporation (DTCC), some trades are still input manually for comparison. It is during this process where the details of the trade reported or input by one party may differ from the details of the trade recognized by the confirming party. These cases can result in trades being unconfirmed. If the firm receiving the details of the trade does not know the terms of the trade as reported, there is an open trade or a "don't know" (DK). The confirming party is required to contact the reporting party by telephone promptly, advising the reporting party that the confirming party does not know the terms of the trade as reported. This phone contact can often lead to a resolution of the unrecognized terms. The issues that may have resulted in the DK may have been a simple input error, or typo. If, however, the terms of the trade remain unrecognized by the confirming party, the confirming party is required to send a written notice return receipt requested to the reporting party within one business day. The reporting broker dealer is then required to send the confirming broker dealer a written notice questioning if a trade did in fact occur between the two parties for the security in question within four business days. If the confirming broker dealer believes that a trade took place but under different terms and conditions, it must once again contact the reporting party by phone and send the reporting party a written notice within one business day failing to confirm the trade details as reported.

> **TAKENOTE!**
>
> If either the reporting broker dealer or the confirming broker dealer believes that the trade was clearly erroneous, it may cancel the trade by reporting it to FINRA and with FINRA's approval. FINRA may also from time to time elect to cancel trades that it deems clearly erroneous. Most of these cancellations will be the result of trades being reported that are clearly unrelated to the market price of a security.

SECURITIES SETTLEMENT OPTIONS

Regular way transactions in corporate stocks and bonds as well as municipal and government debt all settle the next business day, also known as trade date +1 or T+1. However, occasionally either party to the transaction may request an alternative settlement. Other settlement options include:

- Cash
- Seller's option
- Buyer's option
- RVP/DVP/COD

CASH

A transaction done on a cash basis settles the same day. A cash trade requires that the buyer have the funds available for payment and the seller have the securities available for delivery on the day the trade is executed. Cash trades executed prior to 2:00 p.m. EST settle by 2:30 p.m. EST. Trades executed after 2:00 p.m. EST settle within 30 minutes.

SELLER'S OPTION

A seller who wishes to lock in a sale price for the securities but who, for some reason, is not able to deliver the securities, may elect to specify a seller's option settlement. The seller may specify the date on which the securities will be delivered but may not deliver the securities any sooner than the second business day. If the seller wants to deliver the securities earlier than specified in the contract, the seller must give the buyer one day written notice of the intention to settle the trade early.

BUYER'S OPTION

Buyers may specify the date when they will make payment for the securities and accept delivery of the securities, much the same as a seller's option.

RVP/DVP/COD

Many trusts and other fiduciaries will not allow cash to be paid out until the securities they purchased are delivered. Alternatively, in the case of a sale, they will not allow the securities to be delivered until payment is received. A bona fide RVP/DVP account will allow the transaction to settle no sooner than regular way of T + 1 but no later than 35 calendar days. The account is given up to 35 days to settle the transaction. In the case of a purchase, the securities have to be registered in the buyer's name by the transfer agent and delivered. It is the responsibility of the party entering the order for a RVP/DVP account to assure the member executing the order that the bank is aware of the purchase and will make prompt payment when the certificates are presented. When entering an order to sell securities from an RVP/DVP account delivery must be made within 1 business day. Because all of the proceeds and securities are sent to customers the balance in an RVP / DVP account will be zero.

> **TAKENOTE!**
>
> If a broker dealer sells securities for a customer who has physical possession of the certificate, the broker dealer must establish a receivable for the customer's account and will credit the sales proceeds to the customer's account when the certificate is delivered.

WHEN-ISSUED SECURITIES

When a corporate issuer declares a stock split, the stock will trade in the marketplace on a when-issued basis, prior to the distribution of the new shares. Sellers of the stock during this time may sell the stock on a when-issued basis or may deliver the old securities with a due bill attached for the new shares. Corporate securities sold on a when-issued basis will normally settle two business days after the securities are issued. Municipal securities that are sold prior to the certificate being available for delivery are sold on a when-issued basis. The purchaser will receive a when-issued confirmation and a final confirmation two days prior to the certificate's delivery. If for some reason FINRA's Uniform Practice Committee does not determine the settlement date for when issued securities, the transaction will settle when determined by the seller provided that at least 1 business day notice has been provided to the buyer.

ACCRUED INTEREST

Most bonds pay interest semiannually, based on their maturity date. An investor who wishes to sell a bond between the interest payment dates will be owed the interest that has become due or that has accrued during the holding period. Investors who purchase the bonds between interest payment dates will receive the full semiannual interest payment on the bond's next interest payment date. As a result, the purchaser of the bonds must pay the seller the portion of the interest payment that has been earned, which is known as accrued interest. Most bonds trade with accrued interest, which is also known as "and interest." A bond may pay interest on only two dates during the month: the 1st and the 15th of the month. Interest on a new issue of bonds begins to accrue on the dated date. It is not unusual for an investor who purchases a new issue of debt securities to owe accrued interest to the issuer for bonds that are delivered after the dated date. Semiannual interest payments may be made on the 1st or 15th of the following months:

January and July
February and August
March and September
April and October
May and November
June and December

CHAPTER 2   Brokerage Office Procedures and Back-Office Operations

CALCULATING ACCRUED INTEREST

Interest on all bonds accrues from the last interest payment date up to, but not including, the settlement date. Accrued interest calculations for corporate and municipal securities use a 360-day year in which all months contain 30 days. To determine the amount of accrued interest due or owed for corporate and municipal issues, use the following formula:

principal × rate × time

(principal × interest rate) × (number of days/360) = accrued interest

To calculate the accrued interest for a government issue, use the actual number of calendar days in the month and a 365-day year.

CLOSE OUTS

In the case where the selling broker dealer fails to deliver the securities to the buying broker dealer, the buying broker dealer may close out the trade by purchasing the securities in the open market. This is known as a buy in, and the selling broker dealer will be responsible for any loss as a result of the buy in. Notice of the buying broker dealer's intention to buy in the selling broker dealer may be done no sooner than one business day past settlement or trade date plus 2 business days. The broker dealer executing the buy in must send notice to the contra party no later than noon, two business days prior to buying the broker dealer in. The first day that a broker dealer may buy in a security is trade date plus 4 business days. If a selling broker dealer delivers securities in good form to the buying broker dealer and the securities are rejected, the selling broker dealer may sell out the securities immediately. FINRA rules require the mandatory close out of certain naked short positions. If a firm or a customer has a naked short position and fails to deliver the subject securities 13 business days after the settlement date, the position is subject to a mandatory buy in on the 14th day. A special notation next to their symbol on the Nasdaq workstation identifies securities subject to the mandatory buy in. These securities are known as Threshold securities. To be classified as a threshold security the securities must have a net short position of at least 10,000 shares, and the net short position must be at least 0.5% of the issuer's outstanding stock. A full list of all subject securities is available online.

CUSTOMER CONFIRMATIONS

All customers must be sent a confirmation at or before the completion of the transaction. Industry rules consider the completion of the transaction to be the settlement date. For buyers of the security, it is the time when the payment is made. If the customer has the funds available in the account, it is the time when the funds are moved through a bookkeeping entry. For the seller, it is the time when the security is delivered. If the security is delivered prior to its due date, completion will occur when the payment is credited into the account. It is unlawful to settle a transaction without having sent a confirmation of the transaction to the customer. All customer confirmations must include:

- Customer's name and account number
- Description of the transaction, such as buy or sell
- Trade date and settlement date
- Number of shares, bonds, or units
- Price
- CUSIP number
- Amount due or owed
- Commission charged for agency transactions
- Markup charged for riskless principal transactions
- Markup charged for principal transactions in Nasdaq Global market and third-market trades (i.e., reported securities), as required under SEC Rule 10b-10
- Markup charged for Nasdaq Capital market securities stocks under FINRA rules
- Transactions executed for a customer on a net transaction basis only show the net price and not the markup or markdown
- Yield information for bonds
- If bonds or preferred stock is callable
- Whether the firm acted as an agent or principal
- Whether the firm acted as agent for the other side of the transaction, which is known as dual agency
- Amount of commission or markup or markdown
- If the firm makes a market in the security

CHAPTER 2 Brokerage Office Procedures and Back-Office Operations

- If there is a control relationship between the firm and the issuer of the security
- Information regarding where the transaction was executed
- If the firm received payment for executing the order with another firm
- The time of execution or a statement that the time will be furnished upon request

If the customer requests additional information within 30 days of the transaction, as detailed on the confirmation, the firm has five business days to provide it. If the customer's request is made after 30 days the firm may take up to 15 days to provide the information. If the firm receives payment for executing orders with other firms (payment for order flow), the firm must disclose this at the time the customer opens the account and annually thereafter.

RULES FOR GOOD DELIVERY

All securities delivered by a customer or another broker dealer must be in good condition and must:

- Be signed by all owners, and all owners must be alive.
- Be in the correct denominations, such as number of shares or par value of bonds.
- Have all attachments.
- Be accompanied by a uniform delivery ticket.

The owner of a security must endorse the certificate at the time of sale to ensure its negotiability or sign a stock or bond power, also known as a power of substitution. The stock power, when attached to the certificate, will make it negotiable and includes an irrevocable power of attorney. All signatures must be accepted by the transfer agent. To ensure that the transfer agent accepts the signatures on certificates delivered by NYSE member firms, the NYSE started the Medallion Signature Guarantee Program, which allows NYSE members to stamp the certificates with a medallion rather than sign them. This stamp ensures that the transfer agent will accept the certificates for transfer and provides indemnification insurance for fraud. Medallion Program members pay to participate in the program.

Examples of invalid signatures are:

- The signature of a minor
- The signature of a deceased person
- The signature of only one owner if jointly registered
- A forged signature

A member firm may also use the medallion seal to effect the change of ownership for an account, the gifting of shares and for estate matters for the account of a deceased client.

DELIVERY OF ROUND LOTS

Stock certificates must be delivered in denominations that are in round lots or in lots that easily add up to create round lots. Stock certificates for odd lots are cleared separately.

EXAMPLE A customer sells 200 shares of XYZ. The following certificates are considered good delivery:

- One certificate for 200 shares
- Two certificates for 100 shares
- Two certificates for 60 shares and two certificates for 40 shares
- Twenty certificates for 10 shares

The following is not good delivery:

- Five certificates for 40 shares
- One certificate for 130 shares

Certificates that cannot be easily added up to 100 shares are not good delivery. If the selling broker dealer delivers a certificate for a portion of the trade and the remaining shares will add up to one round lot or multiples of round lots, then the buying broker dealer must accept the partial delivery.

DELIVERY OF BOND CERTIFICATES

Bond certificates delivered between broker dealers must be in par values of $1,000 or $5,000 and must be in bearer form unless clearly identified as otherwise at the time of the trade. Partially called bonds are not considered to be good delivery between broker dealers. However, bonds subject to a total call are good delivery. If a bond is delivered with a coupon missing, the buying broker dealer will deduct the value of the coupon payment from the amount delivered to the seller. Municipal bonds delivered without the legal opinion attached must be identified as being traded ex legal in order to be considered good delivery.

REJECTION OF DELIVERY

The buying firm may reject the delivery of securities from the selling member if:

- The certificates are mutilated.
- The certificates are not in the proper denominations.
- All attachments are not present.
- The signatures are invalid.
- The signatures have not been guaranteed.
- The securities are delivered prior to settlement.
- The wrong securities are delivered.
- If the specific bond being delivered has been called and was not identified as being called at the time of the trade.

RECLAMATION

A broker dealer may return or demand the return of securities previously accepted for delivery through a process known as reclamation. A broker dealer using the reclamation process must make the demand by submitting a Uniform Reclamation Form to the contra broker dealer. The reasons for rejecting delivery listed above are also valid reasons for instituting the reclamation process.

MARKING TO THE MARKET

A broker dealer who has an open contractual commitment to another broker dealer will monitor the market value of the securities involved relative to the contract or trade price. This process is known as marking to the market. A broker dealer who is partially unsecured can issue a call or demand for more collateral. If a firm sends a mark to the market demand to another broker dealer, the demand must be met promptly.

> **EXAMPLE** If a broker dealer borrows $20,000 worth of securities for a customer who is executing a short sale for $20,000 worth of ABC, the borrowing broker dealer would have to deposit $20,000 with the lending broker dealer as collateral for the securities. If the market value of ABC increases to $25,000, the broker dealer who loaned the securities may demand that the borrowing broker dealer deposit an additional $5,000 as collateral. Alternatively, if the market value of ABC had fallen to $15,000, the borrowing broker dealer may demand a return of $5,000.

CUSTOMER ACCOUNT STATEMENTS

A customer must receive a statement every month in which there is activity in the account. All customers must receive account statements at least quarterly when there has been no activity in the account. Examples of activity include:

- Purchases and sales
- Dividend and interest received
- Interest charged
- Addition or withdrawal of cash or securities

Customer account statements must show:

- All positions in the account.
- All activity since the last statement.
- All credit and debit balances.

>  **TAKENOTE!**
>
> Customers who have accounts containing penny stocks must receive monthly statements showing the value of each penny stock position.

Brokerage firms that carry customer accounts are required to disclose their financial condition to their clients by sending them a balance sheet every 6 months or on the request of a customer with cash or securities on deposit.

DIVIDEND DISTRIBUTION

If a corporation decides to pay a dividend to its common stockholders, it may not discriminate as to who receives the dividend. The dividend must be paid to all common stockholders of record. Existing stockholders do not need to notify the company that they are entitled to receive the pending dividend—it will be sent to them automatically. However, new purchasers of the stock may or may not be entitled to receive the dividend, depending on when they purchased the stock relative to when the dividend is going to be distributed. Let's now examine the dividend distribution process.

DECLARATION DATE

The declaration date is the day that the board of directors decides to pay a dividend to common stockholders of record. The declaration date is the starting point for the entire dividend process. The company must notify the regulators at the exchange or FINRA, depending where the stock trades, at least 10 business days prior to the record date.

EX-DIVIDEND DATE

The ex-dividend date or the ex date is the first day when purchasers of the security are no longer entitled to receive the dividend that the company has declared for payment. Stated another way, the ex date is the first day when the stock trades without (ex) the dividend attached. The exchange or FINRA set the ex date for the stock, based on the record date determined and announced by the corporation's board of directors. Because it takes one business day for a trade to settle, the ex date is always the same day as the record date announced by the corporation.

RECORD DATE

The record date is the day when investors must have their name recorded on the stock certificate in order to be entitled to receive the dividend that was declared by the board of directors. Stockholders whose names are on the stock certificates (owners of record) will be entitled to receive the dividend. The investor must have purchased the stock before the ex-dividend date in order to be an owner of record on the record date. The record date is determined by the corporation's board of directors and is used to determine which shareholders will receive the dividend.

PAYMENT DATE

This is the day when the corporation actually distributes the dividend to shareholders and it completes the dividend process. The payment date is controlled and set by the board of directors of the corporation and is usually 4 weeks following the record date.

STOCK PRICE AND THE EX-DIVIDEND DATE

It is important to note that the value of the stock prior to the ex-dividend date reflects the value of the stock with the dividend. On the ex-dividend date, the stock is now trading without the dividend attached, and new purchasers will not receive the dividend that had been declared for payment. As a result, the stock price will be adjusted down on the ex-dividend date in an amount equal to the dividend.

EXAMPLE   TRY declares a $.20 dividend payable to shareholders of record as of Wednesday, August 21. The ex-dividend date will be the same day as the record date. In this case, the ex date will also be Wednesday, August 21. If TRY closed on Tuesday, August 20 at $24 per share, the stock would open at $23.80 on Wednesday.

Sunday	Monday	Tuesday	Wednesday	Thursday	Friday	Saturday
				1	2	3
4	5	6	7	8	9	10
11	12	13	14	15	16	17
18	19	20	**21**	22	23	24
25	26	27	28	29	30	31

Dividends for ordinary income earners are subject to a tax rate of 15%. Dividends for high income earners are subject to a tax rate of 20%.

DIVIDEND DISBURSEMENT PROCESS

The corporation's dividend disbursement agent is responsible for the distribution of dividends and will send the dividends to the shareholders of record on the record date. Most investors, for convenience, have their securities held in the name of the broker dealer, also known as the street name. As a result, the dividend disbursement agent will send the dividends directly to the broker dealer. The broker dealer's dividend department will collect the dividends and distribute them to the beneficial owners. The dividend department also handles:

- Stock dividends.
- Stock splits.
- Bond interest payments.
- Rights distributions.
- Warrant distributions.

 TAKENOTE!

It is fair and reasonable for a brokerage firm to charge a fee for the collection of dividends and other services as long as the fee is not excessive and is in line with the fees charged by similar firms.

DUE BILLS

Should the wrong party receive a dividend or any other type of distribution, the buying broker dealer whose customer is owed the dividend will send a due bill to the selling broker for the amount of the dividend owed. In most cases, this would happen when the buyer purchased the stock just prior to the ex date and the security was delivered late to the buyer.

PROXIES

Common stockholders have the right to vote on major corporate issues. Most stockholders, however, do not have the time to attend the meetings and must therefore vote using an absentee ballot, known as a proxy. The Securities

Exchange Act of 1934 requires that all corporations that distribute proxies solicit votes from their shareholders. The corporation will send proxies to the shareholders of record. Stockholders who have their securities held in street name will have the proxies forwarded to them by the brokerage firm. The brokerage firm will then cast the beneficial shareholder's votes as indicated on the proxy as the shareholder of record. Proxies that have been signed and returned without indicating how to vote must be voted in accordance with the issuer's management's recommendation. If a shareholder fails to return the proxy to the member at least 10 days prior to the annual meeting, the member may vote the shares as it sees fit, as long as the matter is not of major importance. If the vote concerns a major issue, such as a merger, the member may never cast the votes. Member firms are required to forward proxies and other corporate communications, such as annual and quarterly reports, to the beneficial owner, and the issuer is required to reimburse the member for reasonable expenses. Brokerage firms may disclose a shareholder's name and contact information to the corporation so that the shareholder may receive proxies and corporate reports directly, if the investor does not object. Investors who allow their names to be disclosed to the corporation are known as nonobjecting beneficial owners. Investors who do not want their information disclosed to the corporation are known as objecting beneficial owners.

OPERATIONS PROFESSIONALS COVERED PERSONS

FINRA has identified three key types of employees who meet the definition of a covered person for purposes of the Series 99 exam. A covered person is any one of the following:

- A member of senior management who supervises or controls covered functions
- Department managers empowered by senior management to oversee covered functions, as well as employees who perform covered functions
- Employees with authority to commit firm capital or agree to the terms of a contract (usually the terms of a trade) as part of a covered function

A covered person who performs a covered function will be required to register as an operations professional. The covered functions are as follows:

- Margin clerk
- Stock loan and stock lending
- Customer account clerk/client on boarding

- Producing or maintaining trade confirmations and account statements
- Handling receipt and delivery of cash and securities
- Handling bank reconciliations including custody
- Performing settlement functions
- Performing prime brokerage services
- Assisting in the preparation of financial reports
- Assisting in the creation or maintenance of general ledgers
- Assisting in financial control functions
- Performing sweep functions for free cash balances
- Performing buy ins and sell outs or segregation duties
- Approving or designing of pricing or valuation models
- Approving trading or validation system for covered functions

In order to be subject to the registration and continuing education requirements of the Series 99 exam, the person must meet the definition of a covered person and perform a covered function. If a person performs a covered function but does not meet the definition of a covered person, he or she is not required to become Series 99 registered.

OPERATIONAL RED FLAGS

Operational personnel should pay particular attention to the activities of brokers, traders, customers, and producing branch office mangers in an effort to identify potential red flags. Some examples to look out for are:

- A producing branch office manager who seems to be submitting a large number of transactions to be canceled from one account and rebilled to another may be showing favoritism to his clients over the clients of the other brokers in the office.
- A registered representative engaging in this practice may also be showing preferential treatment to one customer over another or may be trying to park stock.
- Customers who frequently fail to pay or require extensions to pay for securities may be engaging in free riding.

- A customer who seems to be submitting a large number of requests to journal assets to seemingly unrelated accounts or who engages in a pattern of trading that seems to make no economic sense may be engaging in money laundering.
- A trader or registered representative who seems to be moving a large number of transactions into the firm's error account may be parking stock or trying to shift losses for unprofitable trades to the firm.
- A history of 1035 exchanges for annuity contracts may constitute churning.

CHAPTER 2

Pretest

BROKERAGE OFFICE PROCEDURES AND BACK-OFFICE OPERATIONS

1. When hiring a new employee, which of the following is NOT required of the principal?
    a. The principal must confirm the agent's employment for the last 3 years.
    b. The principal must obtain a U5 directly from the employee.
    c. The principal must attest to the employee's character.
    d. The principal must sign Form U4 prior to submission.

2. As it relates to influencing the employees of member firms, which of the following are true?
    I. The gift may be given to the employee.
    II. A record of the gift must be maintained by the employing firm.
    III. The gift must be given to the employer for distribution.
    IV. A contractual relationship is excluded from the rule.
    a. I and IV
    b. II and III
    c. II, III, and IV
    d. I, II, and IV

3. All of the following personnel are exempt from the registration requirement, EXCEPT:
   a. A manager who acts as a liaison between the firm and the board of directors.
   b. A receptionist who receives calls from clients and takes messages for agents.
   c. The firm's Web designer, who posts information about market conditions on the firm's website.
   d. A sales assistant who occasionally accepts a customer's order.

4. As it relates to securities held in street name, which of the following are true?
   I. The corporation will send proxies to the broker dealer.
   II. The corporation will not reimburse the broker dealer for forwarding the proxies.
   III. The broker dealer may vote blank proxies any way it wishes.
   IV. A shareholder who attends the annual meeting will have their proxies voided.
   a. I and III
   b. II and III
   c. I and IV
   d. II and IV

5. A broker dealer that does not carry customer accounts is required to do all of the following, EXCEPT:
   a. Clear all trades on an omnibus basis.
   b. Forward all securities to the carrying firm.
   c. Forward all checks to the carrying firm.
   d. In the case of market making, have the carrying firm stand behind all trades.

6. Which of the following is NOT a reason to reject delivery?
   a. The signatures are not guaranteed.
   b. The customer has determined that the investment is unsuitable.
   c. The certificate is unclear.
   d. A bond is missing a coupon.

7. A security has been delivered late to the buying member after the record date for a dividend distribution. Which of the following are true?
    I. The seller will keep the dividend.
    II. The buyer will be owed the dividend.
    III. The buying member will send a due bill.
    IV. The selling member will receive the dividend.
    a. I and II
    b. II and III
    c. I only
    d. II, III, and IV

8. A customer who purchased 1,000 shares of XYZ on margin 2 months ago and has not executed any order since must:
    a. Receive a statement this month.
    b. Not receive a statement this month.
    c. Have received a statement for the last 2 months only.
    d. Have received a statement for the last 2 months and must receive one this month as well.

9. A brokerage firm may charge a fee for which of the following?
    I. The safekeeping of securities
    II. The collection of dividends
    III. Lack of activity in the account
    IV. The clipping of coupons
    a. I and II
    b. II and III
    c. I, II, and IV
    d. I, II, III, and IV

10. A wealthy customer has just made a purchase in his margin account. There are substantial assets in the account. The brokerage firm, as a courtesy to the client, may ignore a call for cash for up to:
    a. $1,000.
    b. $10,000.
    c. $5,000.
    d. $500.

CHAPTER 3

Record Keeping, Financial Requirements, and Clearing

> **INTRODUCTION**
>
> All broker dealers are required to prepare and maintain reports and records according to industry regulations. The content and timing of the reports depends on the nature of the report. SEC Rule 17 a-3 sets forth the requirements for broker dealer reporting, timing, and content. SEC Rule 17a-4 sets the retention requirements for those records. Records subject to these rules must be maintained anywhere from 3 years to the life of the firm. Records that are required to be maintained must be readily accessible for the first 2 years. Under SEC Rule 17a-3, a significant number of records must be filed and maintained by broker dealers. The following is a list of those records and their definitions.

BLOTTERS

Blotters are records of original entry and must reflect transactions as of the trade date. Blotters must be prepared no later than the following business day, or T + 1. This would include a historical account of all the daily transactions, such as:

- Purchases and sales of securities.
- Receipts and disbursements of cash.
- Receipts and deliveries of securities.

GENERAL LEDGER

The general ledger reflects the firm's assets, liabilities, income and expenses, and capital accounts. The firm's trial balance and other financial reports can be prepared from this to show the broker dealer's financial condition. It must be prepared monthly.

CUSTOMER ACCOUNTS

Customer accounts are itemized records of each cash and margin account for each customer. This reflects all purchases, sales, receipts, and deliveries of cash and securities for each customer as well as the new account form and margin agreement, if applicable.

SUSPENSE ACCOUNT

The suspense account is an account used to hold open items for which there are unresolved issues or problems. Open items such as unconfirmed trades, fails to receive, and returned deliveries would all be placed in the suspense account until the issues are resolved. The word "suspense" must appear in the account title, and suspense account records must be kept by the firm for 6 years total, with 2 years readily accessible.

SUBSIDIARY (SECONDARY) RECORDS

These are records prepared from the blotter, including:

- Securities in transfer: Securities in the process of being transferred into a customer's name.
- Dividends and interest received: A record of all dividends and interest due to the customer (long) or payable by the customer (short).
- Securities borrowed and loaned: Records of the broker dealer's borrowing or loaning of securities to complete their transactions.
- Monies borrowed, monies loaned: This also includes any collateral used in connection with the loan.

- Securities failed to receive or deliver: These records must show the date due as well as the date received or delivered.

SECURITIES POSITION BOOK (LEDGER) STOCK RECORD

A securities position book or stock record is a record of the long and short position in each security, whether carried for the account of the broker dealer or for the account of a customer. The location of these securities must also be maintained.

ORDER TICKETS

An order ticket, also known as an order memorandum, is a record detailing the terms and conditions of an order to purchase or sell a security. Records must be maintained whether or not the order is executed.

CONFIRMATIONS AND NOTICES

A confirmation is a notice of the terms and conditions of an executed order. Copies of all confirmations and notices of other debits and credits must be maintained.

MONTHLY TRIAL BALANCES AND NET CAPITAL COMPUTATIONS

Monthly trial balances and net capital computations serve as a check on the current status and accuracy of the firm's ledger account and financial condition. Firms are required to file their net capital computations with regulators via the FOCUS form.

EMPLOYMENT APPLICATIONS

A copy of the registration application or Form U4 will suffice as an employment application. Applications must be approved in writing by an authorized representative of the member.

RECORDS REQUIRED TO BE MAINTAINED FOR 3 YEARS

The following is a list or records that must be maintained by the firm for 3 years:

- Retail communication
- Institutional communication
- All changes to the text and content on the firm's website
- Order tickets
- Confirmations
- Option records
- FOCUS reports
- Monthly trial balances
- Subsidiary ledgers
- Long and short securities differences
- Compliance and policy and procedure manuals (kept after changes)
- U4, U5, fingerprints, and employment applications for terminated employees

RECORDS REQUIRED TO BE MAINTAINED FOR 6 YEARS

The following is a list of records that must be maintained by the firm for 6 years:

- Blotters
- General ledgers
- Customer ledgers
- Customer account records
- Stock records/position records
- Suspense account records

RECORDS REQUIRED TO BE MAINTAINED FOR THE LIFE OF THE FIRM

The following records must be maintained for the life of the firm:

- Articles of incorporation
- Corporate stock certificate books
- Minute books from meetings of the board of directors

- Partnership records
- Form BD

OTHER RECORD RETENTION REQUIREMENTS

In addition to the standard 3-year, 6-year, and lifetime record retention requirements certain other records have their own requirements. The various records and requirements are as follows:

- Exception reports from clearing firms – 18 months
- Written customer complaints – 4 years
- Suspicious Activity Reports (SAR) – 5 years
- Information collected to verify customer identity – 5 years
- Currency transaction reports CTR Form 112 – 5 years

The following chart outlines SEC Rule 17a-3 (records that must be kept) and SEC Rule 17a-4 (how long records must be kept):

SEC RULE 17a-3 Records that must be kept current by broker dealers	SEC RULE 17a-4 Time period records must be preserved	SEC RULE 17a-4 Time period records must be kept in a readily accessible place
Subsidiary records	3 years	First 2 years
Trial balance	3 years	First 2 years
Employment applications for associated persons	Until 3 years after person has terminated employment	Until 3 years after person has terminated employment
Order tickets	3 years	First 2 years
Checkbooks, bank statements	3 years	First 2 years
Blotters (records of original entry)	6 years	First 2 years
General ledger	6 years	First 2 years
Security position records (each long and short position)	6 years	First 2 years
Customer ledgers	6 years	First 2 years
Director's minutes	Life of enterprise	First 2 years
Stock certificate books	Life of enterprise	First 2 years
Partnership articles and articles of incorporation	Life of enterprise	First 2 years

SEC Rule 17a-3 requires that the records of a broker dealer be kept current. The following chart summarizes guidelines for what SEC defines as current:

Records	Definition of Current
General ledger	Posted at least monthly no later than 10 business days after month end
Blotter or other original entry records	Prepared no later than business day after trade date
Securities position record	Posted no later than business day after settlement date
Customer purchase and sale transaction	Recorded in their accounts no later than settlement date
Trial balance and capital computation	Prepared no later than 10 business days after month end
Securities failed to deliver or receive ledger	Posted no later than second business day after settlement date
Money borrowed and loaned ledger	Posted no later than second business day after securities are forwarded to transfer agent
Securities transfer ledger	Posted no later than second business day after securities are forwarded to transfer agent
Long and short security differences	Recorded in ledger account no later than seven business days after discovery
Securities borrowed and loaned	Posted no later than two business days after movement of securities
Order tickets	Prepared prior to order execution
Option records	No later than the business day after the option position is open
Confirmations	No later than the business day after the trade date

REQUIREMENT TO PREPARE AND MAINTAIN RECORDS UNDER SEC 17A-3 AND 17A-4

A broker dealer that introduces all of its transactions on a fully disclosed basis is exempt from the preparation and maintenance requirement for most records. The carrying or clearing broker dealer that maintains custody of clients' cash and securities is required to prepare and maintain the records relating customer accounts and securities. If the broker dealer clears its transactions through a bank, the bank must provide the introducing broker with a statement that the records relating to the customers' accounts are the property of the broker dealer. The clearing bank must also provide written notice to the SEC that the records are available to be inspected. If a broker dealer clears its transactions on an omnibus basis, the introducing member will be responsible for the preparation and maintenance of most records. Broker dealers may store records in electronic format provided that they inform their Designated Examining Authority 90 days prior to implementing the electronic system.

FINANCIAL REQUIREMENTS

All broker dealers are required to maintain a minimum level of financial solvency known as net capital. A broker dealer's net capital requirement is contingent upon the type of securities business the firm is engaged in. The SEC sets forth the rules regarding net capital for broker dealers and sets requirements for:

- Determining a firm's net capital.
- Minimum net capital.
- Subordinated loans.
- Maximum aggregate indebtedness.
- Allowable aggregate indebtedness relative to net capital.

General securities broker dealers carrying customer accounts must meet a financial requirement or minimum net capital of $250,000. A broker dealer who carries customer accounts is known as a clearing broker dealer. A clearing broker dealer must be a member of both the Depository Trust & Clearing Corp/DTCC and the National Securities Clearing Corp/NSCC and is qualified to:

- Settle transactions for customer accounts.
- Hold funds and securities.
- Handle variable annuity or mutual fund transactions by wire order or through application.
- Act as market makers for corporate securities.
- Be members of syndicates for any type of underwriting.

Broker dealers who generally do not carry customer accounts have a financial responsibility or minimum net capital of $50,000. These are known as fully disclosed or introducing broker dealers. They:

- May not carry customer accounts or hold customer cash or securities.
- Can only deal in underwritings on a best efforts or all-or-none (AON) basis. If involved in a firm commitment underwriting, the net capital must increase to $100,000.
- Must forward all customers' securities and funds to a carrying broker dealer, with checks made payable to the carrying broker dealer or escrow agent.
- May handle variable annuity or mutual fund transactions by wire order or through application.
- May not act as a market maker.
- Can handle transactions for the firm's personal account.

Broker dealers who engage exclusively in the sale of redeemable shares of registered investment companies and variable contracts, or who do not receive customer cash and securities, or who engage only in transactions relating to a merger or acquisition or direct participation programs, have a financial responsibility of $5,000. These broker dealers:

- May not carry customer accounts or hold customer cash or securities.
- May not receive customer cash or securities.
- May sell variable annuities and mutual funds by application only. No wire orders.
- May not participate in any underwriting.

TAKE**NOTE!**

A broker dealer that handles mutual fund orders on a wire basis must have minimum net capital of $25,000.

The net capital requirements for broker dealers who engage in the sale of options outside of a registered national securities exchange or association is $250,000.

Market makers in OTC securities must maintain net capital in an amount equal to the greater of the following two requirements:

- $100,000

OR

- $2,500 for each security it makes a market with a bid price more than $5, and $1,000 for each such security with a bid price of $5 or less.

The following chart summarizes the minimum dollar amount of net capital for broker dealers:

Type of Broker Dealer	Minimum Net Capital
Mergers and acquisitions or direct participation programs	$ 5,000
Investment companies on a subscription basis only	$ 5,000
Introducing firm that does not receive customer funds or securities	$ 5,000
Purchases investment company securities on a wire basis or sells stock for customers whose proceeds are immediately invested in open-end investment companies	$ 25,000
Introducing firm receiving customer funds or securities for immediate delivery to clearing firm	$ 50,000
Participating in best efforts or all-or-none underwritings only	$ 50,000
Introducing dealer executing more than 10 proprietary trades per year	$ 100,000
Participating in firm commitment underwritings	$ 100,000
Carries customer accounts but does not retain custody of customer funds or securities (K2i firms)	$ 100,000
Market makers	$ 100,000
General securities broker dealer carrying customer accounts (carrying firm)	$ 250,000
Acts as a CQS market maker in listed securities	$ 500,000
Acts as an executing broker for prime brokerage transactions or is a block positioner	$ 1,000,000
Acts as an executing broker for prime brokerage transactions or as a block positioner	$ 1,000,000
Maintains a joint back office between two or more broker dealers for carrying or clearing accounts	$25,000,000

BOX COUNTS

All broker dealers who maintain custody of securities must conduct a quarterly count of the securities they have in their possession or control. Securities that are considered to be in a broker dealer's control are securities in transfer or transit. The quarterly counts must be made no less than 2 months apart and not more than 4 months apart. If a broker dealer's physical count reveals fewer certificates than are recorded on its books, the firm has a short securities difference. A short securities difference will result in a deduction from the broker dealer's net capital if not resolved in seven business days from the time of discovery. On the eighth day from discovery, the broker dealer will have to take a haircut equal to 25 percent of the current market value of the security. After 28 days, the broker dealer must deduct 100 percent of the value of the short securities difference from its net capital. If the short securities difference is not resolved within 45 days the short securities difference must be bought in. If the broker dealer's physical count reveals more certificates than it has on its records the broker dealer has a long securities difference. A long securities difference has no effect on a broker dealer's net capital.

MISSING AND LOST SECURITIES

The Securities Information Center (SIC) is in charge of keeping reports for all lost and stolen securities. SEC Rule 17f-1 outlines the requirements for reporting an inquiry with respect to missing, lost, counterfeit, or stolen securities. When it is believed criminal activity was involved, the theft must be reported within one business day of discovery to the SIC, the registered transfer agent for the issue, and the Federal Bureau of Investigation (FBI). When criminal activity is not believed to be involved and securities have been missing or lost for at least two business days, a report must be made on the third business day to the SIC and the registered transfer agent for the issue. When securities are found to be counterfeit, a report must be made within one business day of discovery to the SIC, the registered transfer agent for the issue, and the FBI. If securities are discovered to be missing after an internal audit or box count, and no criminal activity is suspected, a report must be filed with the SIC within 10 business days of discovery or as soon as the securities can be identified by certificate number. When stolen, missing, lost, or counterfeit securities have been recovered, the appropriate authority must be notified within one business day of the recovery. Required inquiries must be made by the SIC whenever securities come into the possession of a reporting institution, unless:

- The institution compares the securities against bondholder or stockholder lists as part of its business.
- The securities certificate came directly from the issuer or the issuer's agent.

- The securities certificate is received from another reporting institution and is registered in the name of the customer or was previously sold to the customer and verified through internal records.
- The transaction did not exceed a face value of $10,000 for bonds or a market value of $10,000 for stocks.
- The securities certificate is received as part of a normal drop by the reporting institution.

The SIC will accept reports on securities not listed above.
The following securities are not subject to the above provisions:

- Securities without Committee on Uniform Securities Identification Procedures (CUSIP) numbers
- Bond coupons
- Uncertified securities
- A securities issue that is represented by a single master certificate registered in the name of the clearing agency (a global securities issue)
- Securities that do not provide negotiable securities certificates

THE CUSTOMER PROTECTION RULE

The customer protection rule ensures that customer funds held by a broker dealer are maintained in safe areas of the business related to servicing its customers or are deposited in a special reserve bank account. The broker dealer must make the following monthly computation to determine the amount required to be on deposit in its special reserve bank account for the exclusive benefit of the customers:

(credit items − debit items) × 105% = the amount to be deposited in the special reserve account

If the broker dealer computes weekly rather than monthly, only 100% of the credit excess must be deposited in the reserve account. If the broker dealer computes weekly rather than monthly, only 100% of the credit excess must be deposited in the reserve account. A broker dealer must compute weekly if at any time its aggregate indebtedness exceeds 800% of its net capital or if its aggregate funds owed to customers exceeds $1,000,000. Weekly reporting must continue until neither condition occurs for four successive weeks. The required deposit into the special reserve account must be made by 10:00 a.m. Tuesday two business days after the weekly calculation is made. Money placed in the special reserve account is deducted from the broker dealer's aggregate indebtedness. The special reserve bank account may not be used for any of the following purposes:

- To secure a loan to the broker dealer
- Be subject to a lien by a bank against the broker dealer
- Be used to allow bank offset privileges against other accounts of the broker dealer

Also note the following relating to the special reserve account:

- It may only contain cash or U.S. government securities.
- If debit items exceed credit items, no deposit need be made.
- The funds contained in the account reduce the amount of the broker dealer's aggregate indebtedness.
- A broker dealer may withdraw excess beyond required deposit in special reserve account.
- A broker dealer must buy-in all short security differences within 45 calendar days after the date of discovery.

> TAKENOTE!
>
> A broker dealer must obtain notification from the bank that it is informed of these restrictions and that money is being held for the exclusive benefit of customers of the broker dealer.

Exemptions from SEC Rule 15c3-3 are listed under subsections (k)(2)(A) and (k)(2)(B) and are referred to by those section names in the trade. A (k)(2)(A) broker dealer exemption is available if the broker dealer:

- Does not carry margin accounts.
- Promptly transmits all customer funds and delivers all securities received in trade.
- Does not hold funds or securities for clients.

A (k)(2)(B) broker dealer exemption is available if the broker dealer:

- Clears all transactions with a clearing broker dealer.
- Promptly transmits all client funds and securities to a clearing broker dealer who carries the accounts and maintains the books.

The FOCUS report is the fundamental reporting form used by broker dealers to report financial conditions to the regulatory agencies. It is filed electronically and has the following parts:

- FOCUS Part I is a summary of key financial ratios and numbers that is filed monthly within 10 business days after the end of the month by broker dealers who carry customer accounts.
- FOCUS Part II is a balance sheet, income statement, and net capital computation that is filed quarterly. Any broker dealers who clear or carry customer accounts must file Part II within 17 business days from the end of each calendar quarter.
- FOCUS Part IIA is a less comprehensive version than Part II that is filed quarterly. Any broker dealer who does not carry or clear customer accounts must only file FOCUS Part IIA within 17 business days after the end of each calendar quarter.

Rule 17a-5 also requires broker dealers who carry customer accounts to furnish customers with financial statements twice a year. One will be an audited financial statement, which must also be filed with the SEC not more than 60 days after the date of the financial statements. This report must be sent to customers within 45 days of when the report was sent to the SEC. The other report will be an unaudited statement sent approximately 6 months later. Current balance sheets must also be made available to bona fide customers at their request. Broker dealers must also furnish customers with the following information within 105 days after the date of the audited report:

- An unconsolidated balance sheet with appropriate notes prepared in accordance with generally accepted accounting principles
- A statement including the amount of the firm's net capital and its required net capital

- A statement indicating the existence of any material inadequacies in the accounting system, the internal accounting control, or the procedures for safeguarding securities
- A statement indicating that Part I of the FOCUS report is available for copying at the principal office of the broker dealer and at the regional office of the SEC

Reports explaining the situation must be sent to the SEC and FINRA if any of the following circumstances occur (within 15 days of occurrence):

- The services of an accountant are contracted.
- The services of an accountant are terminated.
- A change in the firm's fiscal year. The reason for the change must be supplied and the request must be approved.
- An extension of time is needed to file an annual report.

> **TAKENOTE!**
>
> All firms are required to file an audited FOCUS report II or IIA within 60 days of its year-end in hard copy. The firm must submit two copies to the principal office of the SEC, one copy to the SEC regional office, and one copy to FINRA. A firm may request a maximum extension of 30 days to file the annual report. Under no conditions may the report be filed more than 90 days after year-end. All accountants who provide audit services to broker dealers must be independent from and not under the control of the broker dealer.

FINRA FINANCIAL REQUIREMENTS

FINRA monitors the financial condition of member firms very closely. If FINRA feels that the financial or operational condition of a firm is compromised or is experiencing difficulty, FINRA may take action by restricting or reducing the firm's business. FINRA may require the firm to stop expanding its business if the following conditions persist for more than 15 business days: if its net capital is less than 150% of its minimum required net capital or if AI:NC is greater than 10:1. FINRA may also require the member to reduce its business if the following conditions exist for more than 15 business days: the firm's net capital is less than 125% of its minimum required net capital or AI:NC is greater than 12:1. Indications that the firm is experiencing financial difficulty include the following:

- The firm cannot settle transactions in a timely manner
- The firm cannot demonstrate that it is in compliance with the net capital or customer protection requirements
- The firm fails to maintain its books and records
- The firm's excess net capital has fallen 25% in the last 2 months or 30% in the last 3 months

FINRA may require the firm to:

- File special financial reports.
- Close out or reduce inventory positions.
- Deliver free credit balances and fully paid securities to customers.
- Not open new customer accounts.
- Close branch offices.
- Execute unsolicited orders only.
- Execute liquidating transactions only.
- Restrict payments to officers.
- Undergo an independent audit.
- Eliminate or discontinue unsecured loans.

FIDELITY BONDS

FINRA member firms are required to obtain a fidelity bond that covers the firm's officers and employees. The purpose of the fidelity bond is to protect the firm's customers from:

- Fraudulent acts.
- Loss of securities.
- Check forgery.
- Securities forgery.

The fidelity bond does not cover losses incurred as a result of errors or omissions. The required amount of the fidelity bond is based on the firm's net capital. The minimum required fidelity bond coverage is 120% of the firm's net capital for firms whose required net capital is less than $600,000 with a $25,000 minimum. The minimum fidelity bond requirement is based on 120% of the firm's highest net capital requirement during the preceding 12 months. All firms must review their fidelity bond coverage annually and must make any required changes to the coverage within 60 days of the anniversary date of the bond's issuance. For firms whose minimum required net capital is greater than $600,000, the minimum required fidelity bond coverage is $750,000. The minimum required coverage increases to a maximum of $5 million for a firm whose minimum required net capital is greater than $12 million. The maximum allowable deductible is 25% of the bond's coverage.

CARRYING OF CUSTOMER ACCOUNTS

Not all brokerage firms maintain physical possession of the customers' cash and securities. A brokerage firm that maintains the account of its customers and holds their cash and securities is known as a carrying firm, or a self-clearing member. A broker dealer may find it easier to have another member provide the clearing and custodial functions for its customers' accounts. This type of broker dealer is known as an introducing broker dealer. Anytime a clearing agreement is executed or amended it must be sent to FINRA for review. The clearing member must notify the introducing member of the reports it offers clearing members to monitor customer accounts when it executes the agreement and at least annually no later than July 1. Additionally, the introducing member must notify the clearing member of the reports it needs to supervise customer accounts. The introducing member forwards all cash and securities to the carrying or clearing member for deposit into the customers' accounts. The clearing firm sends the customers' statements and confirmations to the introducing firm's customers. If a firm clears all of their transactions on a fully disclosed basis, all customers of the introducing firm must be notified of the fact in writing when the account is opened. In addition to sending confirmations and account statements, the clearing firm will also provide the following:

- Year-end tax statements/1099s
- Record keeping
- Order execution
- Access to ECNs
- Cashiering functions

- Margin loans
- AML compliance
- Access to software and data services
- Stock loans for short sales

An introducing member may also choose to clear its trades through an omnibus account maintained at the clearing firm. In this case, all transactions are cleared through one account, and the clearing member does not know for whom the trade was executed. The introducing member is required to send customer confirmations and statements if they clear through an omnibus account. Omnibus accounts are not allowed to purchase securities on margin for customers. All securities must be paid for in full.

THE DEPOSITORY TRUST & CLEARING CORPORATION (DTCC)

The DTCC is a centralized securities depository that acts as a national clearinghouse for the settlement of trades in eligible securities. The DTCC is a nonprofit organization owned by members of the securities industry. It is regulated by the SEC and is a member of the Federal Reserve System. The DTCC, through its subsidiaries, transfers securities on a book entry or journal entry basis between buyers and sellers. DTCC-eligible securities include:

- Corporate equity and debt securities
- OTC derivatives
- U.S. Treasury and agency issues
- Municipal bonds
- Money market instruments
- Mortgage-backed bonds
- Some mutual funds and insurance products

The DTCC has created subsidiaries to serve the needs of specific products and markets. The list of subsidiaries includes:

- The Depository Trust Company (DTC)
- The National Securities Clearing Corporation (NSCC)
- The Fixed Income Clearing Corporation (FICC)

THE DEPOSITORY TRUST COMPANY (DTC)

The DTC holds broker dealer non custom funds and securities held in street name in book entry form. The DTC journals trades between the accounts of broker dealers. The DTC does not provide clearing services or hold physical certificates. The DTC, like its parent company, is a member of the Federal Reserve System.

The Depository Trust Company's (DTC) offers a deposit and withdrawal at custodian (DWAC) service that provides participants with the ability to make electronic book-entry deposits and withdrawals of eligible securities into and out of their DTC book-entry accounts using a Fast Automated Securities Transfer service (FAST). DWAC allows participants to instruct DTC regarding deposit and withdrawal transactions being made directly via a FAST transfer agent. Deposits will be credited to the participants account and withdrawals will be debited to from the participant's account. The FAST system eliminates the transfer of physical securities certificates for securities registered in the name of DTC's nominee, Cede & Co, on the transfer agent's books. DTC and its FAST transfer agents reconcile electronic deposits and withdrawals on a daily basis. All DTC participants may use the DWAC service. For securities to be eligible to use the DWAC service the issuer of the securities must use a transfer agent that participates in DTC's FAST program.

THE NATIONAL SECURITIES CLEARING CORPORATION (NSCC)

The NSCC is the clearing and settlement arm of the DTCC. NSCC member firms clear their trades with the NSCC, and the settlement and clearing of all trades are guaranteed by the DTCC. All transactions are cleared on a continuous net settlement basis. All purchases and all sales for each security and for each broker dealer are netted against each other to determine the net amount of each security purchased or sold. The netting process allows the firm to be credited or debited the correct amount of cash or securities for all transactions in each security on a daily basis. In addition to clearing and settlement services, the NSCC provides risk management for the following securities:

- Corporate equity and debt securities
- Exchange-traded funds (ETFs)
- American depositary receipts (ADRs)
- Limited partnerships
- Municipal bonds
- Unit investment trusts (UITs)
- Hedge funds

CHAPTER 3   Record Keeping, Financial Requirements, and Clearing   **103**

- Funds of funds
- Some nontraded real estate investment trusts (REITs)

THE FIXED INCOME CLEARING CORPORATION (FICC)

The FICC provides clearing and settlement services for government and mortgage-backed securities through its government securities division and its mortgage-backed securities division. In addition the FICC provides risk management services, real-time matching, and cash-only settlement services for banks in Treasury bills, notes, bonds, inflation-protected securities, government agency issues, and mortgage-backed securities.

THE OPTION CLEARING CORPORATION (OCC)

The Option Clearing Corporation (OCC) was created and is owned by the exchanges that trade options and is regulated by the SEC. The OCC issues all standardized options and guarantees their performance. The OCC does not guarantee a customer against a loss; it only guarantees the option's performance. The OCC guarantees that if an investor who is short an option is unable to perform its obligation under the contract, the investor who is exercising the contract will still be able to do so without any delay. Without this performance guarantee, the trading of standardized options would be impossible. The OCC issues option contracts the day after the trade date, and all standardized options will settle on the next business day, or T + 1. When an investor closes out a position through either a closing purchase or sale, the OCC will eliminate the closing investor's obligations or rights from its books. All standardized options of the same series are interchangeable or fungible. For example, all XYZ April 50 calls are the same. In order to meet the prospectus requirements of the Securities Act of 1933, the OCC publishes a disclosure document known as The Characteristics and Risks of Standardized Options. All option investors must be given this document prior to or at the time their account is approved for option trading.

AMERICAN VS. EUROPEAN EXERCISE

Two styles of options trade in the United States: American and European. An American-style option may be exercised at any time by the holder during the life of the contract. A European-style option may only be exercised by the holder at expiration.

If an investor who is long an option decides to exercise the option, the OCC will randomly assign the exercise notice to a broker dealer who is short that option. The broker dealer must then assign the exercise notice to a customer who is short that option. The broker dealer may use any fair method approved by the exchange for randomly assigning exercise notices. If the broker dealer uses the FIFO (first in, first out) method of assignment, the customer with the oldest open short position will receive the assignment. Any changes to the broker dealer's assignment practices must be approved by the exchange prior to implementation.

EXPIRATION AND EXERCISE

The OCC has set the following rules for the expiration and exercise of stock and narrow-based index options:

- Options cease trading at 4:00 p.m. EST (3:00 p.m. CST) on the third Friday.
- Option holders who wish to exercise their options must do so by 5:30 p.m. EST (4:30 p.m. CST) on the third Friday.
- All options expire at 11:59 p.m. EST (10:59 p.m. CST) on the third Friday.
- All options held by public customers will automatically be exercised if they are $.01 in the money.
- All options held by broker dealers will automatically be exercised if they are $.01 in the money.
- Any customer who owns an option subject to automatic exercise, who does not want the option to be exercised, must submit negative exercise instructions to the broker dealer. This is usually the case when a retail customer owns an option that is only a few cents in the money.
- The exercise of an equity option results in the delivery of the underlying stock regular way the next business day

The OCC has set the following rules for broad-based option expiration and exercise:

- The exercise of an equity option results in the delivery of the underlying stock regular way the next business day
- Any customer who owns an option subject to automatic exercise, who does not want the option to be exercised, must submit negative exercise instructions to the broker dealer. This is usually the case when a retail customer owns an option that is only a few cents in the money.
- Options cease trading at 4:15 p.m. EST (3:15 p.m. CST) on the third Friday.
- Option holders who wish to exercise their options must do so by 5:30 p.m. EST (4:30 p.m. CST) the third Friday.
- All options expire at 11:59 p.m. EST (10:59 p.m. CST) on the third Friday.

CHAPTER 3

Pretest

RECORD KEEPING, FINANCIAL REQUIREMENTS, AND CLEARING

1. A broker dealer executing customer orders must post activity to the blotter by the end of the:
   a. Trade date.
   b. Settlement date.
   c. Following business day.
   d. Payment date.

2. All of the following records must be maintained for 3 years, EXCEPT:
   a. Order tickets.
   b. General ledgers.
   c. U4 forms.
   d. FOCUS reports.

3. Trial balances must be prepared no later than:
   a. 1 business day after the week's end.
   b. 1 business day after the month's end.
   c. 10 business days after the quarter's end.
   d. 10 business days after the month's end.

4. A broker dealer that does business exclusively in open-end mutual fund shares and transmits customer's orders on a wire basis must have net capital of:
   a. $5,000.
   b. $25,000.
   c. $30,000.
   d. $50,000.

5. Which of the following are true regarding FOCUS Part I reports?
   I. They are filed electronically.
   II. They must be filed within 17 business days of the quarter's end.
   III. They must be filed within 10 days of the end of the month.
   IV. They are filed by both carrying and introducing firms.

   a. II and IV
   b. I and III
   c. I, II, and IV
   d. I, III, and IV

6. A newly formed broker dealer is introducing all of its accounts on a fully disclosed basis to a general securities firm. The firm is receiving customers' cash and securities and is promptly forwarding them to the general securities firm carrying its accounts. What is the new member's minimum net capital requirement?
   a. $5,000
   b. $50,000
   c. $100,000
   d. $250,000

7. The customer protection rule requires broker dealers to deposit how much in a special reserve account?
   a. 105% of customer credit balances
   b. 105% of customer fails to receive
   c. 115% of customer credit balances
   d. 115% of customer fails to receive

8. As it relates to the Depository Trust Company (DTC), which of the following is true?
   a. It holds physical certificates registered in the names of the investors.
   b. It holds and safeguards customers' free credit balances.
   c. It holds securities registered in the name of customers in journal entry from.
   d. It holds securities registered in street name in journal entry form.

9. Which of the following is NOT required to be kept for 6 years?
   a. Blotters
   b. Customer ledgers
   c. General ledgers
   d. Broker dealer bank records

10. The minutes of the board of directors meetings must be kept for:
    a. 3 years, with 2 years readily accessible.
    b. 6 years, with 2 years readily accessible.
    c. The life of the firm, with 2 years readily accessible.
    d. The life of the firm, with 6 years readily accessible.

CHAPTER 4

Issuing Corporate Securities

> **INTRODUCTION**
>
> The Securities Act of 1933 was the first major piece of securities industry regulation. It was brought about largely as a result of the stock market crash of 1929. Other major laws, such as The Securities Exchange Act of 1934, were also enacted to help prevent another meltdown of the nation's financial system. We will start our review with the Securities Act of 1933 because it regulates the issuance of corporate securities.

The Securities Act of 1933 was the first major piece of securities industry legislation, and it regulates the primary market. The primary market consists exclusively of transactions between issuers of securities and investors. In a primary market transaction, the issuer of the securities receives the proceeds from the sale of the securities. The Securities Act of 1933 requires nonexempt issuers (typically issuers of corporate securities) to file a registration statement with the Securities and Exchange Commission (SEC). The registration statement, formerly known as an S-1, is the issuer's full disclosure document for the government. The registration statement must contain detailed information relating to the issuer's operations and financial condition and must include:

- A balance sheet dated within 90 days of the filing of the registration statement.
- Profit and loss statements for the last 3 years.
- The company's capitalization.
- The use of proceeds.

- Shareholders owning more than 10% of the company's securities.
- Biographical information on the officers and directors.

The registration statement will be under review by the SEC for a minimum of 20 days. During this time, known as the cooling-off period, no sales of securities may take place. If the SEC requires additional information regarding the offering, the SEC may issue a deficiency letter or a stop order that will extend the cooling-off period beyond the original 20 days. The cooling-off period will continue until the SEC has received all of the information it has requested. A registered representative may only begin to discuss the potential offering with customers after the filing date.

THE PROSPECTUS

While the SEC is reviewing the securities' registration statement, registered representatives are very limited as to what they may do with regard to the new issue. During the cooling-off period, the only thing that a registered representative may do is obtain indications of interest from clients by providing them with a preliminary prospectus, which is also known as a red herring. The term *red herring* originated from the fact that all preliminary prospectuses must have a statement printed in red ink on the front cover stating: "These securities have not yet become registered with the SEC and therefore may not be sold." An indication of interest is an investor's or broker dealer's statement that it might be interested in purchasing the securities being offered. The preliminary prospectus contains most of the same information that will be contained in the final prospectus except for the offering price, the effective date, and the proceeds to the issuer. The preliminary prospectus will usually contain a price range for the security to be offered. All information contained in a preliminary prospectus is subject to change or revision. The preliminary prospectus must be given in hard copy to expected purchasers at least 48 hours before the sale is confirmed if the company has not been a reporting company under the Securities Exchange Act of 1934. This is done to ensure that the final prospectus is not the first piece of information forwarded to the purchaser.

THE FINAL PROSPECTUS

All purchasers of new issues must be given a final prospectus before any sales may be allowed. The final prospectus serves as the issuer's full-disclosure

CHAPTER 4 Issuing Corporate Securities

document for the purchaser of the securities. If the issuer has filed a prospectus with the SEC and the prospectus can be viewed on the SEC's website, a prospectus will be deemed to have been provided to the investor through the "access equals delivery" rule. Once the issuer's registration statement becomes effective, the final prospectus must include:

- Type and description of the securities
- Price of the security
- Use of the proceeds
- Underwriter's discount
- Date of offering
- Type and description of underwriting
- Business history of issuer
- Biographical data for company officers and directors
- Information regarding large stockholders
- Company financial data
- Risks to purchaser
- Legal matters concerning the company
- SEC disclaimer

PROSPECTUS TO BE PROVIDED TO AFTERMARKET PURCHASERS

Certain investors who purchase securities in the secondary market just after a distribution must also be provided with the final prospectus. The term for which a prospectus must be provided depends on where the issue will be traded in the aftermarket and if the issuer has been reporting financial results as required by the Securities Exchange Act of 1934. If the security has an aftermarket delivery requirement, a prospectus must be provided by all firms that execute a purchase order for the security during the term. The aftermarket prospectus delivery requirements may be met electronically and are as follows:

- For IPOs: 90 days after being issued for nonreporting companies with securities to be quoted on the OTC MKT or in the pink OTC; 25 days for companies to be listed or Nasdaq securities.
- Additional offerings: 40 days for securities quoted on the OTC MKT or in the pink OTC. No aftermarket requirement for listed or Nasdaq securities.

SEC DISCLAIMER

The SEC reviews the issuer's registration statement and the prospectus, but does not guarantee the accuracy or adequacy of the information. The SEC disclaimer must appear on the cover of all prospectuses and states: "These securities have not been approved or disapproved by the SEC nor have any representations been made about the accuracy of the adequacy of the information."

MISREPRESENTATIONS

Financial relief for misrepresentations made under the Securities Act of 1933 is available for purchasers of any security that is sold under a prospectus that is found to contain false or misleading statements. Purchasers of the security may be entitled to seek financial relief from any or all of the following:

- The issuer
- The underwriters
- Officers and directors
- All parties who signed the registration statement
- Accountants and attorneys who helped prepare the registration statement

A due diligence meeting will be held during the cooling-off period to ensure that the information contained in the prospectus is accurate.

TOMBSTONE ADS

SEC Rule 134 allows certain types of advertisements to be run relating to a new issue. Tombstone ads are the only form of advertising that is allowed during the cooling-off period. A tombstone ad is an announcement and description of the securities to be offered. A tombstone ad lists the names of the underwriters, where a prospectus may be obtained, and a statement that the tombstone ad does not constitute an offer to sell the securities and that the offer may only be made by a prospectus. Tombstone ads are traditionally run to announce the new issue, but they are not required and do not need to be filed with the SEC. Tombstone ads may also include:

- The amount of the security to be offered
- The date of sale

CHAPTER 4 Issuing Corporate Securities

- A general description of the issuer's business
- The price of the security

FREE RIDING AND WITHHOLDING/FINRA RULE 5130

A broker dealer underwriting a new issue must make a complete and bona fide offering of all securities being issued to the public and may not withhold any of the securities for:

- The account of underwriters.
- The account of another broker dealer.
- The account of a firm employee or the account of those who are financially dependent on the employee.
- The account of employees of other FINRA members.

> **TAKENOTE!**
>
> An exception to FINRA Rule 5130 applies to employees of limited broker dealers who engage solely in the purchase and sale of investment company products or direct participation programs (DPPs). Employees of limited broker dealers may purchase new issues. This exemption applies only to the employees of the limited broker dealer, not to the firm itself.

These rules are in effect for initial public offerings, but are especially prevalent when dealing with a hot issue. A hot issue is one that trades at an immediate premium to its offering price in the secondary market. A broker dealer may not free ride by withholding securities for its own account or for the accounts of those listed above. FINRA Rule 5130 covers initial offerings of common stock only. Exempt from the rule are offerings of additional issues, bonds, and preferred shares. These offerings may be purchased by registered persons. FINRA Rule 5130 requires that a broker dealer obtain an eligibility statement from all account owners who purchase a new issue of stock within 12 months prior to the purchase. Some people may purchase hot issues as long as the amount is not substantial and they have a history of purchasing new issues. These conditionally approved people are:

- Officers and employees of financial institutions.
- Nonsupported family members.

- Accountants, attorneys, and finders associated with the underwriting.
- Accounts where restricted persons, whose interest is limited to 10% or less or where a maximum of 10% of the allocation of new issue is for the benefit of such persons. This is known as the carve out procedure.

The agreement among the underwriters must clearly state how the syndicate will handle the repurchase of shares trading at a premium. If a client "flips" the hot issue in the secondary market and the shares are repurchased by the book running lead underwriter, those shares must be used to cover any syndicate short position. If no syndicate short position exists, the shares may be used to cover unfilled qualified customer orders at the offering price. Any account to receive these shares must receive the shares through a random allocation process. In the extremely unlikely event that no unfilled orders exist, the syndicate may sell the shares in the market and anonymously donate the profits to an unaffiliated charity. If a purchaser sells the stock (flips) within 30 days of the offering the syndicate may not seek to reclaim any sales credit earned by the agent or member unless the stock was sold back to the syndicate's penalty bid. Issuers who are going public are allowed to direct stock to the officers, directors, and employees of the company. The number of shares directed to the employees of the issuer are part of, and are not in addition to, the number of shares being underwritten.

UNDERWRITING CORPORATE SECURITIES

Once a business has decided that it needs to raise capital to meet its organizational objectives, it must determine how to raise the needed capital. Most corporations at this point will hire an investment banker, also known as an underwriter, to advise them. The underwriter works for the issuer, and it is the underwriter's job to advise the client about what type of securities to offer. The issuer and the underwriter together determine whether stocks or bonds should be issued and what the terms will be. The underwriter is responsible for trying to obtain the financing at the best possible terms for the issuer. The underwriter will:

- Market the issue to investors.
- Assist in the determination of the terms of the offering.
- Purchase the securities directly from the issuer to resell to investors.

CHAPTER 4 Issuing Corporate Securities

The issuer is responsible for:

- Filing a registration statement with the SEC.
- Registering the securities in the states in which it will be sold, also known as blue-skying the issue.
- Negotiating the underwriter's compensation and obligations to the issuer.

TYPES OF UNDERWRITING COMMITMENTS

The agreement between the issuer and the underwriter spells out the underwriter's responsibilities to the issuer. The agreement may take a variety of forms and may include:

- Firm commitment
- Best efforts
- Mini-maxi
- All or none
- Standby

FIRM COMMITMENT

In a firm commitment underwriting, the underwriter guarantees to purchase all of the securities being offered for sale by the issuer regardless of whether it can sell them to investors. A firm commitment underwriting agreement is the most desirable for the issuer because it guarantees the issuer all of the money right away. The more in demand the offering is, the more likely it is that it will be done on a firm commitment basis. If the issue is in extremely high demand and is oversubscribed, the underwriter may exercise the greenshoe provision to cover overallotments. This will allow the underwriter to purchase an additional 15% of the issue from the issuer. In a firm commitment, the underwriter puts its own money at risk if it can't sell the securities to investors.

MARKET-OUT CLAUSE

An underwriter offering securities for an issuer on a firm commitment basis is assuming a substantial amount of risk. As a result, the underwriter will insist on having a market-out clause in the underwriting agreement. A market-out clause would free the underwriter from its obligation to purchase all of the securities in the event of a development that impairs the quality of the securities or that adversely affects the issuer. If a syndicate was underwriting a new issue for a biotech company with a drug in clinical trials and the FDA rejected the drug for use, the underwriters could invoke the market-out clause. Poor market conditions are not a reason to invoke the market-out clause.

BEST EFFORTS

In a best efforts underwriting, the underwriter will do its best to sell all of the securities that are being offered by the issuer, but in no way is the underwriter obligated to purchase the securities for its own account. The lower the demand for an issue, the greater likelihood that it will be done on a best efforts basis. Any shares or bonds in a best efforts underwriting that have not been sold will be returned to the issuer.

MINI-MAXI

A mini-maxi is a type of best efforts underwriting that does not become effective until a minimum amount of the securities have been sold. Once the minimum has been met, the underwriter may then sell the securities up to the maximum amount specified under the terms of the offering. All funds collected from investors will be held in escrow until the underwriting is completed. If the minimum amount of securities specified by the offering cannot be reached, the offering will be canceled and the investors' funds that were collected will be returned to them.

ALL OR NONE (AON)

With an all-or-none underwriting, the issuer has determined that it must receive the proceeds from the sale of all of the securities. Investors' funds are held in escrow until all of the securities are sold. If all of the securities are sold, the proceeds will be released to the issuer. If all of the securities are not sold, the issue is canceled, and the investors' funds will be returned to them.

STANDBY

A standby underwriting agreement will be used in conjunction with a preemptive rights offering. All standby underwritings are done on a firm commitment basis. The standby underwriter agrees to purchase any shares that current shareholders do not purchase. The standby underwriter will then resell the securities to the public.

TYPES OF OFFERINGS

Securities that are being sold under a prospectus may include securities that are part of different types of offerings. The different types of offerings include initial public offerings, subsequent primary offerings, and registered secondary offerings.

INITIAL PUBLIC OFFERING (IPO)/NEW ISSUE
An initial public offering (IPO) is the first time that a company has sold its stock to the public. The issuing company receives the proceeds from the sale minus the underwriter's compensation.

SUBSEQUENT PRIMARY/ADDITIONAL ISSUES
In a subsequent primary offering, the corporation is already publicly owned and the company is selling additional shares to raise new financing.

PRIMARY OFFERING VS. SECONDARY OFFERING
In a primary offering, the issuing company receives the proceeds from the sale minus the underwriter's compensation. In a secondary offering, a group of selling shareholders receives the proceeds from the sale minus the underwriter's compensation. A combined offering has elements of both the primary offering and the secondary offering. Part of the proceeds goes to the company and part of the proceeds goes to a group of selling shareholders.

REVIEW OF UNDERWRITING AGREEMENTS BY FINRA

All underwriting agreements must be submitted to FINRA's Corporate Finance Department for review no later than 3 business days after the filing of any registration with the SEC or with any state regulator. If the offering is not required to be filed at either the federal or state level, the agreement must be filed with FINRA at least 15 business days prior to the anticipated offering date. In most cases, the agreement is submitted by the managing underwriter. FINRA will review the maximum total compensation to the underwriters to ensure that the underwriter's compensation is fair and reasonable in light of the size and complexity of the offering. The submission must include:

- The maximum offering price
- The maximum underwriter's discount
- The maximum estimated reimbursement for underwriter's expenses

UNDERWRITER'S COMPENSATION

The largest percentage of the underwriter's compensation will come in the form of the underwriter's discount. Other items received by the syndicate will also be considered compensation, such as:

- Reimbursement of costs usually not borne by the issuer.
- Options, rights, or warrants.
- Shares of the issuer.
- Finders' fees reimbursed by the issuer.

Expenses that are not considered when looking at the underwriter's compensation would be:

- Printing costs.
- Accounting fees.
- Blue-sky fees.

 TAKENOTE!

If the securities are being sold for a member firm, then the member firm that is the issuer is required to file the underwriting agreement with FINRA.

The following are all exempt from the filing of the underwriting agreement with the Corporate Finance Department:

- U.S. government securities
- Municipal securities

- Redeemable investment company shares
- Variable contracts
- Private placements

EXEMPT SECURITIES

Certain securities are exempt from the registration provisions of the Securities Act of 1933 because of the issuer or the nature of the security. Although the securities may be exempt from the registration and prospectus requirements of the act, none are exempt from the antifraud provisions of the act. Examples of exempt securities are:

- Debt securities with maturities of less than 270 days and sold in denominations of $50,000 or more.
- Employee benefit plans.
- Option contracts, both puts and calls on stocks and indexes.

Examples of exempt issuers are:

- U.S. government
- State and municipal governments
- Foreign national governments
- Canadian federal and municipal governments
- Insurance companies
- Banks and trusts
- Credit unions and savings and loans
- Religious and charitable organizations

 TAKENOTE!

Insurance and bank holding companies are not exempt issuers.

EXEMPT TRANSACTIONS

Sometimes a security that would otherwise have to register is exempt from the registration requirements of the Securities Act of 1933 because of the type of transaction that is involved. The following are all exempt transactions:

- Private placements/Regulation D offerings
- Rule 144
- Regulation S offerings
- Regulation A offerings
- Rule 145
- Rule 147 intrastate offerings

PRIVATE PLACEMENTS/ REGULATION D OFFERINGS

A private placement is a sale of securities that is made to a group of accredited investors where the securities are not offered to the general public. Accredited investors include institutional investors and individuals who:

- Earn at least $200,000 per year if single.

Or

- Earn at least $300,000 jointly with a spouse.

Or

- Have a net worth of at least $1,000,000 without the primary residence.

The SEC has recently added a new category that will allow an individual to qualify as an accredited investor. Individuals who meet certain educational or certification requirements can now meet the definition of an accredited investor. Included in this category are individuals who have an active Series 7, 65 or 82 license. Sales to nonaccredited investors for private placements exceeding $1 million are limited to 35 in any 12-month period. No commission may be paid to representatives who sell a private placement to a nonaccredited investor. All investors in private placements must hold the securities fully paid for at least 6 months and sign a letter stating that they are purchasing the securities for investment purposes. Stock purchased through a private placement is known as lettered stock, legend stock, or restricted stock, because there is a legend on the stock certificate that limits the ability of the owner to transfer or sell the securities. There is no limit as to how many accredited investors may purchase the securities. The limits on the amount of money that may be raised under the various regulation D offerings are as follows:

>Regulation 504 D allows issuers to raise up to $10 million.
>
>Regulation 506 D allows issuers to raise an unlimited amount of capital.

PURCHASER REPRESENTATIVE

A purchaser's representative is an individual designated in writing by the prospective purchaser to represent the buyer when evaluating the suitability of a private placement. A purchaser's representative may not:

- Receive a blanket appointment to represent the investor for all private placements.
- Own more than 10% of the issuer's stock.
- Be an officer, director, employee, or affiliate of the issuer, unless he or she is a close relative of the prospective purchaser.

For private placements exceeding $5 million, the offering will be limited to institutional, accredited, and a limited number of nonaccredited investors who, together with their purchaser's representative, have the financial and business knowledge to evaluate the offering. The issuer in a private placement may not advertise the issue or hold a seminar open to the general public. The JOBS Act now allows investors to view private placement documents online so long as the website requires an investor to submit a questionnaire documenting assets, income, and investment experience. This questionnaire must be reviewed and, if qualified for participation, the issuer or broker dealer may assign the investor a username and password granting them access to view the details of the offerings.

RULE 144

Rule 144 regulates how control or restricted securities may be sold. Rule 144 designates:

- The holding period for the security.
- The amount of the security that may be sold.
- Filing procedures.
- Method of sale.

Control securities are owned by officers, directors, and owners of 10% or more of the company's outstanding stock. Control stock may be obtained by insiders through open-market purchases or though the exercise of company stock options. There is no holding period for control securities. However, insiders are not allowed to earn a short swing profit through the purchase and sale of control stock in the open market. If the securities were held for less than 6 months, the insider must return any profit to the company.

Restricted securities may be purchased by both insiders and investors through a private placement or be obtained through an offering other than a public sale. Securities obtained through a private placement or other nonpublic means need to be sold under Rule 144 in order to allow the transfer of ownership. Restricted stock must be held fully paid for for 6 months. After 6 months, the securities may be sold freely by noninsiders so long as the seller has not been affiliated with the issuer in the last 3 months. It's important to note that Rule 144 imposes a 12 month holding period for the restricted stock of non reporting issuers who fail to meet the requirements of adequate publicly available information. Rule 144 sets the following volume limits for both restricted and control stock during any 90-day period. Securities may be sold under Rule 144 four times per year. The seller must file Form 144 at the time the order is entered, and the order is limited to the greater of:

- The average weekly trading volume for the preceding 4 weeks.

Or

- 1% of the issuer's total outstanding stock.

Stock sold under Rule 144 becomes part of the public float. Form 144 does not need to be filed for orders for 5,000 shares or less and for orders that do not exceed $50,000. If the owner of restricted stock dies, their estate may sell the share freely without regard to the holding period or volume limitations of Rule 144.

> **TAKENOTE!**
>
> There is a 6-month holding period for control stock acquired through a private placement, and control stock is always subject to the volume limitations.

BROKER TRANSACTIONS UNDER RULE 144

A firm handling a customer's sale under Rule 144, except in very limited circumstances, must execute the order on an agency basis for the customer. The broker dealer may execute the order with a market maker, or may inquire with customers who have expressed an unsolicited interest in the securities in the last 10 days or with a broker dealer who has expressed interest in the securities in the last 60 days. Firms that are classified as a bona fide block positioner are allowed to purchase the stock on a principal basis.

RULE 144A

Rule 144A permits the resale of restricted stock to qualified institutional buyers (QIBs). A QIB is defined as a company that owns investments worth at least $100 million and includes:

- Corporations
- Partnerships
- Insurance companies
- Investment companies
- Banks
- Trust funds
- Pension plans
- Registered investment advisers
- Small business development companies

The broker dealer must verify that the customer meets the definition of a QIB. When determining the eligibility for a buyer to participate in a 144A transaction, the broker dealer may use any of the following:

I. The purchaser's most recent, publicly available financial statements
II. The purchaser's most recent publicly available information appearing in documents filed an SRO
III. The most recent publicly available information appearing in a recognized securities manual or filed with a foreign regulator
IV. A certification by the purchaser's chief financial officer or other executive

The broker dealer may not rely on the information on the customer's account card. If shares of restricted stock have been sold under rule 144A, the remainder of the restriction period passes to the buyer and the security remains restricted for 6 months from the original date of purchase.

> **TAKENOTE!**
>
> A broker dealer will be considered a QIB if it owns $10 million worth of securities or if it engages in riskless principal transactions for other QIBs.

To qualify for the exemption provided under Rule 144A, the QIB must purchase the securities for its own account or for the account of other QIBs. Not all securities will be eligible for an exemption under Rule 144A. Ineligible securities include:

- Securities of registered investment companies
- Securities of the same class as those listed on an exchange or Nasdaq
- Certain warrants and convertible securities

All purchasers of securities under Rule 144A must be informed that the seller is relying on the exemption provided under Rule 144A, and the issuer of the securities must be willing to provide financial information to owners and prospective purchasers. The PORTAL Market has been developed to help ensure compliance with Rule 144A and to help facilitate Rule 144A transactions. Transactions that qualify under Rule 144A may be executed without regard to any holding period otherwise imposed so long as the buyer is a QIB.

PRIVATE INVESTMENT IN A PUBLIC EQUITY (PIPE)

Public companies that wish to obtain additional financing without selling securities to the general public may sell securities to a group of accredited investors through a private placement. The accredited investors in most cases will be institutional investors who wish to invest a large amount of capital. Common stock, convertible or nonconvertible debt, rights, and warrants may all be sold to the investors through a PIPE transaction. Obtaining capital through a PIPE transaction benefits the public company in a number of ways, such as:

- Reduced transaction cost
- Term disclosure only upon completion of the transaction
- Increased institutional ownership
- Quick closing

Securities sold through a PIPE transaction are subject to Rule 144. If the issuer files a registration statement after the closing of the offering sales may begin immediately upon the effective date.

REGULATION S OFFERINGS

Domestic issuers who make a distribution of securities exclusively to offshore investors do not have to file a registration statement for the securities under the Securities Act of 1933. In order to qualify for exemption offered under Regulation S, the issuer cannot make offerings of the securities within the United States and cannot announce or distribute literature relating to the securities within the United States. Securities distributed under Regulation S are subject to a distribution compliance period during which the securities may not be resold to domestic investors. The distribution compliance period is 6 months for equities if the issuer is a reporting company and files 10-Qs, 10-Ks, and 8-Ks, and 1 year for nonreporting companies. The distribution compliance period is 40 days for debt. Sales of the securities may take place in offshore markets anytime after the initial sale. Issuers must report the sale of securities under Regulation S by filing Form 8-K.

REGULATION A OFFERINGS

Regulation A allows US and Canadian issuers to raise up to $75 million in any 12 month period. A Regulation A offering provides issuers with an exemption from the standard registration process. This exemption from full registration allows smaller companies access to the capital markets without having to go through the expense of filing a full registration statement with the SEC. The issuer will instead file an abbreviated notice of sale or offering circular known as an S1-A with the SEC. Issuers are required to file 2 years of audited financial statements with the SEC and purchasers of the issue will be given a copy of the offering circular rather than a final prospectus. Purchasers of the issue must have the preliminary or final offering circular mailed to them 48 hours before mailing the confirmation. The same 20-day cooling-off period also applies to Regulation A offerings. Regulation A has two tiers, with Regulation A now sometimes being referred to as Regulation A plus. Tier 1 allows issuers to raise up to $20 million. Of this $20 million, no more than $6 million may be offered by selling shareholders. Tier 2 allows issuers to raise up to $75 million, of which no more than $22.5 million may be offered by selling shareholders. When determining the total amount of money raised through a regulation A offering, the look-back period includes money raised in the past 12 months.

RULE 145

Rule 145 requires that shareholders approve any merger or reorganization of the company's ownership. Any merger or acquisition will be reported to the SEC on Form S-4. Stockholders must be given full disclosure of the proposed transaction or reclassification and must be sent proxies to vote on the proposal. Rule 145 covers:

- Mergers involving a stock swap or offer of another company's securities in exchange for its current stock.
- Reclassification involving the exchange of one class of the company's securities for another.
- Asset transfers involving the dissolution of the company or the distribution or sale of a major portion of the company's assets.

Rule 145 does not cover:

- Stock splits.
- Reverse splits.
- Changes in par value.

RULE 147 INTRASTATE OFFERING

Rule 147 allows an issuer to raise an unlimited amount of capital within one state. Because the offering is being made only in one state, it is exempt from registration with the SEC and is subject to the jurisdiction of the state securities administrator. In order to qualify for an exemption from SEC registration, the issue must be organized and have its principal place of business in the state and meet at least one of the following business criteria:

- 80% of the issuer's income must be received in that state.
- 80% of the offering's proceeds must be used in that state.
- 80% of the issuer's assets must be located in that state.
- A majority of the issuer's employees are based in-state.

All purchasers must be located within the state and must agree not to resell the securities to an out-of-state resident for 6 months.

If the issuer is using an underwriter, the broker dealer must have an office in that state.

The SEC has also adopted Rule 147A, which is largely identical to Rule 147. However, Rule 147A allows companies that are incorporated out of state to utilize the Rule 147 exemption so long as the company's principal place of business is in that state. Rule 147 A also allows issuers to use the internet and to advertise securities being offered through Rule 147. Offers may be made to residents while out of state. However, all sales are still limited to investors residing in the state where the offering is being conducted. Interestingly, an existing domestic partnership made up of partners from both in-state and out-of-state would be allowed to purchase these shares being issued under Rule 147.

RULE 137 NONPARTICIPANTS

Firms that are not participating in a distribution of securities may issue recommendations, information, or opinions relating to the securities that are in registration, if the issuer is a reporting company, as required by the Securities and

Exchange Act of 1934. So long as the broker dealer did not receive compensation from the issuer, a selling shareholder, or a participant in the distribution for issuing the report, it will not constitute an offer of the securities.

RULE 138 NONEQUIVALENT SECURITIES

If a registration statement has been filed for a nonconvertible bond or a nonconvertible preferred stock, a broker dealer who is a participant in a distribution of the securities may in the normal course of business issue recommendations, information, or opinions relating to the issuer's common stock or convertible securities. If the registration statement covers common stock or a convertible security of the issuer, a broker dealer may only issue recommendations, information, or opinions relating to the issuer's nonconvertible debt or preferred stock.

RULE 139 ISSUING RESEARCH REPORTS

A broker dealer who is participating in a distribution may continue to issue research reports relating to the issuer if the issuer is a large reporting company under the Securities and Exchange of 1934 and:

- The company is followed by analysts.
- The information, opinion, or recommendation appears in a regularly published report.
- Information, opinions, or recommendations that are at least as favorable as the current report must have been contained in the previous report.

If the broker dealer is not currently covering the company, the report is not considered to be issued with sufficient regularity. Any projections relating to the company's earnings may not extend past the current fiscal year. Broker dealers may issue reports for smaller issuers if the report contains information relating to a substantial number of issuers in the same industry as the issuer, or a list of securities currently recommended by the broker dealer, so long as the information relating to the registrant is not displayed more prominently than other information in the same report.

If the conditions for continuing to publish research reports are not met, the quiet period for managers and co-managers begins at the time when the issuer files the registration statement and continues until the expiration of the prospectus delivery requirement, 40 days for IPOs and 10 days for additional offerings.

If the company is classified as an emerging growth company with annual review of less than $1 billion, reports may be distributed anytime after the IPO. One additional exception to the quiet period occurs in the event of a material development at the company. Should a material change take place, such as the approval of a new drug, research reports may be published and analyst appearances may take place with the approval of the firm's legal or compliance department.

RULE 415 SHELF REGISTRATION

Rule 415 allows an issuer to register securities that may be sold for its own benefit, for the benefit of a subsidiary, or in connection with business plans in an amount that may be reasonably sold by the issuer within a two-year period. The 2-year window starts from the registration date and allows the issuer and the underwriters flexibility in the timing of the offering. Issuers who qualify as well-known seasoned issuers (WKSI) and who qualify for automatic registration may sell securities for up to 3 years. Rule 415 also allows the issuer to register to sell securities on a continuous basis in connection with an employee benefit plan or upon the conversion of other securities.

> Any post-effective amendment to any registration will be declared effective immediately.

SECURITIES OFFERING REFORM RULES

The SEC has adopted the securities offering reform rules, which are designed to modify and streamline the filing and communication requirements of issuers under the Securities Act of 1933. The rules focus on the following areas:

- The communications related to registered securities offerings
- Registration and other procedures in the offering and capital-formation processes
- The delivery of information to investors, including the timeliness of that delivery

The rules adopted have placed an increased importance on the value of electronic communications and filing and have helped eliminate cumbersome and outdated filing requirements.

SEC RULE 405

SEC Rule 405 defines certain classes of issuers who may be entitled to use a streamlined registration process depending on how the issuer is classified. Well-known seasoned issuers and seasoned issuers may take advantage of automatically effective shelf registration of securities by filing Form S-3 or F-3. The registration of the securities covered under the filing of Form S-3 or F-3 is effective immediately upon filing.

WELL-KNOWN SEASONED ISSUER (WKSI)

A well-known seasoned issuer is an issuer that within 60 days of its eligibility determination has at least $700 million worth of voting and nonvoting common equity held by nonaffiliates or has issued within the last 3 years at least $1 billion in nonconvert- ible securities for cash (excluding common equity). A WKSI also includes a company that is a majority-owned subsidiary of a WKSI. If during the course of an offering the WKSI sees the value of its securities fall below the required levels to be considered a WKSI, the issuer may continue to sell the securities until it files its next 10-K.

SEASONED ISSUER (PRIMARY S-3 ELIGIBLE)

A seasoned issuer is an issuer that has a public float of $75 million meets the requirements of Form S-3 to register a primary offering of securities.

UNSEASONED REPORTING ISSUER (NOT PRIMARY S-3 ELIGIBLE)

An unseasoned reporting issuer is an issuer that is required to report under the Exchange Act but that does not qualify with the requirements of Form S-3 or F-3 to file a primary offering of securities.

INELIGIBLE ISSUER

An ineligible issuer is a reporting issuer that is not current with the filing of reports required under the Securities Exchange Act. Ineligible issuers also include:

- Companies who have filed for bankruptcy within the last 3 years
- Blank check companies
- Shell companies
- Issuers of penny stock
- Issuers that are limited partnerships that don't have a firm commitment underwriting agreement to sell securities
- Issuers that have been subject to a stop order or have been convicted of a felony or misdemeanor under the Exchange Act directly or indirectly through a subsidiary within the last 3 years

ADDITIONAL COMMUNICATION RULES

An issuer who is a reporting company may continue to release regular business communications with forward-looking statements prior to the effective date of an additional offering of securities. A forward-looking statement is one that contains information about what may possibly happen in the future, such as projected sales or new products. If the securities being offered are the subject of an IPO for a nonreporting issuer, only standard factual business communications may be released by the company. Standard factual information contains information relating to products or services and is not intended to be used by potential investors to make an investment decision. These two safe harbors allow the companies to continue to communicate without violating the gun-jumping provisions of the communications rules. The gun-jumping rules are designed to limit communications during the time an issue is in registration and to prevent companies from trying to create more favorable market conditions for the securities than otherwise would exist.

Road shows are designed to help the company communicate the details of the offering to broker dealers and representatives. Road shows have been traditionally held at large hotels in financial centers across the country. More and more these road shows are being conducted over the internet via webinars and are known as electronic road shows. These road shows may be broadcast live and recorded for playback and may be available on demand. If the recorded road show is for an IPO of equity securities, the recorded road show must be filed with the SEC unless at least one version is made available to the public in addition to the financial community. Recorded road shows for additional issues do not have to be filed with the SEC.

If the company is a reporting company under the Securities Exchange Act of 1934, the issuer may use forward looking statements in both their prospectus and annual reports, provided that the statements are clearly identified as forward looking. Key words such as expect, predict, potential, and anticipate are all used to inform the reader that the statements are not facts but projections based on management's beliefs. If the company uses a third party to review the projections it must disclose the nature of any relationship, the qualifications of the reviewer and the extent of the review. The company is under no obligation to have the projections reviewed.

CROWDFUNDING

Crowdfunding has become a popular way for issuers to raise capital from small investors. Issuers may offer securities to investors for purchase through a broker dealer or through a registered crowdfunding portal. The portal must be registered with the SEC and must also be a FINRA member firm. Issuers who raise capital through crowdfunding may not engage directly in crowdfunding as a way to sell shares to investors. Issuers who sell shares through crowdfunding must register the securities with the SEC by filing form C. Because most of the securities are speculative in nature, broker dealers and crowdfunding portals must offer educational material to investors who are considering purchasing securities offered through crowdfunding. The material must detail the risks involved in making investments in companies through the crowdfunding process as well as the fact that the securities have a limited amount of liquidity. Investors who purchase shares through crowdfunding may not sell the shares for 12 months. Shares however may be transferred earlier to a relative or to a trust controlled by the investor or as a result of death or divorce. Early transfer will also be allowed if the purchaser is an accredited investor or if the securities are part of an SEC registered offering. Investors who purchase shares are limited to the amount of securities they may purchase through the crowdfunding process in any 12 month period. Investors who have annual income or a net worth of less than $124,000 are limited to purchasing the greater of $2,500 worth of securities or 5% of their annual income or net worth. If the investor uses the 5% calculation to determine their purchase limit the amount the person may purchase will be the lesser of the two amounts. Investors who have an annual income or a net worth greater than $124,000 may invest the lesser of 10% of their annual income or net worth up to a maximum of $124,000.

CHAPTER 4

Pretest

ISSUING CORPORATE SECURITIES

1. A syndicate has published a tombstone ad prior to the issue becoming effective. Which of the following must appear in the tombstone?

    I. A statement that the registration has not yet become effective.//
    II. A statement that the ad is not an offer to sell the securities.//
    III. Contact information.//
    IV. A no commitment statement.

    a. III and IV
    b. II and III
    c. I and II
    d. I, II, III, and IV

2. During a new issue registration, false information is included in the prospectus to buyers. Which of the following may be held liable to investors?

    I. Officers of the issuer
    II. Accountants
    III. Syndicate members
    IV. People who signed the registration statement

    a. I and III
    b. I, III, and IV
    c. I, II, and III
    d. I, II, III, and IV

3. Corporations may do all of the following, EXCEPT:
   a. Issue preferred stock only.
   b. Issue nonvoting common stock.
   c. Sell stock out of the treasury.
   d. Repurchase its own shares.

4. A firm participating in the offering of a private placement may sell the private placement to no more than:
   a. 12 nonaccredited investors in any 12-month period.
   b. 6 nonaccredited investors in any 12-month period.
   c. 35 nonaccredited investors in any 12-month period.
   d. 15 nonaccredited investors in any 12-month period.

5. Rule 145 covers which of the following?
   a. Stock splits
   b. Stock swaps
   c. Reverse splits
   d. Changes in par value

6. The SEC has been reviewing a company's registration statement and would like clarification on a few items. It would most likely:
   a. Call the company.
   b. Issue a stop order.
   c. Issue a deficiency letter.
   d. Call the lead underwriter.

7. XYZ has just gone public and is quoted on the Nasdaq Capital securities market. Any investor who buys XYZ must get a prospectus for how long?
   a. 30 days
   b. 25 days
   c. 90 days
   d. 45 days

8. A red herring given to a client during the cooling-off period will contain information on all of the following, EXCEPT:
   a. Proceeds to the company.
   b. Use of proceeds.
   c. Biographies of officers and directors.
   d. A notice that all the information is subject to change.

9. For an insider to sell unregistered stock under an exemption from registration with the SEC, Form 144 Notice of Offering, which contains certain information, must be filed with the SEC. The insider can sell securities during the period of time in which the Form 144 Notice of Offering is effective, which is:
   a. 60 days.
   b. 6 months.
   c. 90 days.
   d. 12 months.

CHAPTER 5

Trading Securities

> **INTRODUCTION**
>
> Investors who do not purchase their stocks and bonds directly from the issuer must purchase them from another investor. Investor-to-investor transactions are known as secondary market transactions. In a secondary market transaction, the selling security owner receives the proceeds from the sale. Secondary market transactions may take place on an exchange or in the over-the-counter market known as Nasdaq. Although both facilitate the trading of securities, they operate in a very different manner. We will begin by looking at the types of orders that an investor may enter and the reasons for entering the various types of orders.

TYPES OF ORDERS

Investors can enter various types of orders to buy or sell securities. Some orders guarantee that the investor's order will be executed immediately. Other types of orders may state a specific price or condition under which the investor wants an order to be executed. All orders are considered day orders unless otherwise specified. All day orders will be canceled at the end of the trading day if they are not executed. An investor may also specify that an order remain active until canceled. This type of order is known as *good 'til cancel* or *GTC*.

MARKET ORDERS

A market order will guarantee that the investor's order is executed as soon as the order is presented to the market. A market order to either buy or sell guarantees the execution but not the price at which the order will be executed. When a market order is presented for execution, the market for the security may be very different from the market that was displayed when the order was entered. As a result, the investor does not know the exact price that the order will be executed at.

BUY LIMIT ORDERS

A buy limit order sets the maximum price that the investor will pay for the security. The order may never be executed at a price higher than the investor's limit price. Although a buy limit order guarantees that the investor will not pay over a certain price, it does not guarantee that the order will be executed. If the stock continues to trade higher away from the investor's limit price, the investor will not purchase the stock and may miss a chance to realize a profit.

SELL LIMIT ORDERS

A sell limit order sets the minimum price that the investor will accept for the security. The order may never be executed at a price lower than the investor's limit price. Although a sell limit order guarantees that the investor will not receive less than a certain price, it does not guarantee that the order will be executed. If the stock continues to trade lower away from the investor's limit price, the investor will not sell the stock and may miss a chance to realize a profit or may realize a loss as a result.

> **FOCUSPOINT!**
>
> It is important to remember that even if an investor sees stock trading at the limit price, it does not mean that the order was executed, because there could have been stock ahead of the order at that limit price.

STOP ORDERS/STOP LOSS ORDERS

A stop order, or stop loss order, can be used by investors to limit or guard against a loss or to protect a profit. A stop order will be placed away from the market in case the stock starts to move against the investor. A stop order is not a "live" order; it has to be elected. A stop order is elected and becomes a live order when the stock trades at or through the stop price. The stop price is also known as the trigger price. Once the stock has traded at or through the stop price, the order becomes a market order to either buy or sell the stock, depending on the type of order that was placed.

BUY STOP ORDERS

A buy stop order is placed above the market and is used to protect against a loss or to protect a profit on a short sale of stock. A buy stop order could also be used by a technical analyst to get long the stock after the stock breaks through resistance.

EXAMPLE An investor has sold 100 shares of ABC short at $40 per share. ABC has declined to $30 per share. The investor is concerned that if ABC goes past $32 it may return to $40. To protect the profit, the investor enters an order to buy 100 ABC at 32 stop. If ABC trades at or through $32, the order will become a market order to buy 100 shares, and the investor will cover the short at the next available price.

SELL STOP ORDERS

A sell stop order is placed below the market and is used to protect against a loss or to protect a profit on the purchase of a stock. A sell stop order could also be used by a technical analyst to get short the stock after the stock breaks through support.

EXAMPLE An investor has purchased 100 shares of ABC at $30 per share. ABC has risen to $40 per share. The investor is concerned that if ABC falls past $38 it may return to $30. To protect the profit, the investor enters an order to sell 100 ABC at 38 stop. If ABC trades at or through $38, the order will become a market order to sell 100 shares, and the investor will sell the stock at the next available price.

If the order to sell 100 ABC at 38 stop was entered as GTC, we could have a situation such as this:

> ABC closes at 39.40. The following morning ABC announces that it lost a major contract, and ABC opens at 35.30. The opening print of 35.30 elected the order, and the stock would be sold on the opening or as close to the opening as practical.

STOP LIMIT ORDERS

An investor would enter a stop limit order for the same reasons he or she would enter a stop order. The only difference is that once the order has been elected the order becomes a limit order instead of a market order. The same risks that apply to traditional limit orders apply to stop limit orders. If the stock continues to trade away from the investor's limit, the investor could give back all of the profits or suffer large losses.

OTHER TYPES OF ORDERS

There are several other types of orders that an investor may enter. They are:

- All or none (AON).
- Immediate or cancel (IOC).
- Fill or kill (FOK).
- Not held (NH).
- Market on open (MOO)/market on close (MOC)

ALL-OR-NONE ORDERS

AON orders may be entered as day orders or as GTC. All-or-none orders, as the name implies, indicate that the investor wants to buy or sell all of the securities or none of them. AON orders are not displayed in the market because they require special handling and the investor will not accept a partial execution.

IMMEDIATE OR CANCEL ORDERS

With an IOC order, the investor wants to buy or sell whatever is possible immediately and then cancel whatever is not filled.

FILL OR KILL ORDERS

With an FOK order, the investor wants the entire order executed immediately or the entire order canceled.

NOT-HELD ORDERS

With an NH order, the investor gives discretion to the floor broker as to the time and price of execution.

MARKET ON OPEN/MARKET ON CLOSE ORDERS

With MOO/MOC orders, the investor wants the order executed on the opening or closing of the market or as reasonably close to the opening or closing as practical. If the order is not executed, it is canceled. Partial executions are allowed.

>  **TAKENOTE!**
>
> The SEC has granted permission for the NYSE to eliminate the use of AON orders and FOK orders.

THE EXCHANGES

The most recognized stock exchange in the world is the New York Stock Exchange (NYSE). There are, however, many exchanges throughout the United States that all operate in a similar manner. Exchanges are dual-auction markets. They provide a central marketplace where buyers and sellers come together in one centralized location to compete with one another. Buyers compete with other buyers to be the highest price anyone is willing to pay for a security, and sellers compete with other sellers to be the lowest price at which anyone is willing to sell a security. All transactions in an exchange-listed security that are executed on the exchange have to take place in front of the specialist or designated market maker (DMM) for that security. The specialist/DMM is an exchange member who is responsible for maintaining a fair and orderly market for the stock in which he or she specializes. The specialist/DMM stands at the trading post where all the buyers and sellers must go to conduct business in the security. This is the reason for the crowd that you see on the news and financial reports when they show the floor of the exchange. All securities that trade on an exchange are known as listed securities.

PRIORITY OF EXCHANGE ORDERS

Orders that are routed to the trading post for execution are prioritized according to price and time. If the price of more than one order is the same, orders will be filled as follows:

- **Priority:** The order that was received first gets filled first.
- **Precedence:** If the time and price are the same, the larger order gets filled first.
- **Parity:** If all conditions are the same, the orders are matched in the crowd and the shares are split among the orders.

THE ROLE OF THE DESIGNATED MARKET MAKER

The DMM, formerly known as a specialist, is an independent exchange member who has been assigned a stock or group of stocks for which he or she is the DMM. DMMs are responsible for:

- Maintaining a fair and orderly market for the securities.
- Buying for their own account in the absence of public buy orders.
- Selling from their own account in the absence of public sell orders.
- Acting as an agent by executing public orders left with them.
- Displaying quotes for their own account at the inside market a certain percentage of the time.
- Determining the opening and closing prices for securities and providing price discovery.

A large amount of capital is required in order to fulfill the requirements of a DMM. As a result, most DMMs are employees of DMM firms. Although the DMM is not required to participate in every transaction, every transaction for that security that is executed on the exchange must take place in front of the DMM. The DMM may act as either an agent or as a principal if he or she plays a role in the transaction.

THE DMM ACTING AS A PRINCIPAL

In the absence of public orders, DMMs are required to provide liquidity and price improvement for the stocks in which they, as the designated market maker, are required to trade against the market, and may now trade for their own account at prices that would compete with public orders.

EXAMPLE

If the public market for XYZ is quoted as follows:

	Bid	Offer
10 × 10	20.45	20.55

There is a 20.45 bid for 1,000 shares and 1,000 shares offered at 20.55.

If a public sell order came in to sell the stock, the DMM could purchase the stock for his or her own account at 20.45 because he or she is on parity with the public. The DMM could also purchase the stock for his or her own account at 20.50 and would be improving the price that the seller would be receiving. This is known as price improvement. Alternatively, if a public buy order came in, the DMM could sell the stock from his or her own account at 20.55 because he or she is now allowed to compete with the public. He or she could also sell the stock to the customer at 20.50 because, once again, that would be providing price improvement for the order.

THE DMM ACTING AS AN AGENT

DMMs are also required to execute orders that have been left with them. Orders that have been left with the DMM for execution are said to be "left or dropped on the DMM's book." The DMM is required to maintain a book of public orders and to execute them when market conditions permit. The types of orders that may be left with the DMM are:

- Buy and sell limit orders.
- Stop orders.
- Stop limit orders.
- Both day and GTC orders.
- AON orders.

Market on close/limit on close and limit on close orders may be entered or canceled up until 3:45 p.m. on the NYSE. After 3:45 p.m. market and limit on close orders may only be entered if there is an order imbalance of 50,000 shares or more on the opposite side of the market. A market on close or limit on close that had been entered in error may be canceled up until 3:58 p.m.

DMMs will execute the orders if and when they are able to and will send a commission bill to the member who left the order with them for execution. The fee commission charged by the DMM is usually only a cent or a fraction of a cent per share. The DMM is also required to quote the best market for the security to any party that asks. The best or inside market is composed of the highest bid and the lowest offer. This is made up from bids and offers contained in the DMM's book and in the trading crowd. The inside market is also the market that is displayed to broker dealers and agents on their quote system.

When quoting the inside market, the specialist/DMM will add all of the shares bid for at the highest price and all of the shares offered at the lowest price to determine the size of the market. The following types of orders are not included when determining the inside market:

- Stop orders
- AON orders

A DMM may not accept the following types of orders:

- Market orders
- Immediately executable limit orders
- NH orders
- IOC orders
- FOK orders

Market orders and immediately executable limit orders are filled as soon as they reach the crowd, so there is nothing to leave with the DMM. In the case of an NH order, once a floor broker is given discretion as to time and price, it may not be given to another party.

A DMM's book may look something like the following example:

Buy	XYZ	Sell
5 Goldman	20	
10 Schwab		
	20.05	
	20.10	1 Prudential
		5 Fidelity
	20.15	2 Morgan
5 Merrill Stp	20.20	

The inside market for XYZ based on the DMM's, book would be:

        Bid   **Ask**
15 × 6 20.00 20.10

Buyers are bidding for 1,500 shares and sellers are offering 600 shares of XYZ.

> TAKENOTE!
>
> The buy stop entered over the market by Merrill is not contained in the quote, because the order has not been elected.

CROSSING STOCK

A floor broker from time to time may get an order from both a buyer and a seller in the same security. The floor broker may be allowed to pair off, or "cross" the orders, and execute both orders simultaneously. In order for the floor broker to cross the stock, the specialist must allow it and the floor broker must announce the orders in an effort to obtain price improvement. The floor broker must offer the stock for sale at a price above the current best bid and may purchase the stock using the buy order if no price improvement has been offered. This will then complete the cross, and both orders will be filled.

DO NOT REDUCE (DNR)

GTC orders that are placed underneath the market and left with the specialist for execution will be reduced for the distribution of dividends. Orders that will be reduced are:

- Buy limits.
- Sell stops.

These orders are reduced because when a stock goes ex-dividend its price is adjusted down. To ensure that customer orders placed below the market are only executed as a result of market activity, the order will be adjusted down by the value of the dividend.

EXAMPLE A customer has placed an order to buy 500 XYZ at 35 GTC. XYZ closed yesterday at 36.10. XYZ goes ex-dividend for 20 cents and opens the next day at 35.90. The customer's order will now be an order to purchase 500 XYZ at 34.80 GTC.

If the customer had entered the order and specified that the order was not to be reduced for the distribution of ordinary dividends, it would have remained an order to purchase 500 shares at 35. The order in this case would have been entered as:

Buy 500 XYZ 35 GTC DNR

Orders placed above the market are not reduced for distributions.

ADJUSTMENTS FOR STOCK SPLITS

GTC orders that are left with the specialist must be adjusted for stock splits. Orders that are placed above and below the market will be adjusted so that the aggregate dollar value of the order remains the same.

EXAMPLE A customer has placed a GTC order. Let's look at what happens to the order if the company declares a stock split:

Type of Split	Old Order	New Order
2:1	Buy 100 at 50	Buy 200 at 25
2:1	Sell 100 at 100	Sell 200 at 50
3:2	Buy 100 at 100	Buy 150 at 66.67
3:2	Sell 100 at 60	Sell 150 at 40

Notice that in all of the examples the value of the customer's order remained the same. To calculate the adjustment to an open order for a forward stock split, multiply the number of shares by the fraction and the share price by the reciprocal of the fraction. For example:

Buy 100 at 50 after a 2:1 stock split

$100 \times 2/1 = 200$

$50 \times 1/2 = 25$

The value of the order was $5,000 both before and after the order. If the stock undergoes a reverse stock split, all open orders will be canceled.

SUPER DISPLAY BOOK (SDBK)

Most customer orders will never be handled by a floor broker. Floor brokers usually only handle the large, complex institutional orders. Customer orders will be electronically routed directly to the trading post for execution via the Super Display Book (SDBK) system. The SDBK bypasses the floor broker and sends the order right to the specialist/DMM for execution. If the order can be immediately executed, the system will send an electronic confirmation of the execution to the submitting broker dealer. All listed securities are eligible to be traded over the SDBK system. All preopening orders that can be matched up are automatically paired off by the system and executed at the opening price. Any preopening orders that cannot be paired off are routed to the trading post for inclusion on the SDBK.

SHORT SALES

An investor who believes that a stock price has appreciated too far and is likely to decline may profit from this belief by selling the stock short. In a short sale, the customer borrows the security in order to complete delivery to the buying party. The investor sells the stock high, hoping that it can be bought back at a cheaper price and replaced. It is a perfectly legitimate investment strategy. The investor's first transaction is a sell, and the investor exits the position by repurchasing the stock. The short sale of stock has unlimited risk because there is no limit to how high the stock price may go. The investor will lose money if the stock appreciates past the sales price.

AFFIRMATIVE DETERMINATION

All firms and agents are required to make an affirmative determination for all sell orders entered on behalf of the firm or a customer. All sell orders must be marked either long or short. A person is considered long the security if the investor:

- Has possession of the security.
- Has purchased the security but the trade has not settled.
- Has issued conversion or exercise instructions for a right, warrant, option, convertible bond, or preferred stock.

If the investor owns rights, warrants, options, or a convertible security but has not issued exercise or conversion instructions, the investor is not considered long the security.

The firm must make a determination if the customer is long the security or if the customer is selling short. If the customer is selling short, the firm must determine if the security can be borrowed for delivery.

An investor is only considered long the security to the extent of the investor's net long position in the security. If an investor is long 1,000 shares of

ABC and is short 600 shares of ABC in another account, the investor may only mark a sell ticket for 400 shares of ABC long.

REGULATION SHO

The SEC has adopted new rules relating to the short sale of securities. Regulation SHO has been adopted to update prior short sale regulations. Regulation SHO covers:

- Definitions and order marking.
- Suspension of uptick and plus-bid requirements.
- Borrowing and delivery requirements for securities.

Under Regulation SHO, the SEC has prohibited any SRO from adopting any price criteria as a requirement of executing a short sale.

RULE 200 DEFINITIONS AND ORDER MARKING

Rule 200 updates the definition of who is determined to be long a security. As new derivatives and trading systems and strategies have been introduced, amendments to the short sale rules under the Securities Exchange Act of 1934 needed to be updated. Most of the prior rules and definitions remain unchanged. The new updates under Rule 200 are as follows:

- Investors are considered long the security if they hold a security future contract and have been notified that they will receive the underlying security.
- Broker dealers must aggregate their net positions in securities unless they qualify to allow each independent trading unit to aggregate its positions independently.

A broker dealer may qualify to have its various trading departments determine their net long or short positions independently if:

- Traders are only assigned to one independent trading unit at any one time.
- Traders in each independent trading unit employ their own trading strategies and do not coordinate their trading with other independent trading units.
- The firm has documented each aggregation unit and the independent trading objectives of each unit.
- The firm supports the independent nature of each trading unit.

- At the time a sell order is entered, each independent aggregation unit determines its net position for the security.

The order-marking requirements of Rule 200 require the broker dealer to mark all orders long, short, or short exempt. The definition of long and short include the definitions in the affirmative determination rule and have been expanded to include the following:

- An order may be marked long if the investor or broker dealer has possession of the security and can reasonably be expected to deliver the security by settlement date.
- An order must be marked short if the investor or broker dealer has possession of the security but cannot reasonably be expected to deliver the security by settlement date.
- An order does not need to be marked short exempt if the seller is only relying on a price test exemption under the tick test or bid test rule.

RULE 203 SECURITY BORROWING AND DELIVERY REQUIREMENTS

A broker dealer may not accept an order to sell short an equity security for the account of a customer or for its own account without having borrowed the security, having arranged to borrow the security, or without having a reasonable belief that the security can be borrowed. A broker dealer can rely on an easy-to-borrow list of securities so long as the list is less than 24 hours old. If a security does not appear on the easy to borrow list or if it is on the hard to borrow list, the broker-dealer must specifically obtain a borrow to complete delivery. An interesting test point relating to this information, is the fact that a security that does not appear on the hard to borrow list, should not be assumed to be included on the easy to borrow list. For sell orders that were marked long, the broker dealer must deliver the securities by the settlement date and may not borrow the securities to complete delivery. However, a broker dealer may borrow securities to complete delivery under the following exceptions:

- To complete delivery to the buyer when a customer fails to deliver.
- When the security is being loaned to another broker dealer.

- When a fail to deliver resulting from a good faith mistake and a buy in would create an undue hardship.

A broker dealer must close out all customer fails-to-deliver within 35 days of the trade date. The broker dealer must borrow the securities or buy in the securities of a like kind and quantity.

A broker dealer is exempt from the locating requirements for short sales if:

- The broker dealer has accepted an order to sell short an equity security short from another broker dealer. The broker dealer entering the order is required to locate the securities unless the broker dealer accepting the order has a contractual obligation to comply.
- The transactions are in securities futures.
- The transactions are executed in accordance with bona fide market making.
- The transactions are executed by a specialist, block positioner, or dealer.
- An order where the customer has been determined to be long and will deliver the security when restrictions have been removed or expired. The seller must deliver the securities within 35 calendar days. If the broker dealer does not receive the securities, the broker dealer must buy in the customer or borrow the securities.

RULE 204 CLOSEOUT PROCEDURES

SEC Rule 204 Requires broker dealers who have a failure to deliver as the result of a sale, to close out the failing position promptly. Any broker dealer with an outstanding failure to deliver as the result of a short sale must close out that failure on the business day immediately following the settlement date. If the failure is the result of a long sale, or bona fide market making, the broker dealer must close out the failure no later than 3 business days after settlement. A broker dealer may close out the failure by purchasing securities in the open market or by delivering borrowed securities. Firms that are not in compliance with SEC Rule 204 may not execute and may not accept an order to sell the securities short for any customer or correspondent firm, without first obtaining borrowed securities to complete delivery. A broker dealer must close out a customer's failure to deliver on the 36th day following the trade date. If the customer fails to deliver the securities free from all restrictions by the end of the 35th day, the broker dealer must close out the failure and purchase the securities in the market. The failure to remove the restriction from securities sold under Rule 144 is often the cause of the buy in.

THRESHOLD SECURITIES

The self-regulatory organizations (SROs) are responsible for the inclusion of securities on the threshold securities list. The SROs monitor reports from the National Securities Clearing Corporation (NSCC) to determine which securities meet the definition of a threshold security. The NSCC is the clearing intermediary through which clearing member firms reconcile their securities accounts. A threshold security is an equity security that meets the following criteria:

- The security is registered under Section 12 of the Securities Exchange Act of 1934.
- There is an aggregate fail to deliver position at a clearing firm of 10,000 shares or more for 5 consecutive settlement days and such position represents 0.5% or more of the issuer's outstanding securities.
- The security has been included on the threshold securities list by an SRO and the list has been distributed by the SRO to its members.

A broker dealer who has a fail to deliver in a threshold security at a clearing firm for 13 consecutive settlement days must immediately close out the position by buying securities of a like kind and quantity. A broker dealer with a fail-to-deliver in a threshold security for 13 consecutive settlement dates may not accept an order to sell the security short from another person and may not sell the security short for its own account without having located the security until the fail to deliver has been closed out. Clearing firms that provide clearing services to other broker dealers may allocate or distribute a fail-to-deliver position in threshold securities to its broker dealer customers who are responsible for the fail-to-deliver. By allocating the fail-to-deliver position to its broker dealer customers who established the position, the obligation to close out the position is transferred from the clearing firm to the broker dealer customers who established the position. The 13-day requirement does not apply to any fail-to-deliver position that was established prior to a security becoming a threshold security. If a market maker cannot borrow a threshold security to execute transactions in connection with bona fide market-making activities, then the market maker is entitled to an excused withdrawal from that security.

A security will cease to be considered a threshold security if it does not exceed the specific fails to deliver criteria for 5 consecutive settlement days.

Firms must maintain a record of customer and firm short positions. The firm must file a short-interest report twice per month for short positions that have settled by the 15th and as of the last trading day of each month, using FINRA's Regulation Filing Application (RFA). All reports are required to be filed with the firm's designated examining authority (FINRA or NYSE) by the end of the second business day following the settlement date.

OVER THE COUNTER/NASDAQ

Securities that are not listed on a centralized exchange trade over the counter or on the Nasdaq. Nasdaq stands for National Association of Securities Dealers Automated Quotation System. It is the interdealer network of computers and phone lines that allows securities to be traded between broker dealers. Nasdaq is not a traditional exchange. It is a negotiated market where one broker dealer negotiates a price directly with another broker dealer. None of the other interested parties for that particular security have any idea of what terms are being proposed. The broker dealers may communicate over their Nasdaq workstations or can speak directly to one another over the phone. The normal business hours for the Nasdaq market are from 9:30 a.m. to 4:00 p.m. EST.

MARKET MAKERS

Because there are no specialists for the OTC markets, bids and offers are displayed by broker dealers known as market makers. A market maker is a firm that is required to display a two-sided market. A two-sided market consists of a simultaneous bid and offer for the security quoted through the Nasdaq workstation. The market maker must be willing to buy the security at the bid price, which is displayed, as well as be willing to sell the security at the offering price, which is also displayed. These are known as firm quotes. There is no centralized location for the Nasdaq market; it is simply a network of computers that connects broker dealers throughout the world. Market makers purchase the security at the bid price and sell the security at the offering price. Their profit is the difference between the bid and the offer, which is known as the spread. Rule changes and new trading systems known as ECNs, or electronic communication networks, have narrowed the spreads on stocks significantly in recent years. Firms that act as market makers must continuously display two-sided quotes when displaying quotes. Firms that remain open for extended-hours trading are required to comply with Nasdaq rules.

NASDAQ SUBSCRIPTION LEVELS

Broker dealers will subscribe to the Nasdaq workstation services that meet their firm's requirements. The levels of service are:

- **Level I:** Nasdaq Level I subscription service provides information relating to the inside market, last sale, and daily volume data and provides quotes for registered representatives.
- **Level II:** Nasdaq Level II allows the subscriber to see the inside market, the quotes of all market makers, the total daily volume, and the high and low for the day.
- **Level III:** Nasdaq Level III is the highest level of service offered over the Nasdaq workstation. Level III contains all of the features of Level II and allows the firm to enter and update its own markets. Level III is only for approved market makers.

NASDAQ QUOTES

Most actively traded Nasdaq stocks are quoted by a large number of market makers. As market makers enter their quotes, some will be above or below the best quote, which is known as the inside market. A market maker whose quote is above or below the inside market is said to be away from the market. As the market makers adjust their quotes, the market maker who is publishing the highest bid for the security has its bid displayed at the top of the list and the bid is published as the best bid to anyone with a Nasdaq Level I subscription service or higher. The market maker publishing the lowest offer will have its offer listed at the top of the list and published as the lowest offer to anyone with a Nasdaq Level I subscription service or higher. As a result, the best bid and offer from any two market makers comprise the inside market.

EXAMPLE

	XYAD	
	Bid	**Ask**
	15.00	15.05
MM 1	14.90	15.10
MM 2	15.00	15.20
MM 3	14.85	15.05
MM 4	14.95	15.15
MM 5	14.98	15.18

 TAKENOTE!

Notice how the inside market for XYAD consists of the bid from market maker 2 and the offer from market maker 3. All of the other market makers are away from the inside market.

NOMINAL NASDAQ QUOTES

All quotes published over the Nasdaq workstation are firm quotes. A dealer who fails to honor its quotes has committed a violation known as backing away. Dealers who provide quotes over the phone, which are clearly indicated as being subject or nominal, cannot be held to trade at those prices. Nasdaq qualifiers include:

- "It looks like . . ."
- "It's around . . ."
- "Subject to . . ."
- "Nominal . . ."
- "Work it out . . ."
- "Last I saw . . ."

A response of "it is" would indicate a firm quote. A firm quote is always good for at least one round lot, or 100 shares.

NASDAQ EXECUTION SYSTEMS

Most Nasdaq trades are executed over the Nasdaq workstation using one of its automated execution systems. These systems allow dealers to execute orders without having to speak with one another on the phone.

NASDAQ MARKET CENTER EXECUTION SYSTEM (NMCES)

The Nasdaq Market Center Execution System, also known as NMCES accepts market orders and immediately executable limit orders for both customer and firm accounts. Orders may be entered for up to 999,999 shares per order. The orders will immediately be routed to dealers on the inside market for automatic execution. Larger orders may be split up to meet the maximum order volume. Orders executed through the NMCES are automatically reported to the ACT (Automated Confirmation of Transaction) system. Orders executed through the NMCES are executed based on the priority of price and time. Orders will be executed against the market maker that is quoting the best price first. If more than one market maker is quoting the same price, orders will be executed against the market maker who quoted the best price first. Orders may be entered in the NMCES by both market makers and order entry firms.

 TAKENOTE!

The Series 99 exam may use the terms Nasdaq Market Center Execution System, NMCES, or simply Nasdaq in test questions relating to the Nasdaq order execution and quote systems.

ELECTRONIC COMMUNICATION NETWORKS (ECNs)

Electronic communication networks, or ECNs, operate independently of FINRA. ECNs display and execute third-party orders and are allowed access to the NMCES. ECNs are widely used by both broker dealers and institutional investors to display and execute orders. ECN quotes are included in the Nasdaq quote system, but the ECN is not required to maintain a two-sided market like a market maker and ECNs do not take positions in the security. There are two ways that the ECN may participate in the NMCES. The ECN may be a full-participation ECN or it may be an order delivery ECN. Full-participation ECNs may:

- Display quotes.
- Enter and accept directed and nondirected orders.
- Accept automatic executions.
- Send orders for automatic execution through the NMCES.

An order delivery ECN will display customer orders in the Alternative Display Facility (ADF). If the ECN displays quotes through the ADF, it must provide access to its quotes though a connectivity provider for order execution.

Broker dealers and institutions that subscribe to the ECN may execute orders within the ECN's internal network.

NON-NASDAQ OTC MKT

Non listed securities which were formally traded on the OTC bulletin board are now quoted and traded in marketplaces provided by The OTC Markets Group. The marketplaces broadly referred to as the OTC MKT consist of 3 tiers. These tiers are the OTCQX Best Market, OTCQB Venture Market and the OTC PINK. The quality of the issuer's financial performance, corporate governance and the availability of financial information determine where the company's shares will be quoted and traded. The requirements for the marketplaces from highest to lowest are OTCQX, OTCQB and OTC PINK respectively. Firm priced quotes and unpriced indications of interest (bid or offer wanted) may be published in these markets.

To qualify for the OTCQX market, companies must meet high financial standards, follow best practice corporate governance, demonstrate compliance with U.S. securities laws, be current in their disclosure, and have a professional third-party sponsor introduction.

The OTCQB Venture Market is for entrepreneurial and development stage U.S. and international companies. To be eligible, companies must be current in their reporting and undergo an annual verification and management certification process. Companies must meet a $0.01 bid test and may not be in bankruptcy.

The OTC PINK consists of PINK CURRENT Information and PINK LIMITED Information companies

To qualify for Current Information, Alternative Reporting companies may subscribe to the OTC Disclosure & News Service and publish current information pursuant to OTC Markets' Pink Basic Disclosure Guidelines. This information will be made publicly available on the OTC Markets' website. Companies will be processed for Current Information once the following required documentation has been publicly disclosed:

- Financial Statements: Two most recent annual reports and any subsequent quarterly report
- Disclosure Statement: Most recent annual and any subsequent quarterly reports

- Attorney Letter covering all relevant information for non-audited companies

Additionally, the company must verify its Company Profile through OTCIQ. This includes a complete list of officers, directors, and control persons; service providers; outstanding shares; a business description and contact information.

U.S. banks and bank holding companies that are not SEC reporting may follow OTC Markets' Bank Reporting Disclosure Guidelines.

The Pink Limited Information market tier includes companies that OTC Markets Group determines meet the minimum requirements under Rule 15c2-11, but have limited disclosure and/or financial information publicly available, such as those that may be delinquent in their filing obligations with the SEC, a foreign exchange or regulator, or under the Pink Disclosure Guidelines. PINK LIMITED also includes non-U.S. companies listed on a qualified foreign exchange that does not mandate English language disclosure. U.S. companies providing the following under the Pink Disclosure Guidelines may be designated as "Limited Information":

Financial Statements: Companies must upload financial statements for a completed Fiscal Year within the past 16 months. Financial reports must be prepared according to U.S. GAAP or International Financial Reporting Standards (IFRS) but are not required to be audited.

The Company Profile has been verified through OTCIQ. Required Information includes a complete list of officers, directors, and control persons; service providers; outstanding shares; a business description and contact information.

Securities designated as Limited Information may have additional restrictions for unsolicited quoting.

It is important to note that these markets are not exchanges and the OTC LINK and OTC ECN are SEC registered Alternative Trading Systems (ATS). The OTC LINK system allows broker dealers to view and publish quotes and to negotiate trades with dealers. The OTC ECN allows for anonymous auto execution of trades.

SEC RULE 15C2-11

SEC Rule 15C2-11 (as amended) sets the standards for non listed companies to develop a public market and for broker dealers to publish quotations for the securities. SEC 15c2-11 requires issues to be current when reporting and disclosing financial and other information. The OTC Markets Group acts as a qualified interdealer quotation service (IQDS) and monitors issuer compliance on an ongoing basis to ensure that issuers are current with their disclosures. A broker dealer wishing to quote an OTC security will be able to rely on the current information designation made by the IQDS in lieu of submitting Form 211 with FINRA. In order for an issuer to maintain its designation as being current, SEC reporting issuers must continuously make timely filings of all reports. Companies listed on the OTCQX, OTCQB and PINK Current are subject to this rule. If companies fail to meet this continuing reporting requirement, the security will be deemed ineligible for public quotes. During market hours quotes for these ineligible securities will be shown as zero (0). However, last sale data for the stock will be available at the end of the day. If the security is deemed to be inactive, the issuer must work with the broker dealer to file form 211 with FINRA. Rule 15c2-11 permits additional time (180 days) for Exchange Act reporting companies to continue to be eligible for public broker-dealer quotes. Accordingly, companies that make their annual or quarterly reports publicly available (via EDGAR) within 180 days of the end of the reporting period will still be eligible for broker-dealer proprietary quotes, but will be designated as "Limited Information". Companies who have no information available may be traded on either the OTC Expert market or be forced into the Gray market. The OTC Expert market is where broker dealers may publish unsolicited quotes based on customer limit orders to obtain the best possible execution for the customer. Quotes in the Expert Market are restricted from public view. The Gray market is not an electronic market. The stock of issuers whose securities have been delisted or who are no information companies will be traded over the phone between broker dealers. The Gray market lacks the price discovery made available in electronic markets. Investors should be extremely cautious when considering purchasing securities in either the Expert or Gray market.

THIRD MARKET

The third market consists of transactions in exchange-listed securities that are executed over the counter through the Nasdaq workstation. A broker dealer may wish to simply purchase or sell an exchange-listed security directly with another brokerage firm instead of executing the order on the floor of the exchange. These transactions are known as third-market transactions. All third-market transactions are reported through ACT to the consolidated tape for display. Market makers who enter quotes for exchange-listed securities must enter their quotes through the Consolidated Quotation System (CQS). CQS market makers may not execute an order for an exchange-listed initial public offering prior to the security's opening for trading on its primary exchange.

FOURTH MARKET

A fourth-market transaction is a transaction between two large institutions without the use of a broker dealer. The computer network that facilitates these transactions is known as INSTINET. Large blocks of stock, both listed and unlisted, trade between large institutional investors in the fourth market. Although many trades in the fourth market are executed through the INSTINET system, many large portfolio managers execute internal crosses that go unreported. Proprietary trading systems are not considered part of the fourth market, because these systems are either registered as broker dealers or are operated by broker dealers. Trades executed by large institutions via proprietary networks are sometimes referred to as "dark pools," because the supply or demand for a security is unseen by market participants.

THE CONSOLIDATED AUDIT TRAIL SYSTEM (CATS)

In order to ensure that customer orders are transmitted to the marketplace in a timely manner, FINRA developed the Consolidated Audit Trail system (CATS). CATS tracks an order through each stage of its life, from receipt to execution or cancellation. Each firm is required to synchronize clocks used for electronic order events daily before the market opens to within 50 milliseconds of the National Institute of Standardized Time's atomic clock. These clocks must display and record military time in hours, minutes, seconds and milliseconds. Each clock used solely for manual order events may be synchronized to a tolerance within 1 second of the NIST clock. Each member may record and submit manual order events and allocation reports to the Central Repository in increments of 1 second. Firms are only requested to collect and submit data in nanoseconds if the firm collects the data. Firms are required to submit daily electronic CATS reports to FINRA's Central Repository. The business day for CATS is 4:150:00:01 p.m. to 4:15 p.m. the following business day. CATS reports must be made by 8 a.m. on T+1 on the business day following the trade date. For trades executed on Friday, CATS reports may be submitted on Saturday but must be submitted by 8 a.m. Monday morning. Daily CATS reports must be made for each order and each order must have a unique identifier. CATS reports contain the following information for all customer equity and option orders:

- Customer name, account number, date of birth, address and tax ID.
- Date and time of receipt.
- Order ID.

- Terms of the order (i.e., buy, sell, long, short, security, price, shares, account type, and handling instructions).
- If the order was received manually or electronically.
- If the order was routed manually or electronically
- Where the order was routed for execution.
- Any modifications to the order, including the date and time of any modifications.
- Execution information, including partial executions, price, date, time, and capacity in which the firm acted in the trade.
- MPID of firm routing the order
- MPID of firm were order was routed
- If order is executed internally, the ID of desk or department to which the order is routed

 TAKENOTE!

If an order originates on the firm's trading desk during its normal market making or trading activities the order is not required to be included in the CATS report(s) submitted to the Central Repository.

BROKER VS. DEALER

The term *broker dealer* actually refers to the two capacities in which a firm may act when executing a transaction. When a firm is acting as a broker, it is acting as the customer's agent and is merely executing the customer's order for a fee known as a commission. The role of the broker is simply to find someone willing to buy the investor's securities if the customer is selling or to find someone willing to sell the securities if the investor is looking to buy. The firm acts as a dealer when it participates in the transaction by taking the opposite side of the trade. For example, the firm may fill a customer's buy order by selling the securities to the customer from the firm's own account, or the dealer may fill the customer's sell order by buying the securities for its own account. A brokerage firm is always acting as a dealer or in a principal capacity when it is making markets over the counter.

CHAPTER 5

Broker	Dealer
Executes customer's orders	Participates in the trade as a principal
Charges a commission	Charges a markup or markdown
Must disclose the amount of the commission	Makes a market in the security
	Must disclose the fact that it is a market maker, but not the amount of the markup or markdown

FINRA'S 5% MARKUP POLICY

FINRA has set a guideline to ensure that the prices investors pay and receive for securities are reasonably related to the market for the securities. As a general rule, FINRA considers a charge of 5% to be reasonable. The 5% policy is a guideline, not a rule. Factors that go toward what is considered reasonable are:

- The price of the security.
- The value of the transaction.
- The type of security.
- The value of the members' services.
- Execution expenses.

When a customer is executing an order for a low priced or low total dollar amount, a firm's minimum commission may be greater than 5% of the transaction.

EXAMPLE A customer wants to purchase 1,000 shares of XYZ at $1. If the firm's minimum commission is $100, that would be 10% of the trade, but in this case it would be okay.

Stocks generally carry a higher degree of risk than bonds, and, as a result, stocks justify a higher commission or profit to the dealer. Full-service firms may be able to justify a larger commission simply based on the value of the services they provide.

MARKUPS/MARKDOWNS WHEN ACTING AS A PRINCIPAL

A firm that executes customer orders on a principal basis is entitled to a profit on those transactions. If the firm is selling the security to the customer, it will charge the customer a markup. In the case of the firm buying the securities from the customer, it will charge the customer a markdown. The amount of the markup or markdown that a firm charges the customer is based on the inside market for the security.

EXAMPLE

Let's assume that the brokerage firm is a market maker in ABCD. In the morning, the firm purchased shares of ABCD for its own account at 9.50. The stock has been trading higher all day and is now quoted as follows:

Bid	Ask
10.00	10.05

If a customer wants to purchase 100 shares of ABCD from the dealer, the customer's markup would be based on the current offering price of 10.05. As a result, the maximum amount the firm could charge the customer for the stock would be 10.552 per share, or $1,055.20 for the entire order, which would include a 5% markup. Notice that the markup to the customer did not take into consideration the firm's actual cost.

If a customer wants to sell 100 shares of ABCD, the minimum proceeds to the customer would be 9.50 per share, or $950 for entire order, which would include a 5% markdown.

To determine the maximum or minimum prices for a customer, use the following guidelines:

- 105% of the offer price for customers who are purchasing the security
- 95% of the bid price for customers who are selling the security

When determining the amount of the markup or markdown, the following are excluded:

- The firm's actual cost
- The firm's quote if it is a market maker in the security

RISKLESS PRINCIPAL TRANSACTIONS

If a brokerage firm receives a customer order to buy or sell a security and the firm does not have an inventory position in the security, the firm may still elect to execute the order on a principal basis. If the firm elects to execute the order on a principal basis, this is known as a riskless principal transaction. Because the dealer is only taking a position in the security to fill the customer's order, the dealer is not taking on any risk. As a result, the markup or markdown on riskless transactions will be based on the dealer's actual cost, not on the inside market.

EXAMPLE

Bid	Ask
10.00	10.05

A customer wants to purchase 100 shares of ABCD from the dealer, and the dealer executes the order on a principal basis by purchasing the shares for its own account at $10.02 only to immediately resell the stock to the customer. The markup in this case must be based on the dealer's actual cost of $10.02. The maximum the dealer could charge the customer would be $10.521 per share, or $1,052.10 for the entire order.

NET TRANSACTIONS WITH CUSTOMERS

A broker dealer, when acting as a principal, may execute a transaction for a customer as a net transaction. In a net transaction, the broker dealer will purchase the security in the marketplace at one price and sell it to the customer at a higher price for a profit instead of charging the customer a markup. The profit received by the broker dealer is not reported on the customer's confirmation, which only shows the net price. Because the trades take place at two different prices, both trades must be reported to the tape though the Nasdaq TRF. Individual customers must give the broker dealer written permission for each trade to be executed on a net basis. Institutional customers may approve net transactions orally, in writing, or may give blanket consent by not replying to a negative consent letter, which would allow the institution to opt out of net transactions by replying to the letter.

PROCEEDS TRANSACTIONS

In a proceeds transaction, the customer sells a security and uses the proceeds from that sale to purchase another security on the same day. FINRA's 5% policy states that a firm may only charge the customer a combined commission or markup and markdown of 5% for both transactions, not 5% on each.

FIRM QUOTE RULE

All market makers who publish quotes over the Nasdaq system must execute an order that is presented to the firm at a price and size that is at least equal to its published quote. A market maker's firm quote obligation begins when an order is presented to the firm for execution against its quote either electronically or over the phone. A market maker is not bound by the firm quote rule under the following circumstances:

- The market maker is publishing a quote for a security not covered by the rule.
- The market maker has just affected a trade and is in the process of updating its quote.
- The market maker has just updated and published a new quote and the new quote was published prior to, or at the same time as, the receipt of the order.

TAKENOTE!

A market maker that fails to honor its firm quote has committed a violation known as "backing away."

TRADE COMPLAINTS BETWEEN MEMBERS

A member that feels that a trade was reported in error may have the trade reviewed by Nasdaq Market Operations if it is unable to resolve the issue with the contra broker dealer. The party bringing the complaint must submit a written request to Nasdaq Market Operations by fax or other acceptable means by 10:30 a.m. EST for trades occurring prior to 10:00 a.m. EST and within 30 minutes for trades occurring after 10:00 a.m. EST. Once a complaint has been filed, the firm bringing the complaint has 30 minutes to provide additional documentation. The broker dealer responding to the complaint will receive telephone notification and will be given 30 minutes to submit documentation. Once both parties have indicated that they have submitted all documentation, they may not submit additional documentation. The matter will then be reviewed by a Nasdaq Market Operations hearing officer. The hearing officer may cancel the trade, modify the trade, or allow the trade to stand. Both parties will receive telephone notification and a written report. If the Nasdaq system causes erroneous reports to take place, Nasdaq Market Operations can automatically correct or break the trade within 30 minutes of detection. The Nasdaq may correct trades caused by system malfunctions up to 6:00 p.m. EST on the day after the trade date.

CHAPTER 5

Pretest

TRADING SECURITIES

1. Your brokerage firm acts as a market maker for several high-volume stocks that are quoted on the Nasdaq. What is the firm's consideration for being a market maker?
   a. Commission
   b. Fees
   c. Spread
   d. 5%

2. Which of the following are NOT types of orders?
   I. All or none
   II. Fill or kill
   III. Mini/maxi
   IV. Best efforts
   a. I and II
   b. II and IV
   c. I and IV
   d. III and IV

3. The inside market is made up of which of the following?
   I. Highest offer
   II. Lowest offer
   III. Highest bid
   IV. Lowest bid

   a. II and III
   b. I and II
   c. I and IV
   d. I and III

4. Which of the following is true of specialists/DMMs on the NYSE?
   a. They work for themselves.
   b. They are appointed by a vote of the company's board.
   c. They work for the exchange.
   d. They work for the company whose stock they trade.

5. Which of the following would be considered a firm quote?
   I. A quote for a non-Nasdaq security received from a dealer over the phone
   II. A two-sided quote for a non-Nasdaq DPP
   III. A two-sided bond quote
   IV. A two-sided quote from a dealer listed in the pink OTC

   a. I and II
   b. I and III
   c. II and IV
   d. I, III, and IV

6. An investor enters an order to buy 1,000 ABC MOC. Which of the following is NOT true?
   a. The order will be executed as close to the closing price as possible.
   b. The order will be canceled if trading on the exchange is halted.
   c. The order will be canceled if trading in ABC is halted.
   d. It may be executed at any price within the last 4 minutes of the trading day because it is a market order.

7. ABC Technologies, a very volatile stock, closes at $180 per share. Your customer has placed an order to sell 500 ABC at 165 stop limit 160 GTC. After the close, the company announces bad earnings, and the stock opens at 145. What happened to your customer's order?

   a. It has been canceled because the stock price is below the limit price.
   b. It has been elected and has become a limit order.
   c. It has been elected and executed.
   d. It has been canceled because the stock price is below the stop price.

8. An investor would be considered long a security for the purposes of entering sell order in all of the following circumstances, EXCEPT:

   a. The investor has possession of the security.
   b. The investor has purchased the security but the trade has not settled.
   c. The investor has issued conversion instructions for a convertible bond.
   d. The investor is long in the money call option.

CHAPTER 6

General Supervision

INTRODUCTION

The foundation of a firm's supervisory system is its written supervisory manual, also known as the firm's policy and procedures manual. All members are required to have a policy and procedures manual that outlines the supervisory structure of the firm and that designates a principal to be responsible for each business area of supervision. The policy and procedures manual must include the title, location, and registration status of all supervisors, and a copy of the manual must be kept in each office of the firm where supervised activities are conducted. The purpose of the written policy and procedures manual is to ensure compliance with the firm's rules, as well as the rules of the industry. The manual must be updated to reflect the adoption of new policies, a change in personnel, or new industry regulations. The manual must also clearly outline the way the periodic compliance examinations are conducted and documented. Both the SEC and FINRA can take action against a firm or principal for failing to supervise its operations and agents.

THE ROLE OF THE PRINCIPAL

Prior to being admitted as a member of FINRA, a firm must have at least two principals to supervise the firm's activities. At a minimum, one must be a principal to supervise employees and the other must be a financial operations principal, or FINOP, to supervise the financial and operational activities of the firm. It is the principal's responsibility to ensure that all rules in the policy and procedures manual are followed by the firm's employees. It is also the responsibility of the principal to review and approve all of the following:

- New accounts
- Retail communication
- Transactions

The principal reviews and approves the above listed items in writing by signing or initialing the item. In the case of transactions, a principal may initial each ticket or initial a daily trade run. This supervisor's initials will evidence the fact that the trades have been reviewed and approved. As most firms now execute orders using electronic "tickets" the principal may review the trade runs electronically and check a box for approval. There is no requirement that a principal approve a trade prior to its execution, but the trade must be reviewed and approved promptly. Each registered representative must be assigned to a specific supervisor. A firm may also employ a risk based review system designed to identify trades that pose the greatest financial or regulatory risks to the firm or its customers. Monitoring trades executed in certain products, or by producing managers or representatives with disciplinary history may all be considerations for the risk based system. A principal of a member firm who fails to supervise the actions of the agents under their control may be subject to action by both FINRA and the SEC. A principal will not be subject to action if there are written procedures in place that are designed to detect and prevent violations. These procedures must have been enacted, and the supervisor must not have reason to believe the system is not operating properly. Additionally, the principal will not be found to have failed to supervise if an agent has employed extreme measures to conceal his or her actions. Each member firm must designate at least one principal to establish and review the firm's supervisory control systems. This person is responsible for recommending changes in the system to the firm's senior management and reporting the effectiveness of the firm's compliance system, at least once per year. This person must be identified to FINRA as the principal in charge of reviewing the firm's compliance control systems. One key feature of the system must be to supervise the daily customer-related activity for producing branch office managers.

SUPERVISOR QUALIFICATIONS AND PREREQUISITES

People who supervise or train agents generally must register as a principal with FINRA and qualify by training or experience. Prior to taking a principal exam, the individual must have successfully completed the appropriate registered representative examination. A principal of a FINRA member firm will usually take the General Securities Principal exam, known as the Series 24. Series 24 general securities principals may manage or supervise the firm's corporate securities business, including investment banking, direct participation programs, investment company products, and variable contracts. A Series 24 does not qualify an individual as any of the following:

- Registered options principal
- General securities sales supervisor for options or municipal securities
- Municipal securities principal
- Financial and operations principal
- Introducing broker dealer financial and operations principal

All portions of FINRA-administered exams are proprietary and to be held in the strictest of confidence. FINRA considers it a violation of its rules for any individual to:

- Disclose exam questions or content to anyone.
- Reproduce exam questions.
- Receive exam questions or content from anyone.
- Compromise the content of any exam.
- Remove any portion of an exam from the exam location.

CONTINUING EDUCATION

All registered agents and principals are required to participate in industry-mandated continuing education programs. The continuing education program consists of a firm element, which is administered by the broker dealer, and a regulatory element, which is administered by the regulators.

FIRM ELEMENT

Every FINRA member firm at least annually must identify the training needs of its covered employees and develop a written training plan based on its employees' needs. A covered employee is a registered person who engages in sales of securities to customers, trading, and investment banking, and that person's immediate supervisors. The firm, at a minimum, should institute a plan that increases the covered employees' securities knowledge and should focus on the products offered by the firm. The plan should also highlight the risks and suitability requirements associated with the firm's investment products and strategies. The firm is not required to file its continuing education plan with FINRA unless it is specifically requested to do so. However, firms that fail to adequately document their continuing education programs, including their covered agents' compliance with the program, may be subject to disciplinary action.

REGULATORY ELEMENT

FINRA has made substantial changes to its regulatory continuing education requirements. Registered agents and principals will now be required to complete FINRA's regulatory continuing education program annually by December 31st. This schedule replaces the former CE cycle, administered on the second and fifth anniversary of registration and every 3 years thereafter. The courses to be administered will be tailored to each representative or principal registration category held by the individual. FINRA and the CE Council will publish the targeted learning topics for each registration category no later than October 1st of the previous year. These courses replace the S101 and S201 courses administered to agents and principals respectively. Agents who fail to complete the required regulatory CE training program by December 31st will be placed into inactive status. During this time the individual may not act in any capacity that requires an active registration. Agents will not be allowed to receive commissions or interact with customers until the regulatory requirement is satisfied. Each participant will complete the training through FINRA's online FinPro system. The employing firm will be copied on system generated notifications to track compliance.

MAINTAINING QUALIFICATIONS PROGRAM

FINRA has implemented a continuing education program designed to allow eligible agents and principals to maintain their qualifications for up to 5 years from the date of termination. It is important to note that this program does not eliminate the 24 month window. It provides terminated individuals with the option to maintain their licenses during extended absences from the industry. Through the maintaining qualifications program or MQP. Eligible persons who leave to start families or to pursue other interests will be allowed to reenter the industry without being required to requalify by exam. It also allows active agents who have one or more of their registrations terminated through the filing of a partial U5 to maintain the terminated registration. To be eligible to participate individuals must:

- Have been registered in the terminated category for at least 1 year prior to the termination

- Elect to participate in MQP within 2 years of terminating the registration

- Complete all CE requirements by their assigned due date

Individuals who have been inactive for more than 2 years or who have been or who subsequently become statutorily disqualified will be deemed ineligible. The MQP requires individuals to complete annual CE courses containing both regulatory and practical element training and to pay annual fees to participate. Participants in the MQP program will access the courses through the FinPro system.

TAPE RECORDING EMPLOYEES

Certain firms may be subject to special supervision requirements if a significant amount of its registered agents came from a firm or firms that have been disciplined by regulators. A firm that is subject to the taping rule must implement special written procedures and begin taping the conversations of its registered personnel and customers within 60 days of being notified by FINRA that the firm has become subject to the taping rule. The firm also must implement written procedures to retain, review, and classify the recordings. Firms that fall into the following categories must tape their employees:

- Has more than 5 but fewer than 10 registered representatives and 40% or more have come from disciplinary firms within the last 3 years.

- Has at least 10 but fewer than 20 registered representatives and 4 or more have come from disciplinary firms within the last 3 years.

- Has 20 or more employees and at least 20% have come from disciplinary firms within the last 3 years.

A broker dealer that has been notified by FINRA that it is subject to the taping rule has a one-time option to reduce its number of registered representatives. If the firm elects to reduce a portion of the subject agents to eliminate the taping requirement, the firm may not rehire the subject agents who were eliminated for 180 days.

HEIGHTENED SUPERVISORY REQUIREMENTS

In addition to having to record agents under certain conditions, FINRA has enacted rules to ensure that heightened supervision is in place for:

- Representatives who have been sanctioned by FINRA.
- Managers who turn a blind eye to violations.
- Complex structured or proprietary products.
- Producing managers who generate 20% or more of the production where they supervise, based on the trailing 12 months, commissions at the location.

Individuals who supervise producing managers must be financially independent of the managers they supervise. These supervisors should be located at an office that is independent from the office of the producing manger they supervise and they must have the authority to correct the actions of the manager including terminating the manager. Firms must maintain written policies and procedures to detect red flags and to implement heightened supervision where required. A key red flag for producing branch office managers would be an unusual number of cancel and rebill transactions, where trades are cancelled out of one account and placed in another after execution.

INFORMATION OBTAINED FROM AN ISSUER

If a broker dealer obtains information during the performance of duties from an issuer of securities, it may not use that information to solicit business. A broker dealer may obtain information from an issuer while acting as:

- An underwriter.
- A transfer agent.
- A paying agent.
- An investment banker.

CUSTOMER COMPLAINTS

All written complaints received from customers or from individuals acting on behalf of customers must be reported promptly to the principal of the firm. The firm is required to:

- Maintain a copy of the complaint at a supervising office of supervisory jurisdiction for four years.
- Electronically report all complaints to FINRA within 15 days of the end of each calendar quarter. If no complaints were received, no report is due.
- Report complaints within 10 days to FINRA if the complaint alleges misappropriation of funds or securities or forgery.

The firm must maintain a separate customer complaint folder even if it has not received any written customer complaints. If the firm's file contains complaints, the file must state what action was taken by the firm, if any, and it must disclose the location of the file containing any correspondence relating to the complaint.

 TAKENOTE!

A principal is required to review all written customer complaints, but there is no required timeframe to respond or take action.

INVESTOR INFORMATION

All broker dealers that carry customer accounts must send their customers information detailing FINRA's BrokerCheck public disclosure program at least once per calendar year. The BrokerCheck program, accessible via the FINRA website, provides detailed registration and disciplinary history for firms and agents and is maintained at the central registration depository (CRD). The information must contain the program's 800 number, FINRA's website address, and a statement that an investor brochure includes the same information and is available.

MEMBER OFFICES

As a member's business grows, it will often wish to open new offices. The classification of the additional offices depends on the type of activity that is conducted. The three types of offices that a member may open are:

1. An office of supervisory jurisdiction.
2. A branch office.
3. A satellite office.

OFFICE OF SUPERVISORY JURISDICTION

A member firm must inform FINRA which offices it has identified as being an office of supervisory jurisdiction, or an OSJ. An OSJ is any office that conducts one or more of the following activities at that location:

- Has custody of customer funds or securities
- Has final approval for advertising or sales literature
- Has final approval of customer accounts
- Reviews and approves customer orders
- Executes orders or makes markets in securities
- Forms or structures offerings
- Supervises employees at other branch offices

At least one resident principal must manage the OSJ. The resident principal must enforce the policies and procedures of the firm, review all customer activity, and inspect the branch offices within his or her jurisdiction. Each OSJ should have one resident onsite principal who is assigned to the office and who maintains a consistent physical presence at the office. FINRA's guidelines assume that each principal will have supervisory reasonability for only one OSJ. However, if a member's business requires it to assign the supervisory responsibilities for more than one OSJ to a principal, the member must document the supervisory arrangement in its written supervisory procedures manual. FINRA would not be required to approve the arrangement but the member should give special consideration to the experience level of the principal, the geographic location of the offices, the number of representatives and if the principal is a producing agent. An office that solely has final approval over the issuance of research reports need not be classified as an OSJ so long as it does not engage in the activities of an OSJ detailed above.

> **TAKENOTE!**
>
> A copy of the firm's policy and procedures manual, as well as a copy of the *FINRA Manual*, must be kept in each OSJ. The *FINRA Manual* must be made available to a customer upon request. The manual may be provided to the customer in hard or electronic copy.

BRANCH OFFICES

A branch office is any location that is identified to the public as being a place where the member conducts business but does not engage in any of the activities that would require it to be considered an OSJ. Branch offices are inspected by an OSJ. A branch office may operate without a resident principal. A registered representative may act as the branch manager. The supervisory responsibility is with the OSJ. An office of convenience; such as temporary office space provided by an office sharing company for a daily rate, a temporary office maintained as part of the firm's business continuity plan, an insurance sales office where less than 25 securities transactions take place per year, or an office where only back office functions are conducted would not be considered to be branch offices and are classified as non-branch locations. A branch office with the responsibility to supervise the acclivities of non-branch locations would be classified as a supervising branch office. Should the member firm move or relocate a branch office, whether a traditional office, houseboat, or yacht, FINRA must be notified in 30 days.

SATELLITE OFFICES

A satellite office is usually a smaller office that does not meet the definition of a branch. A satellite office may not have any signs or advertising. The home office of a registered representative who works out of their house would be considered a satellite office.

ANNUAL COMPLIANCE REVIEW

At least once per year the member must conduct a compliance review of each OSJ, supervising branch office, and each registered representative. Non-supervising branch offices should be directly reviewed every 3 years. The individuals who conduct the review are generally prohibited from being assigned to the office being inspected. The person inspecting the office should not directly or indirectly report to or be supervised by anyone at the office being inspected. Persons assigned excursively to the firm's compliance department and supervised by the compliance department are generally excluded from this rule. When the member reviews the OSJ, the member is automatically inspecting the activities of the branch offices under the jurisdiction of the OSJ. Each member must designate a principal to test the firm's supervisory and compliance controls. This principal must file a report with senior management detailing the results of these tests. Controls must be in place to provide daily supervision of any producing managers.

BUSINESS CONTINUITY PLAN

One of the regulations developed as a result of the attack on 9/11 is the requirement for FINRA member firms to develop and maintain plans and backup facilities to ensure that the firm can meet its obligations to its customers and counterparties in the event that its main facilities are damaged, destroyed, or are inaccessible. The plan must provide for alternative means of communication between the firm, its employees, customers, and regulators as well as a data backup. The plan must provide for data backup in both hard copy and electronic format. All mission critical functions including financial and operational systems and regulatory reporting must be addressed in the plan. The plan must be approved and reviewed annually by a senior member of the firm's management team and must provide plans to ensure that customers have access to their funds. The plan must be provided to FINRA upon request. Should the firm's business materially change, the business continuity plan should be updated promptly to reflect the change in the member's business. The plan must identify two members of senior management as emergency contacts, one of whom must be a registered principal with the firm. Should one of the contact people change, FINRA must be notified in 30 days. Customers of the firm must be advised of the business continuity plan at the time the account is opened and in writing upon request. The plan must also be posted on the firm's website. Small firms with one office should provide a contact number to the clearing firm. Each member firm is required to evaluate its potential vulnerabilities as well as any areas of weakness that may arise from its relationships with other firms and service providers. The firm's business continuity plan must adequately address each of these issues. A significant business disruption event may require the firm to go out of business temporarily or permanently and customers must be informed of this fact.

The firm must inform customers how they will have access to their assets in such an event.

CURRENCY TRANSACTIONS

The Bank Secrecy Act requires that all member firms must guard against money laundering. Every member must report any currency receipt of $10,000 or more from any one customer on a single day. The firm must fill out and submit a currency transaction report, also known as Form 4789, to the IRS within 15 days of the receipt of the currency. Multiple deposits that total $10,000 or more will also require the firm to file a currency transaction report (CTR). Additionally, the firm is required to maintain a record of all international wire transfers of $3,000 or greater.

THE PATRIOT ACT

The Patriot Act as part of the Bank Secrecy Act requires broker dealers to have written policies and procedures designed to detect suspicious activity. The firm must designate a principal to ensure compliance with the firm's policies and to train firm personnel. The firm is required to file a Suspicious Activity Report (SAR) for any transaction of more than $5,000 that appears questionable. Anti-money-laundering rules require that all firms implement a customer identification program to ensure that the firm knows the true identity of its customers. All customers who open an account with the firm, as well as individuals with trading authority, are subject to this rule. The firm must ensure that its customers do not appear on any list of known or suspected terrorists. A firm's anti-money-laundering program must be approved by senior management. Should the approving member of management leave the firm the plan should be re-approved by the new member of senior management. All records relating to the SAR filing, including a copy of the SAR report, must be maintained by the firm for 5 years. FINRA Rule 3310 requires member firms to identify to FINRA the name of the person in charge of the firm's AML program as well as the name and full contact details of the person(s) who are to oversee the day-to-day operation of the AML program. Any changes to AML persons identified to FINRA must be updated within 30 days. Members must also conduct an annual independent test of the program. The person conducting the test may not perform the daily AML duties at the firm or report to anyone in charge of the program.

The person should have substantial knowledge of the Bank Secrecy Act and its related rules and regulations.

The money-laundering process begins with the placement of the funds. This is when the money is deposited in an account with the broker dealer. The second step of the laundering process is known as layering. The layering process will consist of multiple deposits in amounts less than $10,000. The funds will often be drawn from different financial institutions; this is known as structuring. The launderers will then purchase and sell securities in the account. The integration of the proceeds back into the banking system completes the process. At this point, the launderers may use the money to purchase goods and services, with the money appearing to have come from legitimate sources. Firms must also identify the customers who open the account and make sure that they are not conducting business with anyone on the OFAC list. This list is maintained by the Treasury Department's Office of Foreign Assets Control. It consists of known and suspected terrorists, criminals, and members of pariah nations. Conducting business with anyone on this list is strictly prohibited. Individuals and entities who appear on this list are known as Specially Designated Nationals and Blocked Persons. Registered representatives who aid the laundering of money are subject to prosecution and face up to 20 years in prison and a $500,000 fine per transaction. The representative does not even have to be involved in the scheme or even know about it to be prosecuted. FinCEN is a bureau of the U.S. Department of the Treasury. FinCEN's mission is to safeguard the financial system, guard against money laundering, and promote national security. FinCEN collects, receives, and maintains financial transactions data; analyzes and disseminates that data for law enforcement purposes; and builds global cooperation with counterpart organizations in other countries and with international bodies.

U.S. ACCOUNTS

Every member must obtain the following from U.S. customers:

- A Social Security number/documentation number
- Date of birth
- Address
- Place of business

FOREIGN ACCOUNTS

All non-U.S. customers must provide at least one of the following:

CHAPTER 6 General Supervision

- A passport number and country of issuance
- An alien ID number
- A U.S. tax ID number
- A number from another form of government-issued ID and the name of the issuing country

IDENTITY THEFT

The fraudulent practice of identity theft may be used by criminals in an attempt to obtain access to the assets or credit of another person. The Federal Trade Commission (FTC) requires banks and broker dealers to establish and maintain written identity theft prevention programs. A broker dealer's written supervisory procedures manual must reference its identity theft program. The program must be designed to detect red flags relating to the known suspicious activity employed during an attempt at identity theft. The identity theft prevention program should be designed to allow the firm to respond quickly to any attempted identity theft to mitigate any potential damage. The three common variations of identity theft, prevalent in the financial services and securities industry are family fraud, classic account takeover, and alias fraud. Family fraud includes instances where individuals who are relatives of the victim use personal knowledge of the account holder to gain unauthorized access to the account. A classic account takeover involves someone unknown to your customer who has gained access to the customer's account at the broker dealer, investment adviser or bank. In this scenario the perpetrator attempts to liquidate and transfer assets. It should be recognized that all types of fraud can be used in money laundering schemes. However, the most common to money laundering is alias fraud; Alias fraud is used by identity thieves who use ill-gotten money, but someone else's identity to open the account through which they intend to launder the funds.

INFORMATION SECURITY

Information security has become a large issue for both broker dealers and investment advisers. There are three levels of information firms must protect: public, restricted, and confidential. Note that confidential information is also referred to as secret information. Public information is defined as that which can be made available freely to the public with approval by someone in a managerial position. For securities firms such as broker dealers, this would be a principal. The following are examples of public information; marketing materials, press releases, annual reports (after their release), firm websites and advertisements. Financial firms must take great care when protecting customer and firm information. Firms are expected to deal with two types of sensitive information. Sensitive information is categorized as firm specific, aka branded and customer information. Branded sensitive information includes the firm's business models / plans, training materials, presentations, memos and operational procedures. Branded sensitive information is deemed to be restricted and should not be made available to anyone outside of the firm. Some information, if lost or leaked from a financial institution could result in significant damage, such as that causing financial loss, a lost opportunity to the firm or have a negative impact on shareholders. Such information should be subject to confidential access (aka secret) only. Included under the heading of sensitive customer information would be; customer Social Security or Tax ID number, name, address, account balance, account number, PIN, account access password, phone number, full (not partial) credit card number, or other financial information. To guard against a breach it is recommended that a firms employ the following best practices:

- Access to combinations and codes should be limited to only those with a legitimate need to know and should be changed every 6 months.
- Computer passwords for those working in the financial industry should be at least 8 characters long, consisting of both upper and lowercase letters, numbers and special characters and changed on a regular basis.
- For office security, including branches, file cabinets should be locked until access is required and locked again immediately after use. This would be one of the criteria for principals conducting a proper branch office inspection.

FINRA RULE 3241

FINRA Rule 3241 is designed to address the potential conflicts of interest that can arise when a registered person is named as a beneficiary, Trustee, or executor of a client's estate. The intent of this rule is to ensure that registered individuals act appropriately and that the employing member carefully supervises the actions of registered individuals. A multitude of conflicts can arise when a registered person is named as a beneficiary or is placed in a position of trust over a client's estate. One of the greatest concerns are cases where a registered person subjects an elderly client to undo or inappropriate influence. In these instances the representative may use this influence to be named as a beneficiary or to be placed in a position of trust upon the death of the client. The impact of this undue influence may not be known or realized by the client's family for years. FINRA Rule 3241 establishes a

National Standard to protect individuals and to provide a consistent policy for member firms to follow. A registered person should decline being named as a beneficiary of, or placed in a position of trust over a client's estate. If the registered person does not decline, the registered person must provide written notification to his / her employer and receive his / her employer's written approval to receive the bequest or to accept the appointment as trustee or executor. Upon being notified that a registered person is going to be named to a position of trust or is being named as a beneficiary, the member firm the member firm is required to:

Perform an assessment of the risks created by the registered person being named as a beneficiary or to a position of trust. Specific emphasis should be placed upon evaluating whether such a scenario will interfere with or compromise the registered person's responsibilities to the customer.

Make a determination to approve or disapprove the representative's acceptance or to limit the registered persons activities by placing conditions upon the acceptance.

FINRA further States that That the following factors should be carefully evaluated:

- The customer's age
- The length and type of relationship between the customer and the registered person
- The size of the bequest relative to the size of the customers estate
- If the representative has been named as a beneficiary or has received bequests from other customer accounts or estates
- An evaluation of the customer's mental capacity and ability to protect their own interests. specific weight should be given to any observations the member has made during the course of the relationship with a customer
- Any red flags observed in the management of the customer's account such as excessive trading
- Any red flags observed relating to instances of undue influence on the part of the registered rep

Member firms are well within their right to prohibit representatives from accepting bequests or appointments from clients. However, if the member firm allows representatives to receive bequests or appointments, the member firm must have clear policy and procedures designed to meet the national standards and to supervise such matters. When evaluating the potential risks associated with the acceptance of a bequest or an appointment, the relationship between the representative and the client is a significant matter. For example, the risk associated with the acceptance or appointment being made by a client who has no other relationship with a representative other than that of a client is far greater than that being made by someone who is a lifelong friend of the representative who also happens to be a client.

Should the member firm allow the representative to accept the appointment or bequest, the firm must carefully supervise the registered person's activities and compliance with any limitations placed on the representative's acceptance.. An interesting situation may arise if a registered person is allowed to serve in a position of trust over a client's estate for which the registered person is being compensated. The registered representative is now engaging in an outside business activity and as a result, the activity would be required to be disclosed and supervised by the member firm. The member firm is required to maintain all documents relating to notifications, approvals, denials, bequests and appointments for 3 years from the date of the bequest or the termination of the position of trust or termination of the registered rep by the member firm, whichever occurs first.

All estate matters of the registered person's immediate family are specifically excluded from this rule. Further, this rule does not apply to registered persons who do not manage customer accounts. A registered representative may not circumvent the rules by resigning from managing the customer's account or transferring the customer's account to another associated person. Other attempts to circumvent the rules, such as having the client name the registered representative's spouse or child as a beneficiary are also prohibited. If the registered person is unaware that he / she has been named as a beneficiary or appointed to a position of trust for a client's estate, the registered person will not have violated the disclosure rules. However, once the registered representative becomes aware of the bequest or appointment the knowledge of such triggers the disclosure and compliance requirements.

CHAPTER 6

Pretest

GENERAL SUPERVISION

1. A branch office may do which of the following?
    I. Advertise in the phone book
    II. Approve new accounts
    III. Execute customer orders on a wire basis
    IV. Conduct the member's business with the public
    a. I and IV
    b. II and III
    c. I, II, and IV
    d. I, II, III, and IV

2. A member would be required to record which of the following as part of its anti-money-laundering efforts?
    a. A customer's large transactions executed on a cash basis
    b. A customer's purchase of $70,000 of stock for next-day settlement
    c. A wire transfer from a Canadian client for $4,800
    d. The firm transferring $7,000 to its trading account

3. An office of supervisory jurisdiction may conduct which of the following activities?
   I. Final approval of advertising
   II. Execution of customer orders
   III. Structuring of investment banking
   III. Review of branch offices
   a. I and III
   b. II and IV
   c. I, II, and IV
   d. I, II, III, and IV

4. A satellite office may do which of the following?
   a. Advertise its location.
   b. Transact business with the public.
   c. Conduct compliance reviews of its agents.
   d. Approve new accounts.

5. Which of the following is true?
   I. An OSJ must have at least two resident principals.
   II. An OSJ is responsible for the activities of the branch offices in its area.
   III. A registered representative may act as the manager of a branch office.
   IV. An OSJ must have a resident FINOP.
   a. I and III
   b. II and III
   c. I and IV
   d. II and IV

6. As it relates to a member firm's annual compliance review, which of the following is NOT true?
   a. All branch offices must be directly inspected by the member.
   b. All registered representatives are subject to the review.
   c. All OSJs must be directly inspected by the member.
   d. All branch offices do not need to be directly inspected by the member.

7. A general securities firm carrying customer accounts must do which of the following?

    I. Advise customers of FINRA's public disclosure program.

    II. Give the investors the 800 number for the public disclosure program.

    III. Provide customers with the address for FINRA's website.

    IV. Provide all of the items listed in writing twice per year.

    a. I and III
    b. II and IV
    c. I, II, and III
    d. I, II, III, and IV

8. A Suspicious Activity Report must be filed for questionable actions exceeding:

    a. $3,000.
    b. $5,000.
    c. $10,000.
    d. $15,000.

9. A firm's anti-money-laundering program must be approved by which of the following?

    a. The resident principal at the OSJ
    b. The branch manager
    c. A compliance officer
    d. The senior compliance official only

CHAPTER 7

Customer Accounts

INTRODUCTION

Prior to opening an account for any new customer, a registered representative must complete and sign a new account form. Account ownership is divided into five main types:

1. Individual
2. Joint
3. Corporate
4. Trusts
5. Partnerships

OPENING A NEW CUSTOMER ACCOUNT

When opening a new account, the registered representative should try to obtain as much information about the customer as possible. The representative should obtain the following information about the customer:

- Full name and address
- Home and work phone numbers
- Social Security or tax ID number
- Employer, occupation, and employer's address
- Net worth
- Investment objectives

- Estimated annual income
- Bank/brokerage firm reference
- Whether the customer is employed by a bank or broker dealer
- Any third-party trading authority
- Citizenship
- Legal age
- How the account was obtained
- Whether the client is an officer, director, or 10% stockholder of a publicly traded company

At the time a registered representative opens a new account for a retail customer, the rep should attempt to obtain the name and contact information for a trusted contact for the client. The trusted contact must be at least 18 years old and the firm may contact this individual if they have been unable to reach the customer after multiple attempts, the account may have been subject to fraud or exploitation or if the customer appears to be suffering from diminished mental capacity. If a new retail customer does not wish to provide a trusted contact, the representative should make note of that fact. and the account may still be open by the firm. All new accounts must be accepted and signed by a principal of the firm. The principal must accept the account in writing for the firm either before or promptly after the first trade is executed. The principal accepts the account by signing the new account card. The representative also must sign the new account card as evidence that he or she introduced the account to the firm. The customer never has to sign anything to open a new cash account. Some firms have the customer sign a customer agreement upon opening a new account, but this is not required. The customer agreement will state the policies of the firm and will usually contain a predispute arbitration clause. The predispute clause requires that any potential dispute arising out of the relationship be settled in binding arbitration. The predispute arbitration clause must be presented in a certain format and include the following disclosures:

- That arbitration is final and binding
- That the findings of the arbitrators are not based on legal reasoning
- That the discovery process is generally more limited than the discovry process in a legal proceeding

CHAPTER 7 Customer Accounts

- That the parties are waiving their right to a jury trial
- That the customer must be provided with a copy of the predispute clause and must verify its receipt with a signature
- That a minority of the arbitration panel will be affiliated with the securities industry

If the predispute clause is contained in the customer agreement, there must be a highlighted disclosure just above the signature line.

A firm may also have the customer sign a signature card. A signature card will allow the firm to verify the customer's written instructions that are sent in to the firm or the fund sponsor. A copy of the information collected on the customer's account must be sent to the customer within 30 days of opening the account or with the next statement. Firms must also reconfirm the customer's information no later than 36 months from the time the information was last sent to the customer. The information must contain the customer information that was collected at the time the account was opened, as well as the definitions of the terms used to describe investment objectives. Any changes in the customer's investment objectives, name, or address must be confirmed within 30 days or when the next statement is sent. Customers who do not wish to disclose financial information may still open an account if there is reason to believe that the customer can afford to maintain the account. All registered representatives should update the customer's information regularly and note any changes in the following:

- Address
- Phone number
- Employer
- Investment objectives
- Marital status

Registered representatives are also required to maintain an accurate and up-to-date listing of all of their customer's transactions and investment holdings.

HOLDING SECURITIES

Upon opening an account, the investor must decide how the securities will be held. The following methods are available:

- Transfer and ship
- Transfer and hold in safekeeping
- Hold in street name

TRANSFER AND SHIP

Securities that are to be transferred and shipped will be registered in the customer's name and the certificates will be sent to the customer's address of record.

TRANSFER AND HOLD IN SAFEKEEPING

Securities that are to be transferred and held in safekeeping will be registered in the customer's name and will be held by the brokerage firm. The broker dealer may charge a fee for the safekeeping of the securities. Customers may now elect to hold securities registered in their name electronically in book entry form through the Direct Registration System (DRS). The DRS, which is offered through the Depository Trust Corporation (DTC), enables investors to hold their securities on the books of the issuer or the transfer agent. Investors who hold securities with the DRS will receive a statement from the issuer or transfer agent.

HOLD IN STREET NAME

Securities that are held in street name are registered in the name of the brokerage firm as the nominal owner of the securities, and the customer is the beneficial owner. Most securities are held in this manner to make transfer of ownership easier.

At this time the customer will also decide how to handle distributions from the account. Investors may have the distributions sent directly to them or they may have them reinvested or swept into a money market account.

> **TAKENOTE!**
>
> Many large customers will issue Standard Settlement Instructions (SSIs) which refer to a legal entity's settlement instructions for which key information remains the same from one cash settlement to another; for example, the bank, account number, and account name where cash is to be sent.

MAILING INSTRUCTIONS

All confirmations and statements will be sent to the customer's address of record. Statements and confirmations may be sent to an individual with power of attorney if the duplicates are requested in writing. A customer's mail may be held by a brokerage firm for up to 2 months if the customer is traveling within the United States and for up to 3 months if the customer is traveling outside the United States. If the customer has a valid reason and submits a written request, the broker dealer may hold the customer's mail for up to 6 months. A customer who is in the military and going to be deployed for an extended period of time with no fixed address should be advised to open a military post office box where statements may be sent.

TYPES OF OWNERSHIP

Brokerage accounts may be owned by one or more individuals, partnerships, trusts, or corporations. Orders may only be entered for the account by the owners of the account or by individuals with written trading authorization for the account.

INDIVIDUAL ACCOUNT

An individual account is an account that is owned by one person. That person makes the determination as to what securities are purchased and sold. In addition, that person receives all of the distributions from the account.

JOINT ACCOUNT

A joint account is an account that is owned by two or more adults. Each party to the account may enter orders and request distributions. The registered representative does not need to confirm instructions with both parties. Joint accounts require that the owners sign a joint account agreement prior to the opening of the account. All parties must endorse all securities, and all parties must be alive. Checks drawn from the account must be made out in the names of all of the parties.

JOINT TENANTS WITH RIGHTS OF SURVIVORSHIP (JTWROS)

In a joint account with rights of survivorship (JTWROS), all the assets are transferred into the name of the surviving party in the event of one tenant's death. The surviving party becomes the sole owner of the assets in the account. Both parties on the account have an equal and undivided interest in the assets in the account.

JOINT TENANTS IN COMMON (JTIC)

In a joint account that is established as tenants in common, the assets of the tenant who has died become the property of the decedent's estate. They do not become the property of the surviving tenant. An account registered as joint tenants in common allows the assets in the account to be divided unequally; for example, one party on the account could own 60% of the account's assets.

 TAKENOTE!

Any securities registered in the names of two or more parties must be signed by all parties and all parties must be alive to be considered good delivery.

TRANSFER ON DEATH (TOD)

An account that has been registered as a transfer on death (TOD) account allows the account owner to stipulate to whom the account is to go in the event of his or her death. The party who will become the owner of the account in the event of the account holder's death is known as the beneficiary. The beneficiary may only enter orders for the account if he or she has power of attorney for the account. Unlike an account that is registered as JTWROS, the assets in the account will not be at risk should the beneficiary become the subject of a lawsuit, such as in a divorce proceeding.

DEATH OF A CUSTOMER

If an agent is notified of the death of a customer, the agent must immediately cancel all open orders and mark the account "deceased." The representative must await instructions from the executor or administrator of the estate. In order to sell or transfer the assets, the agent must receive the following:

- Letters testamentary
- Affidavit of domicile
- Inheritance tax waivers
- Certified copy of the death certificate

The death of a customer with a discretionary account automatically terminates the discretionary authority.

TAKENOTE!

In the event an account owner cannot be located after a significant effort by the dealer, the account will be considered to be abandoned and the state will claim the account through the escheatment process. The state will hold the account as a bookkeeping entry, against which the former account owner or his/her estate may make a claim.

PARTNERSHIP ACCOUNTS

When a professional organization, such as a law partnership, opens an account, the registered representative, in addition to the standard paperwork, must obtain a copy of the partnership agreement. The partnership agreement will state who may enter orders for the account. If the partnership wishes to purchase securities on margin, it must not be prohibited by the partnership agreement.

TRUSTS

There are two types of trusts that an individual may establish: revocable and irrevocable. With a revocable trust the individual who established the trust, known as the grantor, may, as the name suggests, revoke the trust and take the assets back. The income generated by a revocable trust is generally taxed as income to the grantor. If the trust is irrevocable the grantor may not revoke the trust and take the assets back. With an irrevocable trust, the trust usually pays the taxes as its own entity or the beneficiaries of the trust are taxed on the income they receive. If the income is not all distributed to the beneficiaries, the trust will pay the taxes on income that is not distributed. The grantor of an irrevocable trust is generally not taxed on the income generated by the trust, unless the assets in the trust are held for the benefit of the grantor, their spouse, or if that grantor has an interest in the income of the trust of greater than 5%.

CORPORATE ACCOUNTS

Corporations, like individuals, purchase and sell securities. In order to open a corporate account, the registered representative must obtain a corporate resolution that states which individuals have the power to enter orders for the corporation. If a corporation wants to purchase securities on margin, the registered representative must obtain a corporate charter that states that the corporation may purchase securities on margin.

TRADING AUTHORIZATION

From time to time, someone other than the beneficial owner of the account may be authorized to enter orders for the account. All discretionary authority must be evidenced in writing for the following accounts:

- Discretionary accounts
- Custodial accounts
- Fiduciary accounts

If a customer dies, any trading authorization is automatically canceled.

DISCRETIONARY ACCOUNTS

A discretionary account allows the registered representative to determine the following, without consulting the client first:

- The asset to be purchased or sold
- The amount of the securities to be purchased or sold
- The action to be taken in the account (i.e., whether to buy or sell)

Prior to exercising discretionary authority the discretionary papers must be received and approved by the firm.

OPERATING A DISCRETIONARY ACCOUNT

A discretionary account allows the registered representative to determine the following, without consulting the client first:

- The asset to be purchased or sold.
- The amount of the securities to be purchased or sold.
- The action to be taken in the account, whether to buy or sell.

The principal of the firm must accept the account and review it more frequently to ensure against abuses. The customer is required to sign a limited power of attorney that awards discretion to the registered representative. The limited power of attorney is good for up to three years. The customer is bound by the decisions of the representative, but may still enter his or her own orders. A registered representative may be given discretion over the time and price at which to execute an order without having first obtained discretionary authority over the account. These orders should be executed during the same trading day. If time / price discretion is given to a representative for a period of more than one day, the customer must provide written instructions regarding the order. It is important to note that a registered representative may not exercise discretionary authority when purchasing direct participation programs. The representative must get the client's prior written approval for each purchase and may not obtain a blanket approval for the purchase of any / all programs. Additionally, if a control relationship exists between the broker dealer and an issuer, a rep with discretionary authority must get the customer's written permission to purchase shares of the issuer. For example, Bank of America, owns Merril Lynch. If a rep at Merrill Lynch wanted to purchase shares of Bank of America in a discretionary account, the client would have to approve the purchase in writing. The full details of the control relationship must be provided to the client in writing prior to settlement of the transaction (usually on or with the confirmation). Once discretion is given to the representative, the representative may not give discretion to another party. If the representative leaves the firm or stops managing the customer's account, the discretionary authority is automatically terminated. A full power of attorney allows an individual to deposit and withdraw cash and securities from the account. A full power of attorney is usually not given to a registered representative. A full power of attorney is more appropriate for fiduciaries, such as a trustee, custodian, or a guardian.

A standard power of attorney will terminate upon the death or incapacitation of the grantor. A durable power of attorney will remain in full force during the incapacitation of the grantor and will only terminate upon the grantor's death. A durable power of attorney is traditionally granted to a family member or friend to ensure that a person's needs are taken care of in the event of the loss of mental acuity. Registered representatives are granted a standard limited power of attorney to purchase and sell securities on the client's behalf. This authority terminates upon the earlier of the onset of mental incompetence or death. Discretion may not be exercised by the representative until the power of attorney has been received and approved. A registered representative may be given discretion over the time and price at which to execute an order without having first obtained discretionary authority over the account. These orders should be executed during the same trading day. If time / price discretion is given to a representative for a period of more than one day, the customer must provide written instructions regarding the order. For example, a customer may instruct a representative to purchase 500 shares of SIA "whenever the price is right." In this instance the customer has identified the action (buy) amount (500 shares) and the asset (SIA). The representative may accept this order without having discretionary authority over the account.

MANAGING DISCRETIONARY ACCOUNTS

All discretionary accounts must have the proper paperwork kept in the account file. Discretionary orders require the following:

- The order must be marked as being discretionary.
- The order must be approved promptly by a principal.
- A designated principal must review the account.
- A record of the transaction must be kept.

THIRD PARTY AND FIDUCIARY ACCOUNTS

A fiduciary account is one that is managed by a third party for the benefit of the account holder. The party managing the account has responsibility for making all of the investment decisions and other decisions relating to the account. The individual with this responsibility must act as a prudent person would and may not speculate. This is known as the prudent man rule. Many states have an approved list of securities, known as the legal list, that may be purchased by fiduciaries. The authority to transact business for the account must be evidenced in writing by a power of attorney. The fiduciary may have full power of attorney, also known as full discretion, under which he or she may purchase and sell securities as well as withdraw cash and securities from the account. Under a limited power of attorney, or limited discretion, the fiduciary may only buy and sell securities and may not withdraw assets. The fiduciary has been legally appointed to represent the account holder and may not use the assets in the account for his or her own benefit. The fiduciary may, however, be reimbursed for expenses incurred in connection with the management of the account.

Examples of fiduciaries include:

- Administrators
- Custodians
- Receivers
- Trustees
- Conservators
- Executors
- Guardians
- Sheriffs/marshals

When opening a third party or fiduciary account, the registered representative is required to obtain documentation of the individual's appointment and authority to act on behalf of the account holder. Trust accounts require that the representative obtain a copy of the trust agreement. The trust agreement will state who has been appointed as the trustee and any limitations on the trust's operation. Most trusts may only open cash accounts and may not purchase securities on margin unless specifically authorized to do so in the agreement. When opening an account for a guardian, the representative must obtain a copy of the court order appointing the guardian. The court order must be dated within 60 days of the opening of the account. If the court order is more than 60 days old, the representative may not open the account until a new court order is obtained. Guardians are usually appointed in cases of mentally incompetent adults and orphaned children.

> **TAKENOTE!**
>
> In the case of a person who is deemed mentally incompetent, the registered representative will need a certificate of incumbency dated within 60 days of the account opening.

UNIFORM GIFTS TO MINORS ACT (UGMA)

Minors are not allowed to own securities in their own name because they are not of age to enter into legally binding contracts. The decision to purchase or sell a security creates a legally binding contract between two parties. The Uniform Gifts to Minors Act (UMGA) regulates how accounts are operated for the benefit of minors. All UMGA accounts must have:

- One custodian.
- One minor.
- UGMA and the state in the account title.
- Assets registered to the child's name after the child reaches the age of majority.

All securities in the UGMA account will be registered in the custodian's name as the nominal owner for the benefit of the minor, who is the beneficial owner of the account. For example, the account should be titled: Mr. Jones as custodian for Billy Jones under New Jersey Uniform Gifts to Minors Act.

Only one custodian and one minor are allowed on each account. A husband and wife could not be joint custodians for their minor child. If there is more than one child, a separate account must be opened for each. The same person may serve as custodian on several accounts for several minors, and the minor may have more than one account established by different custodians. The donor of the security does not have to be the custodian for the account, and if neither of the parents are the custodian of the account, they have no authority over the account.

RESPONSIBILITIES OF THE CUSTODIAN

The custodian has a fiduciary duty to manage the account prudently for the benefit of the minor child within certain guidelines:

CHAPTER 7 Customer Accounts

- No margin accounts may be included.
- No high-risk securities, such as penny stocks, may be included.
- The custodian may not borrow from the account.
- No commodities may be included.
- No speculative option strategies may be included.
- The custodian may not give discretion to a third party.
- All distributions must be reinvested within a reasonable time.
- The custodian may not let rights or warrants expire; they must be exercised or sold.
- The custodian must provide support for all withdrawals from the account.
- Withdrawals may only be made to reimburse the custodian for expenses incurred in connection with the operation of the account or for the benefit of the minor.

CONTRIBUTIONS TO A UGMA ACCOUNT

Gifts of cash and securities or other property may be given to the minor. There is no dollar limit as to the size of the gift that may be given. The limit on the size of the tax-free gift is $18,000 per year. An individual may give gifts valued up to $18,000 to any number of people each year without incurring a tax liability. Once a gift has been given, it is irrevocable. Gifts to a UGMA account carry an indefeasible title and may not be taken back for any reason. The custodian may, however, use the assets for the minor's welfare and educational needs.

UGMA TAXATION

The minor is responsible for the taxes on the account. However, any unearned income that exceeds $2,200 per year will be taxed at the parents' marginal tax rate if the child is younger than 14 years old. For gifts that exceed $18,000 per year, the tax liability is on the donor of the gift, not on the minor.

DEATH OF A MINOR OR CUSTODIAN

If the minor dies, the account becomes part of the minor's estate. It does not automatically go to the parents. If the custodian dies, a court or the donor may appoint a new custodian.

UNIFORM TRANSFER TO MINORS ACT

Some states have adopted the Uniform Transfer to Minors Act (UTMA) rather than the Uniform Gifts to Minors Act. The main difference is that with a UTMA account, the custodian may determine when the assets become the property of the child. The maximum age is 25 years old.

>  TAKENOTE!
>
> No evidence of custodial rights is required to open a UGMA or UTMA account.

ACCOUNTS FOR EMPLOYEES OF OTHER BROKER DEALERS

If an account is opened for the employee of another FINRA member firm or for the spouse or minor child of the employee, the opening firm will:

- Notify the employer in writing.
- Send duplicate copies of confirmations and statements upon written request.

FINRA Rule 3210 governs the opening of accounts for employees of other broker-dealers. This rule requires that an employee of a broker dealer who wishes to open an account at another broker dealer to obtain the employer's written permission prior to opening the account. The employee must present written notification to the broker dealer opening the account that he/she is employed by a FINRA member firm at the time the account is opened. This rule is in effect for the employee or any of the employees immediate family members. This rule will also require the employee to obtain the employer's written permission for accounts that were opened within 30 days of the start of employment. Excluded from this rule are accounts opened by the employee where no transactions may take place in individual securities such as accounts opened to purchase open end mutual funds, variable annuities and UITs.

NUMBERED ACCOUNTS

A broker dealer, at the request of the customer, may open an account that is simply identified by a number or a symbol, as long as there is a statement signed by the customer attesting to the ownership of the account.

PRIME BROKERAGE ACCOUNTS

A prime brokerage account allows the customer to utilize several broker dealers to execute its orders while designating a central or main firm to maintain custody of its assets. The firm that carries and receives the customer's cash and securities is known as the prime broker. Prime brokerage accounts are usually established by institutional investors and larger retail investors. In order to open a prime brokerage account, the client must have at least $500,000 in equity. If the account is managed by a registered investment adviser, the minimum account equity is $100,000. A prime brokerage account will allow the client to receive execution and research reports from a variety of broker dealers, known as executing brokers. The executing broker will buy and sell securities for the customer, and the customer will report the trade to its prime broker. The trade will then be entered into the customer's account at the prime broker. The executing broker will confirm the trade through the DTC institutional ID system, and the prime broker will affirm the trade.

ACCOUNT TRANSFERS

Clients from time to time will wish to have their accounts transferred from one brokerage firm to another. This is usually accomplished through the Automated Client Account Transfer Service (ACATS). The ACAT process may only be used between FINRA member firms and may not be used to transfer an account to a non member. The ACAT provides transfer and delivery instructions to the firm, which will be required to deliver the account to the client's new firm. A client wishing to transfer multiple accounts (Single, Joint, IRA) must sign an ACAT or Transfer Initiation Form (TIF) for each account. Once transfer instructions are received and validated, the account will be frozen, no new orders may be accepted, and all open orders must be canceled, except for open orders for options that expire within seven days. The firm that receives the transfer instructions, known as the carrying member, is required to validate the instructions or take exception to them within one business day. Upon validation, the transfer instructions must be sent back to the receiving firm with a list of the positions to be transferred. Once the instructions have been validated, the firm has another three business days to complete the account transfer. A firm may only take exception to the instructions for the following reasons:

- The customer's signature is missing or invalid (both live and electronic signatures are valid).
- The account title does not match the carrying firm's account title.
- The account contains no assets (AKA Flat)
- The Social Security number does not match.
- The account number is wrong.
- In extreme cases a broker-dealer may protest the transfer of a client's account if the client has any unsatisfied judgments, tax liens or is subject to a court order.
- A receiving firm may reject delivery if the account to be received is operating outside its credit or risk policies.

A difference in securities positions and free credit balances is not a reason to take exception to the transfer instructions. From time to time, certain investment positions will not be able to be transferred from the old firm to the new firm. The customer must be informed of this fact in writing, and the customer is required to give specific instructions as to what should be done with that investment. The customer may elect to:

- Leave the investment at the old firm.
- Have it liquidated.
- Have it shipped.

A customer who owns a proprietary product that can only be held at the carrying firm or who owns a mutual fund when the receiving firm does not maintain a selling agreement with the fund, are two of the reasons positions may be deemed nontransferable. If the position is liquidated, the proceeds must be forwarded to the customer within five business days. The carrying broker dealer is required to continue to forward any and all residual credits received for 6 months from the date of transfer. All credits must be forwarded to the new firm within 10 business days. If the customer is transferring an account that has a checking account, debit card, or credit card connected to the account, the customer must return or destroy the checks and/or card. If a registered representative leaves a broker-dealer during the term of a non-compete clause prohibiting the representative from soliciting existing clients, the firm may not dispute the transfer of a customer's account once valid transfer instructions have been received. A firm may seek a temporary restraining order against the former rep in order to stop the solicitation of clients. However, even with the existence of the temporary restraining order, the firm may not delay or dispute the transfer of the customers' accounts. Broker dealers that engage in partial account transfers from one broker dealer to another use the DTC to settle the transfers. If the old firm fails to deliver a position to the new firm, the old firm has a fail to deliver and the new firm has a fail to receive. Any disputes between the two firms must be resolved within 5 business days. FINRA does not allow customer accounts to be transferred or the broker of record to be changed through a negative consent letter.

Variable contracts and redeemable mutual fund shares held at the issuer (fund company or annuity company) may not use a negative consent letter to change the broker of record. Customers must provide affirmative consent to change the broker of record.

A firm may in limited circumstances use a negative consent letter to bulk transfer customer accounts. A negative consent letter may be used in cases where an introducing broker dealer is changing clearing firms so long as the letter is sent giving the customer 30 days' notice. The letter must explain the reason for the change and if any charges may be incurred by the customer. The customer must also be notified of the option to move his or her account to another firm. The firm sending the negative consent letter may not share any customer personal confidential information with the receiving firm unless the sharing of the information is in line with Regulation S-P. If a broker dealer is going out of business or is at risk of going out of business, closing a line of business, or is merging or acquired by another firm, a negative consent letter may be used to accomplish a bulk account transfer. A firm seeking to use a negative consent letter must file an application with FINRA regarding the proposed transfer and must have received the approval of the proposed transfer, prior to sending the negative consent letter.

BULK ACCOUNT TRANSFERS

In certain situations, a broker dealer may need to transfer such a large number of accounts that obtaining written transfer instructions of each and every customer would be impractical. If there is a material change in the business of a broker dealer, thousands of accounts may need to be transferred at one time. Such business changes can include:

- The loss of a clearing agreement by an introducing broker dealer.
- A change of clearing firms by an introducing broker dealer.
- The insolvency of a broker dealer.
- The insolvency of a clearing firm.
- The merger or acquisition of two broker dealers.

In these situations, a broker dealer may affect a bulk account transfer of customer accounts by sending out a negative response letter. This letter will inform the customer of:

- The reason for the proposed account transfer.
- The timing of the transfer.
- Where the account will be transferred to.
- The time by which the account holder must object to stop the transfer.

If the customer does not object by the date on the negative response letter, the customer is deemed to have given their consent to the transfer. The letter must explain the reason for the change and if any charges may be incurred by the customer. The customer must also be notified of the option to move his or her account to another firm. The firm sending the negative consent letter may not share any customer personal confidential information with the receiving firm unless the sharing of the information is in line with Regulation S-P. A firm seeking to use a negative consent letter must file an application with FINRA regarding the proposed transfer and must have received the approval of the proposed transfer, prior to sending the negative consent letter. Variable contracts and redeemable mutual fund shares held at the issuer (fund company or annuity company) may not use a negative consent transfer to change the broker of record. Customers must provide affirmative consent to change the broker of record.

TAKENOTE!

A registered representative who is leaving one firm to join a new firm may not use a negative response letter to transfer their customer accounts.

MARGIN ACCOUNTS

A margin account allows the investor to purchase securities without paying for the securities in full. The investor is required to deposit a portion of the securities' purchase price and may borrow the rest from the broker dealer. The portion of the securities' purchase price that an investor must deposit is called margin. The amount of the required deposit, or margin, is controlled by the Federal Reserve Board under Regulation T of the Securities Exchange Act of 1934. Regulation T gave the Federal Reserve Board the authority to regulate the extension of credit for securities purchases.

The FRB controls:

- Which securities may be purchased on margin.
- The amount of the initial required deposit.
- Payment dates.

Customers who purchase securities on margin must receive a separate margin disclosure statement at the time the account is opened and annually thereafer detailing the risks of purchasing securities on margin. If the broker-dealer allows customers to open accounts online, the margin disclosure statement must be clearly displayed on the firm's website. The customer will be asked to sign the following:

- A credit agreement
- A hypothecation agreement
- A loan consent

THE CREDIT AGREEMENT

The credit agreement states the terms and conditions under which credit will be extended to the customer. It will include information about how interest is charged as well as information about the rates that will be charged. A margin loan does not amortize, meaning that the principal is not paid down on a regular schedule. The brokerage firm simply charges interest to the account.

THE HYPOTHECATION AGREEMENT

The hypothecation agreement pledges the customer's securities that were purchased on margin as collateral for the loan. It also allows the brokerage firm to take the same securities and repledge, or rehypothecate, them as collateral for a loan at a bank to obtain a loan for the customer.

THE LOAN CONSENT

By signing a loan consent agreement, the customer allows the brokerage firm to lend out the securities to customers who wish to sell the securities short. This is the only part of the margin agreement that the customer is not required to sign. The credit and hypothecation agreements must be signed prior to the account being approved to purchase securities on margin.

All securities purchased in a margin account will be held in street name, that is, the name of the brokerage firm, so that the broker dealer may sell the securities to protect itself if the value of the securities falls significantly.

GUARANTEEING A CUSTOMER'S ACCOUNT

A customer may guarantee the account of another customer, as long as the guarantee is received by the member in writing. The most likely case for using a customer's account to guarantee the account of another customer is to provide the proper equity for a margin account. Both accounts will be closely monitored to ensure that proper equity is maintained in both accounts.

DAY TRADING ACCOUNTS

Day trading is an investment strategy defined by the entering of roundtrip orders, consisting of both a buy and sell order on the same day for the same security. Firms that promote the use of day trading strategies to individual investors must adhere to special account opening requirements. A broker dealer will be considered to be promoting day trading strategies if it holds seminars, advertises, or uses another company to promote its services. If the firm promotes day trading, it must provide the customer with a risk disclosure document and approve the account for day trading. If the customer is not approved for day trading, the customer may still open an account so long as the firm obtains a written statement from the customer stating that he or she will not be engaging in day trading strategies.

> **TAKENOTE!**
>
> A firm will be considered to be promoting day trading if the registered representatives promote day trading strategies with the knowledge of the firm's principal.

COMMINGLING CUSTOMER'S PLEDGED SECURITIES

A broker dealer may not commingle a customer's pledged securities with that of another customer's pledged securities as joint collateral to obtain a loan from a bank without both customers' written authorization. This authorization is required by SEC Rule 15c2-1 and is part of most margin agreements. A customer's securities may never be commingled with the firm's securities.

WRAP ACCOUNT

A wrap account is an account that charges the customer a set annual fee for both advice and execution costs. The fee is based on the assets in the account. Wrap account holders must be given a Schedule H, which details the fees and charges, prior to opening the account. Broker dealers offering wrap accounts must also be registered as investment advisers. Wrap accounts and other asset-based fee accounts are usually not appropriate for clients who trade infrequently and use a buy and hold strategy.

REGULATION S-P

Regulation S-P requires that the firm maintain adequate procedures to protect the financial information of its customers. Firms must guard against unauthorized access to customer financial information and employ policies to ensure its safety. Special concerns arise over the ability for a person to hack into a firm's customer database by gaining unauthorized access. Firms must develop and maintain specific safeguards for their computer systems and WiFi access. Regulation S-P was derived from the privacy rules of the Gramm-Leach-Bliley Act. A firm must deliver:

- An initial privacy notice to customers when the account is opened.
- An annual privacy notice to all customers.

The annual privacy notice may be delivered electronically via the firm's website, as long as the customer has agreed in writing to receive it electronically and it is clearly displayed. The privacy notice must describe the type of information that is collected and the type of nonaffiliated parties with whom it may be shared. Regulation S-P also states that a firm may not disclose non-public personal information to nonaffiliated companies for clients who have opted out of the list. The method by which a client may opt out may not be unreasonable. It is considered unreasonable to require a customer to write a letter to opt out. Reasonable methods are e-mails or a toll-free number. The rule also differentiates between who is a customer and who is a consumer. A *customer* is anyone who has an ongoing relationship with the firm (i.e., has an account). A *consumer* is someone who is providing information to the firm and is considering becoming a customer or who has purchased a product from the firm and has no other contract with the firm. The firm must give the privacy notice to consumers prior to sharing any nonpublic information with a nonaffiliated company. Regulation S-AM prohibits broker dealers from soliciting business based upon information received from affiliated third parties unless the potential marketing has been clearly disclosed to the potential customer and the potential customer was provided an opportunity to opt out but did not opt out.

 TAKENOTE!

A client of a brokerage firm may not opt out of the sharing of information with an affiliated company.

REGULATION BEST INTEREST

Regulation Best Interest (Reg BI) was adopted by the SEC in June of 2019 as an amendment to the Securities Exchange Act of 1934. All broker dealers, investment advisers, and agents are subject to standards of conduct that require the firm and its agents to act in the best interest of retail customers.

Regulation BI covers all recommendations to effect securities transactions as well as all recommendations regarding account establishment. That is to say, when recommending that a client open a joint, transfer on death, trust, or fee-based account, the type of account established must be in the client's best interest. In June of 2020, as part of Regulation BI, all broker dealers and investment advisers will be required to provide retail clients with a client relationship summary (CRS) and will be required to post the CRS on their publicly available website. The CRS may be provided in hardcopy or electronically. If the CRS is provided in hardcopy, the CRS may not be more than two pages long and the CRS must be the first page among any documents sent in the same package. The following rules are in place relating to the CRS:

- The CRS must be written in plain English using everyday terms.
- The CRS should be written using "active voice" with a strong, direct, and clear meaning.
- The CRS must follow the standard format and order as detailed by the SEC.
- The CRS should be written as if speaking to the retail investor directly.
- The CRS must be factual and avoid boilerplate, vague, or exaggerated language.
- The CRS may not include disclosures other than those required under Regulation BI.
- Electronic CRSs should use graphs and charts, specifically dual column charts to compare services.
- Electronic CRSs may use videos and popups and must provide access to any referenced information via hyperlink or other means.
- Electronic CRSs may be delivered via email provided that the email contains a direct link to the CRS.

Some of the required disclosures are referred to as "conversation starters." These conversation starters should be in bold or in other text to ensure that they are more noticeable than other disclosures. These conversation starters include questions such as:

1. Who is my primary contact and does he or she represent a broker dealer or an investment adviser?
2. Who can I speak to about how the person is treating me?
3. Given my financial situation, should I choose a brokerage service? Why or why not?

4. Given my financial situation, should I choose an investment advisory service? Why or why not?
5. How will you choose investments to recommend to me?
6. What is your relevant experience, including licenses, education, and qualifications? What do these qualifications mean?
7. What fees will I pay?
8. How will these fees affect my investments? If I give you $10,000, how much will go toward fees and expenses and how much will be invested for me?
9. What are your legal obligations to me when providing recommendations (broker dealer)?
10. What are your legal obligations to me when acting as my investment adviser?
11. How else does your firm make money?
12. How do your financial professionals make money?
13. What conflicts of interest do you have?
14. Does the firm or its financial professionals have legal or disciplinary history?

Both broker dealers and investment advisers are required to adhere to the standards of conduct under Regulation BI. As such, both must disclose that they must put the interests of the client ahead of theirs when making a recommendation and that the way the firm makes money for providing the services causes a conflict of interest. These conflicts include recommending proprietary products, receiving payments from third parties, principal trading, or revenue sharing.

Online broker dealers who only provide access to trading, as well as investment advisers who only offer automated services and who do not offer access to specific registered individuals, must disclose this fact in the CRS and must provide a section on their website that answers questions relating to the conversation starters. If a broker dealer or investment adviser provides both online services and access to registered personnel, a registered person must be made available to discuss the conversation starters.

Broker dealers are required to provide the CRS to customers before or upon the earlier of recommending the type of account to establish or an investment strategy or upon opening an account or placing an order. Investment advisers must provide the CRS to clients prior to or at the time the contract is entered into even if the contract is oral. The CRS is now known as ADV part 3. For entities who are registered as both a broker dealer and as an investment adviser, the CRS must be delivered upon the earliest requirement for either registration. Any changes required to be made to the CRS must be completed within 30 days and an updated CRS clearly reflecting the changes must be sent to existing customers within 60 days. All broker dealers and investment advisers are required to file the CRS along with any changes with the SEC. Broker dealers will file through the Central Registration Depository (CRD) system and investment advisers will file through the Investment Adviser Registration Database (IARD). The relationship summary must be provided to a client upon request within 30 days.

CHAPTER 7

Pretest

CUSTOMER ACCOUNTS

1. Which of the following is the nominal owner of a UGMA account?
   a. Custodian
   b. Minor
   c. Donor
   d. Parent or guardian

2. A customer and his spouse have an account registered as joint tenants in common. If the customer dies, what would happen to the account?
   a. The spouse would get the assets in the account.
   b. The decedent's assets will be distributed according to his will.
   c. All of the assets in the account will be distributed according to the trustee.
   d. The executor of the estate will determine how all of the assets are to be distributed.

3. All of the following are required in the account title for a custodial account, EXCEPT:
   a. The minor's Social Security number.
   b. The state.
   c. UGMA.
   d. The name of the custodian.

4. An investor has given his representative the authority to purchase and sell securities in his account without first consulting him. Which of the following is NOT true?
   a. The authority must be evidenced in writing.
   b. The account must be reviewed more frequently.
   c. All transactions must be approved by a principal prior to execution.
   d. The investor is bound by the transactions made by the representative.

5. The assets in a UTMA account can:
   a. Remain there until the custodian decides to transfer them to the beneficial owner.
   b. Be invested more aggressively than those in a UGMA.
   c. Remain in the account until the beneficial owner reaches the age of 25.
   d. Remain in the account until the beneficial owner reaches the age of 21.

6. Joint accounts are allowed in all of the following, EXCEPT:
   a. A registered representative and a customer.
   b. A registered representative and a spouse.
   c. A registered representative and a friend.
   d. A registered representative and his 16-year-old child.

7. Which of the following is NOT true of the ACAT process?
   a. The customer must be informed in writing that certain positions may not be able to be transferred.
   b. The instructions must be validated in 1 day.
   c. The account must be transferred within 3 days of validation.
   d. The receiving firm need not send a position report to the new firm.

CHAPTER 7 Pretest

8. As it relates to the management of a discretionary account, which of the following is true?
   a. The client may reject the agent's selections after he has reviewed the transaction.
   b. The agent may give discretion to another agent while on vacation.
   c. The discretionary authority given to the agent is a special power of attorney that survives the death of a client so that the agent may liquidate the account for the estate.
   d. All tickets must clearly state whether discretion was exercised.

9. An agent has just been informed of the death of a client. All of the following must be done by the agent, EXCEPT:
   a. Cancel all open orders.
   b. Mark the account deceased.
   c. Inform the IRS and request inheritance tax waivers.
   d. Await instructions from the executor.

10. A broker dealer carrying customer accounts and providing credit to customers for margin purposes may jointly pledge customers' securities as joint collateral:
    a. Under no circumstances.
    b. Only if it benefits the customers by offering them a lower interest rate.
    c. Only if the margin loans are amortized.
    d. If all parties agree in writing.

CHAPTER 8

Margin Accounts

> **INTRODUCTION**
>
> Investors may borrow a portion of a security's purchase price directly from the broker dealer to establish a position. Investors who borrow money to purchase securities are said to be buying on margin. The term *margin* refers to the portion of the security's purchase price that must be deposited by the customer to establish the position.

REGULATION OF CREDIT

One of the main reasons the stock market crashed in 1929 was the aggressive lending of money to investors who wanted to purchase securities on margin. In an effort to ward off future excessive lending practices, authority was given to the Federal Reserve Board to regulate the extension of credit for securities purchases. Regulation T (Reg. T) of the Securities Exchange Act of 1934 allowed the Federal Reserve Board to regulate the extension of credit by broker dealers.

REGULATION T

Once a customer has established a margin account, Reg. T sets the minimum initial requirement that must be met by the customer to purchase securities on margin. Reg. T currently requires that the customer deposit 50% of the securities' purchase price. However, the NYSE and FINRA require that a customer meet a minimum initial equity requirement of $2,000 before a firm may lend money to an investor. In order to establish a position in a new margin account, the investor must deposit the greater of $2,000 or 50% of the securities' purchase price. The broker dealer may pledge, or rehypothecate, the customer's securities to obtain a loan at a bank for the customer. The broker dealer may pledge the customer's securities with a value of 140% of the customer's debit balance to obtain the loan for the customer. All excess margin securities must be segregated.

EXAMPLE

Purchased	Minimum Equity	Reg. T at 50%	Required Deposit
1,000 ABC at 10	$2,000	$5,000	$5,000
1,000 XYZ at 5	$2,000	$2,500	$2,500
1,000 RTY at 3	$2,000	$1,500	$2,000
100 KLM at 15	$2,000	$750	$1,500

 TAKENOTE!

A customer may never be required to deposit more than the purchase price of the securities.

Investors who purchase securities on margin are charged interest monthly on the amount of the loan. An investor, in theory, may hold the securities on margin indefinitely and will be required to repay the principal amount of the loan upon the sale of the securities. Investors purchasing securities on margin must hypothecate, or pledge, the securities they purchased as collateral for the loan. All securities purchased on margin will be held in the name of the broker dealer (i.e., street name). Holding the securities in the name of the broker dealer will allow the firm to liquidate the securities to protect its loan if the securities fall too far in value. Reg. T also establishes which securities may be purchased on margin. Marginable securities include:

- All exchange-listed stocks and bonds
- All Nasdaq Global and Capital Market stocks
- All securities on the Federal Reserve Board's approved list

Investors who purchase securities on margin must deposit the required amount within four business days. If the investor is unable to make the deposit by the 4th business day, the broker dealer can apply for an extension on behalf of the customer. The broker dealer must request the extension by writing a letter to either the NYSE or FINRA by the expiration of the fourth business day. An investor may meet a margin requirement by:

- Depositing cash equal to the requirement.

Or

- Depositing marginable securities with a loan value equal to the amount of the requirement.

> **TAKENOTE!**
>
> Broker dealers may waive a call for $1,000 or less.

A marginable security's loan value is equal to the complement of Reg. T. When Reg. T is 50%, the security's loan value is 50%.

EXAMPLE An investor purchasing $20,000 worth of securities in a margin account may meet the Reg. T requirement by:

- Depositing $10,000.
- Depositing $20,000 worth of fully paid for marginable securities.

Nonmarginable securities include:

- Non-Nasdaq OTC securities
- Options
- IPOs and new issues for 30 days
- When-issued, nonexempt securities

Certain securities are exempt from the margin requirements of Reg. T. Although an investor may still borrow money from the broker dealer to purchase these securities, the investor is not required to deposit 50% of the purchase price. Securities exempt from Reg. T include:

- U.S. government securities
- U.S. government agencies
- Municipal securities

- Nonconvertible corporate debt

The initial margin requirement for exempt securities is set by the NYSE or FINRA. The initial margin requirement for U.S. government securities is 1–7% of the par value. For municipal securities, it is the greater of 7% of par or 15% of the market value.

HOUSE RULES

A broker dealer may elect to increase the minimum amount of margin that must be deposited by the investor, or it may elect not to extend credit to customers at all. A broker dealer may never lower the amount of the required deposit below Reg. T or below the requirements of the NYSE or FINRA.

ESTABLISHING A LONG POSITION IN A MARGIN ACCOUNT

A customer's long margin account will consist of the customer's equity and the loan amount or debit balance. The customer's equity represents the portion of the securities that the customer has paid for in full. The customer's debit balance represents the portion of the securities purchase price that was loaned by the broker dealer. To determine the customer's equity in the account, use the following formula:

equity = long market value − debit

EXAMPLE

A customer in a new margin account purchases 1,000 shares of XYZ at $40 per share and makes the required deposit when Reg. T is 50%. The investor's margin account will now look like this:

LMV	Debit
40,000	20,000

EQ 20,000

The long market value of the stock is $40,000. The customer has a debit balance, or has borrowed $20,000 and has equity of $20,000.

In order to gain an understanding of the debit balance and equity components, one could compare a long margin account to home ownership. The homeowner's equity represents the portion of the home's market value that

CHAPTER 8

is fully paid for. The mortgage balance is the amount of money owed on the home. As the home's market value changes, so does the homeowner's equity. The mortgage balance, however, does not change as a result of a change in the market value of the home. A long margin account operates in much the same way. As the long market value of the account increases, so does the account holder's equity. Alternatively, if the long market value of the account falls, the account holder's equity falls with it. The customer's debit balance, or the amount that the customer has borrowed, does not change as a result of a change in the market value of the securities. A broker dealer will closely monitor the relationship between the purchase price of the securities and the current market value of the securities through a process known as marking to the market.

AN INCREASE IN THE LONG MARKET VALUE

As the long market value in a margin account increases, the customer's equity will also increase. Let's look at our original example and see what happens to our customer's account if XYZ increases in value to $50 per share.

Original Position

LMV	Debit
40,000	20,000

EQ 20,000

XYZ at $50

LMV	Debit
50,000	20,000

EQ 30,000

As the long market value increased by $10,000, the customer's equity also increased by $10,000. Notice that the debit balance, or the amount of the customer's loan, was not affected. As the long market value increases, the rise in value creates excess equity for the customer. Excess equity is the amount of the customer's equity that exceeds the initial Reg. T requirement at the current market value. Using our current example, the customer's excess equity is calculated as follows:

LMV	Debit
50,000	20,000

EQ 30,000
Reg. T 25,000
EE 5,000

The customer may do all of the following with the excess equity:

- Withdraw an amount equal to the excess equity.
- Use the excess equity to purchase two times the amount of marginable securities.
- Use the excess to purchase an equal amount of nonmarginable securities.

A customer may request that the brokerage firm send a check in an amount equal to the excess equity. Withdrawing the excess equity will increase the customer's debit balance. If the customer in our example withdraws the excess equity, the account will look as follows:

LMV	Debit
50,000	25,000

EQ 25,000
Reg. T 25,000
EE   0

The customer's debit balance increased by the amount of the excess equity that was withdrawn. The customer may also use the excess equity to purchase marginable stock. To determine the customer's buying power, use the following formula:

buying power = excess equity/complement of Reg. T

Or, when Reg. T is 50%,

buying power = excess equity × 2

If the customer uses the excess equity to purchase $10,000 worth of marginable stock, the account would appear as follows:

LMV	Debit
60,000	30,000

EQ 30,000
Reg. T 30,000
EE   0

The long market value and the debit have increased by the amount of the purchase.

SPECIAL MEMORANDUM ACCOUNT (SMA) FOR A LONG MARGIN ACCOUNT

When a customer's equity increases to over 50% of the long market value, it is credited to the special memorandum account, or SMA. A customer's SMA is like a line of credit. Once SMA has been created, it will remain in place until it is used by the customer. A customer may use SMA to:

- Purchase additional securities.
- Have the amount sent by check.

A decline in the long market value in the account will not affect the customer's SMA. A customer may always use SMA, unless doing so would cause the account to fall below the minimum equity requirement. SMA will be created by any of the following:

- An increase in the long market value.
- A nonrequired cash deposit.
- Dividends and interest received.
- A nonrequired deposit of fully paid for marginable securities.
- A sale of securities 50% will be credited to SMA.

> **TAKE**NOTE!
>
> A customer's SMA is the greater of the excess equity or the amount of SMA already established by the account.

EXAMPLE A customer's margin account is as follows:

LMV	Debit
60,000	40,000

EQ 20,000
Reg. T 30,000
EE   0
SMA 5,000

The customer's margin account is restricted because the equity is below the Reg. T requirement. If the customer in this case uses the SMA of $5,000 to purchase $10,000 worth of stock, the account will look as follows:

LMV	Debit
70,000	50,000

EQ 20,000
Reg. T 35,000
EE 0
SMA 0

The customer was able to use the SMA to purchase the stock because doing so did not cause the account to fall below the minimum equity requirement of 25%. An investor may never use SMA to meet a margin call.

A DECREASE IN THE LONG MARKET VALUE

A decrease in the long market value of the securities in a margin account will cause the customer's equity to fall. Should the equity in the customer's account fall below 50% of the current market value, the account becomes restricted. A customer whose account is restricted may still:

- Buy additional marginable securities and deposit 50%.
- Sell securities and withdraw 50% of the proceeds.
- Withdraw securities by depositing 50% of their value in cash or by depositing securities with a loan value of 50%.

 TAKENOTE!

If a customer wants to withdraw cash from a restricted margin account, the customer must deposit marginable securities with a loan value equal to the amount of the cash withdrawn from the account.

MINIMUM EQUITY REQUIREMENTS FOR LONG MARGIN ACCOUNTS

Once the Reg. T deposit has been made by the investor, the NYSE/FINRA set the minimum account equity that must be maintained by the investor. An investor is required to maintain a minimum equity equal to 25% of the long market value of the account. If the equity falls below the minimum, the investor will receive a margin, or maintenance call. A maintenance call can be met by:

- Depositing cash.
- Depositing marginable securities with a loan value equal to the call.
- Selling securities.

All margin calls must be met promptly. If the investor fails to meet the call, the firm will liquidate enough of the customer's securities to satisfy the call.

To determine the minimum equity at a given long market value, use the following formula:

minimum equity = long market value × 25%

EXAMPLE

A customer has a margin account with a long market value of $50,000. The customer's minimum equity would be found as follows:

$50,000 × .25 = $12,500

To determine how far a customer's account value can fall in order to be at the minimum equity requirement, use the following formula:

minimum equity = debit balance/.75

If a customer purchased $40,000 worth of securities and made the required deposit, the account would look as follows:

LMV	Debit
40,000	20,000

EQ 20,000

Using the above formula to determine how low the market value could fall for the account to be at the minimum equity, we get:

$20,000/.75 = $26,667

At the $26,667 level, the account is at the minimum equity of 25%. If the value falls any lower, the investor will receive a margin call.

ESTABLISHING A SHORT POSITION IN A MARGIN ACCOUNT

All short sales must be done in a margin account. Prior to establishing the short position, the customer must first borrow the stock to be sold short. The customer is required to deposit 50% of the market value of the borrowed shares to ensure that resources are available to repurchase the shares if the stock's price rises. The customer's deposit establishes the customer's equity in the account. The customer may meet the Reg. T requirement by depositing cash or fully paid for marginable securities with a loan value equal to the Reg. T requirement. In order to establish a short position in a new margin account, the investor must deposit the greater of $2,000 or 50% of the borrowed securities' market value. Special rules are in place for customers who want to sell low priced stocks short. If the stock sold short is less than $5 per share the required deposit is the greater of 100% of the market value or $2.50 per share.

EXAMPLE

Sold Short	Minimum Equity	Reg. T at 50%	Required Deposit
1,000 ABC at 50	$2,000	$25,000	$25,000
1,000 XYZ at 20	$2,000	$10,000	$10,000
100 RTY at 30	$2,000	$1,500	$2,000
100 KLM at 15	$2,000	$750	$2,000
1,000 FGTK at 3	$2,000	$1,500	$3,000

The credit balance in a short margin account remains constant while the short market value changes. To determine the equity in a short margin account, use the following formula:

equity = credit balance – short market value

Let's look at the account of a customer who sells 1,000 XYZ short at $40 per share. The account will look as follows:

Credit	SMV
40,000	20,000

EQ 20,000

> **TAKE NOTE!**
>
> The credit of $60,000 was created from the proceeds from the short sale of 1,000 XYZ at 40 and the investor's Reg. T deposit of $20,000.

A DECREASE IN THE SHORT MARKET VALUE

Customers who sell stock short hope that the value of the stock will fall and that they will be able to buy it back cheaper and replace it. As a result, as the short market value of the account falls, the investor's equity will increase. The credit balance in a short margin account remains constant while the short market value changes.

Let's look at what happens to the same account if XYZ falls to $30 per share:

Original Position

Credit	SMV
60,000	40,000

EQ 20,000

XYZ at $30

Credit	SMV
60,000	30,000

EQ 30,000

Notice that as the short market value of the account fell from $40,000 to $30,000, the investor's equity increased from $20,000 to $30,000.

SPECIAL MEMORANDUM ACCOUNT (SMA) FOR A SHORT MARGIN ACCOUNT

When a customer's equity increases to over 50% of the short market value, it is credited to the special memorandum account, or SMA. A customer may use SMA in a short margin account to:

- Sell short additional securities.
- Have the amount sent out by check.

To determine if the customer has excess equity in a short margin account, use the following formula:

excess equity = customer's equity − Reg. T requirement of SMV

Let's look at the account again after XYZ has fallen to $30 per share:

Credit	SMV
60,000	30,000

EQ 30,000
Reg. T at 30 15,000
EE 15,000
SMA 15,000

As the short market value of the account has fallen, the investor's equity has increased. The customer's excess equity is credited to SMA, just as in a long margin account. In this case, the customer may sell short an additional $30,000 worth of securities based on the SMA.

Let's look at the account if the investor sells short additional securities valued at $30,000.

Credit	SMV
90,000	60,000

EQ 30,000
Reg. T 30,000
EE 0
SMA 0

The customer's account has exactly 50% equity, as required by Reg. T.

Let's look at the account if the customer withdraws the excess equity instead of selling additional securities short:

Credit	SMV
45,000	30,000

EQ 15,000
Reg. T at 30 15,000
EE 0
SMA 0

AN INCREASE IN THE SHORT MARKET VALUE

An increase in the short market value in a short margin account will cause the investor's equity to fall. Should the equity in the customer's account fall below 50% of the current short market value, the account becomes restricted. A customer whose account is restricted may still:

- Sell short additional securities and deposit 50%.
- Cover the short securities and withdraw 50%.

An increase in the short market value of the account will not affect the customer's SMA. The customer's SMA will be the greater of:

- The excess equity.

Or

- The SMA already established.

MINIMUM EQUITY REQUIREMENTS FOR SHORT MARGIN ACCOUNTS

Once the Reg. T deposit has been made by the investor, the NYSE/FINRA set the minimum account equity that must be maintained by an investor who sells securities short. Because selling stock short involves unlimited risk, a higher level of minimum equity is required to be maintained. An investor is required to maintain a minimum equity equal to 30% of the short market value of the account. If the equity falls below the minimum, the investor will receive a margin, or maintenance call. A maintenance call can be met by:

- Depositing cash.
- Depositing marginable securities with a loan value equal to the call.
- Repurchasing securities.

All margin calls must be met promptly. If the investor fails to meet the call, the firm will repurchase enough of the customer's securities to satisfy the call.

To determine the minimum equity at a given short market value, use the following formula:

minimum equity = SMV × 30%

> **EXAMPLE**
>
> A customer has a margin account with a short market value of $50,000. The minimum equity would be:
>
> $50,000 × .30 = $15,000
>
> To determine how high the short market value can rise in order to be at the minimum equity requirement, use the following formula:
>
> **minimum equity = total credit balance/1.30**
>
> If a customer sold short $50,000 worth of securities and made the required deposit, the account would look as follows:
>
> | Credit | SMV |
> |--------|--------|
> | 75,000 | 50,000 |
>
> EQ 25,000
>
> Using the above formula to determine how high the market value could rise for the account to be at the minimum equity, we get:
>
> $75,000/1.3 = $57,693
>
> At the $57,693 level, the account is at the minimum equity of 30%. If the value rises any higher, the investor will receive a margin call. If the investor has sold short low-priced securities, the minimum is as follows:
>
> - 100% of the market value or $2.50 per share, whichever is greater for stock under $5.
> - 30% of the market value or $5 per share, whichever is greater for stock over $5.

MARGIN REQUIREMENTS FOR DAY TRADING

Special margin requirements are in place for pattern day traders. A pattern day trader is one who day trades four or more times in a 5-day period. A day trade is defined as a purchase and sale entered for the same security on the same day for the same number of shares, which is referred to as a round trip. The customer is flat at the end of the day. Also included in determining a day trade are positions held overnight and closed out the next day prior to establishing another position. The minimum initial equity requirement for a pattern day trader increases from $2,000 to $25,000. A pattern day trader's buying power is four times the trader's maintenance margin excess. If this limit is exceeded during the course of a day, the trader will receive a day trading margin call. The trader must meet the call within 5 business days. During the time the call is outstanding, the trader's buying power is limited to twice the maintenance excess. If the call is not met within 5 business days, the account will become restricted for 90 days, and the buying power will be limited to the available cash in the account. All deposits used to meet a day trading margin call must remain in the account for at least 2 business days. Pattern day traders may not use cross guarantees. This means that the resources of the day trading account must meet the requirements for that account independently. Day traders may not use the accounts of others or use other accounts owned by the day trader to meet the obligations in the day trading account.

 TAKENOTE!

If a customer meets the requirements of a pattern day trader but the number of day trades in a 5-day period is 6% or less of all the trades in the account, the individual will not be considered a pattern day trader.

COMBINED MARGIN ACCOUNTS

Investors may wish to purchase securities that they feel will rise and sell short other securities that they feel will fall. An investor establishing both long and short positions in a margin account is said to have a combined account. The investor will have to determine:

- The Reg. T requirement on the long side.
- The Reg. T requirement on the short side.
- The minimum equity on the long side.
- The minimum equity on the short side.

Let's look at a combined account that has the following:

LMV = $60,000
Debit = $25,000
SMV = $40,000
Credit = $62,000

To determine the customer's equity in a combined account, use the following formula:

(LMV − Debit) + (Credit − SMV)

Using the above example, we get:

(60,000 − 25,000) + (62,000 − 40,000) = $57,000

If you are asked to determine the minimum equity for a combined account, you must determine the minimum equity on the long side and the minimum equity on the short side, and then add them together.

PORTFOLIO MARGIN ACCOUNTS

Broker dealers may offer sophisticated investors who properly hedge their positions portfolio-based margin. In contrast to strategy-based margin, which calculates the margin requirement for all positions in the account separately, portfolio-based margin calculates the potential losses in the account based on all of the positions and offsetting hedges to determine the investor's margin requirement. An institutional investor who is long a basket of S&P 500 stocks and short S&P 500 futures has dramatically lower risk than an investor who is outright long with no hedges. Broker dealers will use an SEC-approved risk-modeling system to determine both the risk to the portfolio and the amount of margin required to hold the positions. Portfolio-based margin calculations generally result in lower overall margin requirements and increased leverage. As a result, portfolio margin is only offered to the largest and most sophisticated investors, such as hedge funds, broker dealers, members of a futures exchange, and accounts with $5 million in equity that have been approved for uncovered option writing. If an account approved for portfolio margin receives a margin call, it must be met in 3 business days.

SECURITIES BACKED LINES OF CREDIT

Some broker dealers allow customers to have a line of credit attached to their account which allow the investor to borrow funds based on the value of the fully paid for assets in the account. This is not a margin loan used to purchase securities. In some ways it functions like a home equity line of credit that allows the investor to borrow from the broker dealer to meet their cash needs or to pay for a large purchase such as a home renovation. Firms must have proper procedures in place to make sure the customers and the representatives understand the loan restrictions and features. Customers must understand how a fall in the market value of the securities in the account can impact their ability to borrow. Additionally a significant fall in the value may also require additional collateral or a portion of the loan to be repaid.

MINIMUM MARGIN FOR LEVERAGED ETFs

To determine the minimum equity requirement for an exchange traded fund that employs leverage to return a multiple of the performance or inverse performance of an index, you must multiply the minimum equity requirement by the leverage factor. Therefore, buying an ETF that uses a leverage factor of 2:1 or 200% would have a minimum equity requirement of 50%. (25% × 2). Buying an ETF that uses a leverage factor of 3:1 would have a minimum equity requirement of 75% (25% × 3). Investors who sell a leveraged ETF short would be subject to the 30% minimum requirement times the leveraged factor. Therefore selling an ETF short with a leverage factor of 3:1 or 300% would have a minimum equity requirement of 90% (30% × 3).

CHAPTER 8

Pretest

MARGIN ACCOUNTS

1. Minimum maintenance is set in a new margin account by:
   a. The Federal Reserve Board.
   b. Regulation T.
   c. The NYSE/FINRA.
   d. The Brokerage firm.

2. The initial minimum for a new margin account is:
   a. 50% of the purchase price.
   b. The greater of $2,000 or 50% of the purchase price.
   c. Set by the Federal Reserve Board.
   d. Set by the MSRB.

3. A margin customer must sign which of the following to pledge securities as collateral for a loan?
   a. Loan consent
   b. Rehypothecation agreement
   c. Hypothecation agreement
   d. Collateral agreement

4. An investor has an open margin account with $48,000 in market value and a debit balance of $10,000. His minimum equity at this level is:
   a. $24,000.
   b. $14,000.
   c. $13,333.
   d. $10,000.

5. The initial margin requirement for municipal bonds is set by:
   a. The NYSE.
   b. Regulation T.
   c. The MSRB.
   d. The Federal Reserve Board.

6. You have the following positions in your margin account:

   Long 500 ABC at 27

   Long 1,500 XYZ at 42

   Long 250 MCX at 80

   You have a debit balance of $28,200. What is your minimum maintenance?
   a. $24,125
   b. $48,250
   c. $22,500
   d. $37,600

7. Your customer buys $100,000 principal amount of New York Bridge and Tunnel revenue bonds at 54 in a margin account. The customer must deposit:
   a. $7,000.
   b. $27,000.
   c. $54,000.
   d. $8,100

CHAPTER 8

8. An investor in a new margin account purchases 200 XYZ at 20 and deposits $2,000. XYZ falls to $18, and the investor's equity falls to $1,600. Which of the following is true?

   a. The investor will receive a margin call for $200.

   b. No action by the investor is required at this time.

   c. The investor must deposit $550 to maintain the $2,000 minimum equity requirement.

   d. The position could be liquidated if the investor doesn't meet the current margin call.

9. You have an open margin account with a long market value of $125,000 and a debit balance of $54,000. How low can the value of the securities drop before you get a margin call?

   a. $72,000

   b. $100,000

   c. $67,500

   d. $93,750

10. Which of the following is true if a client uses SMA to withdraw $2,500 from a margin account?

    a. The SMA is reduced, and the debit balance is reduced.

    b. The SMA is increased, and the debit balance is increased.

    c. The SMA is reduced, and the debit balance is increased.

    d. The SMA is reduced, and the debit balance is not affected.

CHAPTER 9

Investment Companies

INTRODUCTION

In this chapter, we will look at how an investment company pools investors' funds in order to purchase a diversified portfolio of securities. Series 99 operations professionals provide support to firms that transact business in investment company products, so it is imperative that candidates have a complete understanding of this material. Some of the test focus points will be on:

- Types of investment companies.
- Investment company structure.
- Investment company registration.
- Investment company taxation.
- Investment strategies and recommendations.
- Investor benefits.

INVESTMENT COMPANY PHILOSOPHY

An investment company is organized as either a corporation or as a trust. Individual investors' money is then pooled together in a single account and used to purchase securities that will have the greatest chance of helping the investment company reach its objectives. All investors jointly own the portfolio that is created through these pooled funds, and each investor has an undivided interest in the securities. No single shareholder has any right or claim that exceeds the rights or claims of any other shareholder, regardless of the size of the investment. Investment companies offer individual investors the opportunity to have their money managed by professionals who may otherwise only offer their services to large institutions. Through diversification, the investor may participate in the future growth or income generated from the large number of different securities contained in the portfolio. Both diversification and professional management should contribute significantly to the attainment of the objectives set forth by the investment company. There are many other features and benefits that may be offered to investors that will be examined later in this chapter.

TYPES OF INVESTMENT COMPANIES

All investment company offerings are subject to the Securities Act of 1933, which requires the investment company to register with the SEC and to give all purchasers a prospectus. Investment companies are also subject to the Investment Company Act of 1940, which sets forth guidelines on how investment companies must operate. The Investment Company Act of 1940 breaks down investment companies into three different types:

1. Face-amount companies.
2. Unit investment trusts (UITs)
3. Management investment companies (mutual funds).

FACE-AMOUNT COMPANY/ FACE-AMOUNT CERTIFICATE

An investor may enter into a contract with an issuer of a face-amount certificate to receive a stated or fixed amount of money (the face amount) at a stated date in the future. In exchange for this future sum, the investor must deposit an agreed lump sum or make scheduled installment payments over time. Face-amount certificates are rarely issued these days, because most of the tax advantages that the investment once offered have been lost through changes in the tax laws.

UNIT INVESTMENT TRUST (UIT)

A unit investment trust (UIT) will invest either in a fixed portfolio of securities or a nonfixed portfolio of securities. A fixed UIT will traditionally invest in a large block of government or municipal debt. The bonds will be held until maturity, and the proceeds will be distributed to investors in the UIT. Once the proceeds have been distributed to the investors, the UIT will have achieved its objective and will cease to exist. A nonfixed UIT will purchase mutual fund shares in order to reach a stated objective. A nonfixed UIT is also known as a contractual plan. Both types of UITs are organized as trusts and operate as a holding company for the portfolio. UITs are not actively managed, and they do not have a board of directors or investment advisers. Both types of UITs issue units or shares of beneficial interest to investors that represent an undivided interest in the underlying portfolio of securities. UITs must maintain a secondary market in the units or shares to offer some liquidity to investors.

MANAGEMENT INVESTMENT COMPANY (MUTUAL FUND)

A management investment company employs an investment adviser to manage a diversified portfolio of securities designed to obtain its stated investment objective. The management company may be organized as either an open-end company or as a closed-end company. The main difference between an open-end company and a closed-end company is how the shares are purchased and sold. An open-end company offers new shares to any investor who wants to invest. This is known as a continuous primary offering. Because the offering of new shares is continuous, the capitalization of the open-end fund is unlimited. Stated another way, an open-end fund may raise as much money as investors are willing to put in. An open-end fund must repurchase its own shares from investors who want to redeem them. There is no secondary market for open-end mutual fund shares. The shares must be purchased from the fund company and redeemed to the fund company. A closed-end fund offers common shares to investors through an initial public offering (IPO), just like a stock. Its capitalization is limited to the number of authorized shares that have been approved for sale. Shares of the closed-end fund will trade in the secondary market in investor-to-investor transactions on an exchange or in the OTC market, just like common shares.

OPEN END VS. CLOSED END

Although both open-end and closed-end funds are designed to achieve their stated investment objective, the manner in which they operate is different. The following is a side-by-side comparison of the important features of open-end and closed-end funds:

Feature	Open End	Closed End
Capitalization	Unlimited continuous primary offering	Single fixed offering through IPO
Investor may purchase	Full and fractional shares	Full shares only
Securities offered	Common shares only	Common and preferred shares and debt securities
How shares are purchased and sold	Shares are purchased from the fund company and redeemed to the fund company	Shares may be purchased only from the fund company during IPO; secondary market transactions are between investors
Share pricing	Shares are priced by formula: NAV + SC = POP	Shares are priced by supply and demand
Shareholder rights	Dividends and voting	Dividends, voting, and preemptive

INVESTMENT COMPANY REGISTRATION

Investment companies are regulated by the Securities Act of 1933 and the Investment Company Act of 1940. An investment company must register with the SEC if the company operates to own, invest, reinvest, or trade in securities. A company must also register with the SEC as an investment company if the company has 40% or more of its assets invested in securities other than those issued by the U.S. government or one of the company's subsidiaries.

REGISTRATION REQUIREMENTS

Before an investment company may register with the SEC, it must meet certain minimum requirements. An investment company may not register with the SEC unless it has the following:

- Minimum net worth of $100,000
- At least 100 shareholders
- Clearly defined investment objectives

An investment company may be allowed to register without having 100 shareholders and without a net worth of $100,000 if it can meet these requirements within 90 days.

Investment companies must file a full registration with the SEC before the offering becomes effective. The investment company is considered to have registered when the SEC receives its notice of registration. The investment company's registration statement must contain:

- The type of investment company (open end, closed end, and so forth).
- Biographical information on the officers and directors of the company.
- Name and address of each affiliated person.
- Plans to concentrate investments in any one area (such as a sector fund).
- Plans to invest in real estate or commodities.
- Plans to borrow.
- Conditions under which investment objectives may be changed through a vote by shareholders.

Once registered the investment company may:

- Raise money through the sale of shares.
- Lend money to earn interest.
- Borrow money on a limited basis.

An investment company obtains its investment capital from shareholders through the sale of shares. Once it is operating, it may lend money to earn interest, such as by purchasing bonds or notes. An investment company may not, however, lend money to employees. An investment company may borrow money for such business purposes as to redeem shares. If the investment company borrows money, it must have $3 in equity for every dollar that it wants to borrow. Another way of saying this is that the investment company must maintain an asset-to-debt ratio of at least 3:1, or at least 300%.

An investment company is prohibited from:

- Taking over or controlling other companies.
- Acting as a bank or a savings and loan.
- Receiving commission for executing orders or for acting as a broker.
- Continuing to operate with less than 100 shareholders or less than $100,000 net worth.

Unless the investment company meets strict capital and disclosure requirements, it may not engage in any of the following:

- Selling securities short
- Buying securities on margin
- Maintaining joint accounts
- Distributing its own shares

Regardless of the makeup of their investment holdings, all of the following are exempt from the registration requirements of an investment company:

- Broker dealers
- Underwriters
- Banks and savings and loans
- Mortgage companies
- Real estate investment trusts (REITs)
- Security holder protection committees

INVESTMENT COMPANY COMPONENTS

Investment companies have several different groups that serve specialized functions. Each of these groups plays a key role in the investment company's operation. They are:

- The board of directors.
- The investment adviser.
- The custodian bank.
- The transfer agent.

BOARD OF DIRECTORS

Management companies have an organizational structure that is similar to that of other companies. The board of directors oversees the company's president and other officers who run the day-to-day operations of the company. The board and the corporate officers concern themselves with the business and administrative functions of the company. They do not manage the investment portfolio. The board of directors:

- Defines the company's investment objectives.
- Hires the investment adviser, custodian bank, and transfer agent.
- Determines what type of funds to offer, such as growth or income.

The board of directors is elected by a vote of the shareholders. The Investment Company Act of 1940 governs the makeup of the board. The Investment Company Act of 1940 requires that at least a majority of the board be noninterested persons. A noninterested person is a person whose only affiliation with the fund is as a member of the board. Therefore, a maximum of 49% or less than 50% of the board may hold another position within the fund company or may otherwise be interested in the fund. An affiliated person is anyone who could exercise control over the company, such as:

- Officers, directors, and employees of the investment company.
- The investment adviser.
- A company in which the investment company owns at least 5% of the voting stock.
- Any entity owning 5% or more of the investment company's voting stock.
- The person who deposits the assets of a UIT into the custodian bank.

An interested person includes:

- All broker dealers.
- Anyone who has been an attorney, investment adviser, affiliated person, or the principal underwriter for the investment company within the last 2 years.
- The principal underwriter.
- Employees of the investment adviser.
- Most affiliated persons.
- Immediate family of an affiliated person.
- Anyone else the SEC designates.

Both affiliated and interested parties are prohibited from selling securities or property to the investment company or any of its subsidiaries. Anyone who has been convicted of any felony or securities-related misdemeanor or who has been barred from the securities business may not serve on the board of directors.

BONDING OF KEY INVESTMENT COMPANY EMPLOYEES

The investment company is required to obtain a bond to cover itself and each officer, director, and employee with access to the investment company's assets. The company may obtain a bond for each employee or may obtain a blanket bond for all employees that are required to be bonded. In the case of a blanket bond, the company must list the names of the employees to be covered. The bond only covers the employees for negligence. Any criminal acts or acts of bad faith are not covered.

INVESTMENT ADVISER

The investment company's board of directors hires the investment adviser to manage the fund's portfolio. The investment adviser is a company, not a person. The investment adviser must also determine the tax consequences of distributions to shareholders and ensure that the fund's investment strategies are in line with the stated investment objectives. The investment adviser's compensation is a percentage of the net assets of the fund, not a percentage of the profits, although performance bonuses are allowed. The investment adviser's fee is typically the largest expense of the fund, and the more aggressive the objective, the higher the fee. The investment adviser may not borrow from the fund and may not have any security-related convictions. The investment adviser's contract requires initial approval and then annual reapproval by a majority vote of the board of directors and the outstanding shares.

CUSTODIAN BANK

The custodian bank, or the exchange member broker dealer that has been hired by the investment company, physically holds all of the fund's cash and securities. The custodian holds all of the fund's assets for safekeeping and provides other bookkeeping and clerical functions for the investment company, such as maintaining books and records for accumulation plans for investors. All fund assets must be kept segregated from other assets. The custodian must ensure that only approved persons have access to the account and that all distributions are done in line with SEC guidelines.

TRANSFER AGENT

The transfer agent for the investment company handles the issuance, cancellation, and redemption of fund shares. The transfer agent also handles name changes and may be part of the fund's custodian or a separate company. The transfer agent receives an agreed fee for its services.

MUTUAL FUND DISTRIBUTION

Most mutual funds do not sell their own shares directly to investors. The distribution of the shares is the responsibility of the underwriter. The underwriter for a mutual fund is also known as the sponsor or distributor. The underwriter is selected by the fund's board of directors and receives a fee in the form of a sales charge for the shares it distributes. As the underwriter receives orders for the mutual fund shares, it purchases the shares directly from the fund at the net asset value (NAV). The sales charge is then added to the NAV as the underwriter's compensation. This process of adding the sales charge to the NAV is responsible for the mutual fund pricing formula, which is NAV + SC = public offering price (POP). The underwriter may purchase shares from the mutual fund only to fill customer orders. It may not hold mutual fund shares in inventory in anticipation of receiving future customer orders.

SELLING GROUP MEMBER

Most brokerage firms maintain selling agreements with mutual fund distributors, which allows them to purchase mutual fund shares at a discount from the POP. Selling group members may then sell the mutual fund shares to investors at the POP and earn part of the sales charge. In order to purchase mutual fund shares at a discount from the POP, the selling group member must be a member of FINRA. All non-FINRA members and suspended members must be treated as members of the general public and pay the POP.

DISTRIBUTION OF NO-LOAD MUTUAL FUND SHARES

No-load mutual funds do not charge a sales charge to their investors. Because there is no sales charge, the mutual fund may sell the shares directly to investors at the NAV.

DISTRIBUTION OF MUTUAL FUND SHARES

The following drawing details the variety of ways in which mutual fund shares may be distributed to investors:

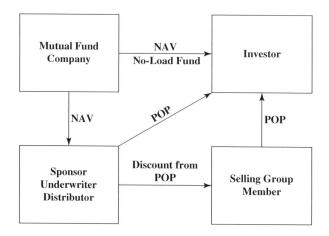

MUTUAL FUND PROSPECTUS

The prospectus is the official offering document for open-end mutual fund shares. The prospectus, or information on where to obtain a prospectus, must be presented to all purchasers of the fund either before or during the sales presentation. The prospectus is the fund's full-disclosure document and provides details regarding:

- The fund's investment objectives.
- Sales charges.
- Management expenses.
- Fund services.
- Performance data for the past 1, 5, and 10 years or for the life of the fund.

The prospectus, which is given to most investors, is the summary prospectus. If investors want additional information regarding the mutual fund, they may request a statement of additional information. The statement of additional information will include details regarding the following as of the date it was published:

- Securities holdings
- Balance sheet
- Income statement

- Portfolio turnover data
- Compensation paid to the board of directors and investment advisory board

A summary prospectus that contains past performance data is known as an advertising prospectus. A mutual fund prospectus:

- Should be updated by the fund every 12 months.
- Must be updated by the fund every 13 months.
- May be used by a representative for up to 16 months.
- Should be discarded after 16 months from publication.

 TAKENOTE!

The date of the financial information is the date that is used to calculate when a mutual fund prospectus must be updated and how long it may be used. This is not always the same date that is on the cover of the prospectus.

Mutual funds are also required to disclose the following either in the prospectus or in the annual report to shareholders:

- A performance comparison graph showing the performance of the fund
- Names of the officers and directors who are responsible for the portfolio's day-to-day management
- Disclosure of any factors that materially affected performance over the latest fiscal year

All mutual fund investors must receive an annual audit report and a semiannual update. The annual report must include:

- A balance sheet.
- An income statement.
- The valuation of all securities held in the investment company's portfolio.
- A complete statement regarding compensation to the board of directors, officers, and investment adviser.
- A statement detailing the total value of all securities purchased and sold.

Mutual funds are required to include summary information at the front of its statutory prospectus. The purpose of this summary information is to clearly convey all of the most pertinent information an investor would require to make an informed decision about the fund. The terms to be detailed in the summary information include the fund's investment objectives, past performance, costs and the biographical information for the management of the fund. Also covered in the summary information will be the principal investment strategies, compensation, purchase and redemptions and tax implications. Mutual funds may use this information to create a "mutual fund profile" for investors. Investors may use the profile- to purchase the mutual fund shares but the investor must be given information on where to obtain a statutory prospectus and the statement of additional information for the fund.

ADDITIONAL DISCLOSURES BY A MUTUAL FUND

An open-end mutual fund must disclose in its statement of additional information how it votes the proxies it receives for securities held by the fund. A closed-end fund will disclose this on Form N-CSR. All management companies must file their complete proxy voting record annually by August 31 for the 12 months ending June 30. They will file the information on Form N-PX. Shareholders that request this information must be sent a copy within 3 business days.

ANTI-RECIPROCAL RULE

A mutual fund may not select a broker dealer to execute the orders for its portfolios based on the dollar amount of the mutual fund that the broker dealer sells. The fund's selection of broker dealers to execute orders and to provide other services must be solely based on the merits of the broker dealer performing the service. Alternatively, a brokerage firm may not recommend a mutual fund to a client based on the amount of commission the firm receives from executing the mutual fund's securities transactions. A broker dealer also may not:

- Allow registered representatives to share in the commission revenue generated by the execution of the fund's order to induce them to sell more mutual fund shares.
- Use the amount of sales of the fund as a way to leverage a higher rate on the fund's execution business.
- Create a list of preferred funds based on the amount of commission business that the funds give the clients.

MONEY MARKET FUNDS

Money market funds invest in short-term money market instruments such as bankers' acceptances, commercial paper, and other debt securities with less than 1 year remaining to maturity. Money market funds are no-load funds that offer the investor the highest degree of safety of principal as well as current income. The NAV for money market funds is always equal to $1; however, this is not guaranteed. Investors use money market funds as a place to hold idle funds and to earn current income. Interest is earned by investors daily and is credited to their accounts monthly. Most money market funds offer check-writing privileges, and investors must receive a prospectus prior to investing or opening an account.

VALUING MUTUAL FUND SHARES

Mutual funds must determine the net asset value of their funds' shares at least once per business day. Most mutual funds will price their shares at the close of business of the NYSE (4:00 p.m. EST). The mutual fund prospectus will provide the best answer as to when the fund calculates the price of its shares. The calculation is required to determine both the redemption price (NAV) and the purchase price (POP) of the fund's shares. The price that is received by an investor who is redeeming shares and the price that is paid by an investor who is purchasing shares will be based on the price that is next calculated after the fund has received the investor's order. This is known as forward pricing. To calculate the fund's NAV, use the following formula:

assets − liabilities = net asset value (NAV)

To determine the NAV per share, simply divide the total net asset value by the total number of outstanding shares:

$$\frac{\text{total NAV}}{\text{total \# of shares}}$$

MUTUAL FUND SALES CHARGES

Mutual funds may assess a number of different sales charges.

SALES CHARGES FOR OPEN-END FUNDS

The maximum allowable sales charge that an open-end fund may charge is 8.5% of the POP. The sales charge that may be assessed by a particular fund will be detailed in the fund's prospectus. It is important to note that the sales charge is not an expense of the fund; it is a cost of distribution, which is borne by the investor. The sales charge pays for the following:

- Underwriters' commission
- Commission to brokerage firms and registered representatives

SALES CHARGES FOR CLOSED-END FUNDS

Closed-end funds do not charge a sales charge to invest. An investor who wants to purchase a closed-end fund will pay the current market price, plus whatever the brokerage firm charges to execute the order.

FRONT-END LOADS

A front-end load is a sales charge that the investor pays when purchasing shares. The sales charge is added to the NAV of the fund and the investor purchases the shares at the POP. The sales charge, in essence, is deducted from the gross amount invested, and the remaining amount is invested in the portfolio at the NAV. Shares that charge a front-end load are known as "A" shares.

EXAMPLE

XYZ mutual fund has an NAV of $9.50, a POP of $10, and a sales charge of 5%. How much in sales charges would an investor pay if he were to invest $10,000 in the fund?

$10,000
× 5%
$500 = sales charge

$10,000
− $500
$9,500 invested in the portfolio at NAV

BACK-END LOADS

A back-end load is also known as a contingent deferred sales charge (CDSC). An investor in a fund that charges a back-end load will pay the sales charge at the time of redemption of the fund shares. The sales charge will be assessed on the value of the shares that have been redeemed, and the amount of the sales charge will decline as the investor's holding period increases. The following is a hypothetical back-end load schedule:

CHAPTER 9 Investment Companies

Years Money Left in Portfolio	Sales Charge
1	8.5%
2	7%
3	5%
4	3%
5	1.5%
5 years or more	0%

The mutual fund prospectus will detail the particular schedule for back-end load sales charges. Mutual fund shares that charge a back-end load are also known as "B" shares. Investors who purchase B shares must receive a confirmation containing a statement that upon selling the shares the investor may pay a sales charge.

OTHER TYPES OF SALES CHARGES

There are other ways in which a mutual fund assesses a sales charge. Shares that charge a level load based on the NAV are known as level-load funds, or "C" shares. Shares that charge an asset-based fee and a back-end load are known as "D" shares.

12B-1 FEES

Most mutual funds charge an asset-based distribution fee to its shares to cover expenses related to the promotion and distribution of the fund's shares. The amount of the fee will be determined annually as a percentage of the NAV or as a flat fee. The 12B-1 fee will be charged to the shares quarterly and will reduce the investor's overall return on the fund. Because a 12B-1 fee reduces the return of the investor, a 12B-1 fee is a type of sales load. 12B-1 fees cover such things as the printing of prospectuses and certain sales commissions to agents.

SALES CHARGE REDUCTIONS

The maximum allowable sales charge that may be assessed by an open-end mutual fund is 8.5% of the public offering price. If a mutual fund charges 8.5%, it must offer the following three privileges to investors:

1. Breakpoint sales charge reductions that reduce the amount of the sales charge based on the dollar amount invested

2. Rights of accumulation that will reduce the sales charge on subsequent investments based on the value of the investor's account
3. Automatic reinvestment of dividends and capital gains at the NAV

If a mutual fund does not offer all three of these benefits to investors, the maximum allowable sales charge that may be charged drops to 6.5%. Although a mutual fund that charges 8.5% must offer these features, most mutual funds that charge less than 8.5% also offer them. If the mutual fund pays a service fee to broker dealers for providing ongoing services to shareholders, the maximum sales charge that may be charged by the fund is 7.25%. FINRA members are prohibited from selling mutual funds that charge a service fee in excess of .25%.

BREAKPOINT SCHEDULE

As an incentive for investors to invest larger sums of money into a mutual fund, the mutual fund will reduce the sales charge based on the dollar amount of the purchase. Breakpoint sales charge reductions are available to any "person," including corporations, trusts, couples, and accounts for minors. Breakpoint sales charge reductions are not available to investment clubs or to parents and their adult children investing in separate accounts. The following is an example of a breakpoint schedule that a family of funds might use:

Dollar Amount Invested	Sales Charge
$1–$24,999	8.5%
$25,000–$74,999	7%
$75,000–$149,999	5%
$150,000–$499,999	3%
$500,000 or greater	1.5%

A breakpoint schedule benefits all parties—the fund company, the investor, and the representative. It is important to note that the fund's distributor will keep track of the investor's contributions to determine if the investor qualifies for a breakpoint. If the same investor holds the fund at different broker dealers the value of both accounts will be combined to determine breakpoint eligibility.

LETTER OF INTENT

An investor who might not be able to reach a breakpoint with a single purchase may qualify for a breakpoint sales charge reduction by signing a letter of intent. A letter of intent will give the investor up to 13 months to reach the dollar amount to which the investor has subscribed. The letter of intent is binding only on the fund company, not on the investor. The additional shares that will be purchased as a result of the lower sales charge will be held by the fund company in an escrow account. If the investor fulfills the letter of intent, the shares are released to the investor. Should the investor fail to reach the breakpoint, a sales charge adjustment will be charged. The investor may choose to pay the adjusted sales charge by either sending a check or by allowing some of the escrowed shares to be liquidated.

BACKDATING A LETTER OF INTENT

An investor may backdate a letter of intent up to 90 days to include a prior purchase, and the 13-month window starts from the back date. For example, if an investor backdates a letter of intent by the maximum 90 days allowed, then the investor has only 10 months to complete the letter of intent.

BREAKPOINT SALES

A breakpoint sale is a violation committed by a registered representative who is trying to earn larger commissions by recommending the purchase of mutual fund shares in a dollar amount that is just below the breakpoint that would allow the investor to qualify for a reduced sales charge. A breakpoint violation may also be considered to have been committed if a representative spreads out a large sum of money over different families of funds. A registered representative must always notify an investor of the availability of a sales charge reduction, especially when the investor is depositing a sum of money that is close to the breakpoint.

RIGHTS OF ACCUMULATION

Rights of accumulation allow the investor to qualify for reduced sales charges on subsequent investments by taking into consideration the value of the investor's account, including the growth. Unlike a letter of intent, there is no time limit and, as the account grows over time, the investor can qualify for lower sales charges on future investments. The sales charge reduction is not retroactive and does not reduce the sales charges on prior purchases. To qualify for the breakpoint, the dollar amount of the current purchase is calculated into the total value of the investor's account.

> **EXAMPLE**
>
> Using the breakpoint schedule presented above, let's look at an investor's account over the last 3 years:
>
> | Year | Deposit | Sales Charge |
> |---|---|---|
> | 1 | $5,000 | 8.5% |
> | 2 | $5,000 | 8.5% |
> | 3 | $5,000 | 8.5% |
>
> Let's assume that the investor's account has increased in value by $7,000, making the total current value of the account $21,000. The investor has another $5,000 to invest this year. Because there is a sales charge reduction available at the $25,000 level, the investor will pay a sales charge of 7% on the new $5,000.

AUTOMATIC REINVESTMENT OF DISTRIBUTIONS

Investors may elect to have their distributions automatically reinvested in the fund and use the distributions to purchase more shares. Most mutual funds will allow investors to purchase the shares at the NAV when they reinvest distributions. This feature has to be offered by mutual funds charging a sales charge of 8.5%. However, it is offered by most other mutual funds as well.

COMBINATION PRIVILEGES

Most mutual fund companies offer a variety of portfolios to meet different investment objectives. The different portfolios become known as a "family" of funds. Combination privileges allow an investor to combine the simultaneous purchases of two different portfolios to reach a breakpoint sales charge reduction.

> **EXAMPLE**
>
> An investor purchases $15,000 worth of an income fund and at the same time invests $40,000 in a growth portfolio offered by the same fund company. If the fund company offers a breakpoint sales charge reduction at $50,000, the investor would qualify for the lower sales charge under combination privileges.

CONVERSION OR EXCHANGE PRIVILEGES

Most mutual fund families will offer conversion or exchange privileges that allow the investor to move money from one portfolio to another offered by the same fund company without paying another sales charge. Another way of looking at this is that the fund company allows the investor to redeem the shares of one portfolio at the NAV and use the proceeds to purchase shares of another portfolio at the NAV. The IRS sees this as a purchase and a sale, and the investor will have to pay taxes on any gain on the sale of portfolio shares.

Other exchange conditions are as follows:

- The dollar value of the purchase may not exceed the sales proceeds.
- The purchase of the new portfolio must occur within 30 days.
- The sale may not include a sales charge refund.
- No commission may be paid to a registered representative or broker dealer.

EXAMPLE An aggressive investor has $20,000 invested in ABC high growth fund that has an NAV of $12 and a POP of $12.60. The investor wants to move the money into the ABC biotech fund, which has an NAV of $17.20 and a POP of $17.90. ABC offers conversion privileges, so the investor will redeem the shares of the growth portfolio at $12 and will purchase 1,162.79 shares of the biotech portfolio at $17.20.

 TAKENOTE!

If a client redeems his or her mutual fund shares within 7 business days of purchase, the sales charge earned by the broker dealer and the representative is returned to the fund company.

VOTING RIGHTS

Mutual fund investors have the right to vote on major issues regarding the fund. All votes are won by a simple majority; that is, 51% of the outstanding shares will win the vote. It is important to distinguish that shares vote, not shareholders. An investor with 5,000 shares has five times as many votes as an investor with 1,000 shares, even though they are both shareholders. Among the major issues to be voted on are:

- Changing capitalization (going from an open-end to a closed-end fund).
- Changing sales load (going from a loaded fund to a no-load fund).
- Changing or terminating business.
- Changing investment objectives.
- Lending money.
- Entering into real estate transactions.
- Issuing or underwriting other securities.
- Changing borrowing policies.
- Electing the board of directors.
- Electing the investment adviser.
- Setting 12B-1 fees.

PORTFOLIO TURNOVER

Portfolio turnover rates will tell you how long the fund holds its securities. The higher the rate, the shorter the fund's holding period. Higher portfolio turnover causes the fund to incur additional expenses in the form of execution charges. A turnover rate of 100% means that the fund replaces its portfolio annually.

RECOMMENDING MUTUAL FUNDS

Mutual funds are designed to be longer-term investments and are generally not used to time the market. When determining suitability for investors the registered representative must first make sure that the investment objective of the mutual fund matches the investor's objective. Once several funds have been selected that meet the client's objective the representative must then compare costs, fees, and expenses among the funds. Priority should be given to any fund company with whom the investor maintains an investment. If the client's objective has changed, the fund most likely offers conversion privileges which will allow the investor to move into another portfolio without paying any sales charge. If the investor is committing new capital, the fund company most likely offers combination privileges and rights of accumulation which will help the investor reach a sales charge reduction. Switching fund companies and/or spreading out investment dollars among different fund companies are red flags for breakpoint sales, violations, and abusive sales practices. The amount of time the investor is seeking to hold the investment will be a determining factor as to which share class is the most appropriate. Investors who have longer holding periods may be better off in B shares that assess a sales charge upon redemption based on their holding period. Investors who have shorter time horizons will be better of choosing A shares over B shares as the expenses associated with B shares tend to be higher. Important to note is that making a large investment in class B shares is a red flag for a breakpoint sales violation as the large dollar amount would have most likely resulted in a reduced sales charge for the investors. Investors with relatively short holding periods or who want to actively move money between funds to try to time the market would be best off with C shares which charge a level load each year.

EXCHANGE TRADED FUNDS/ETFs

In recent years exchange traded funds, or ETFs, have gained a lot of popularity. ETFs are created through the purchase of a basket of securities that are designed to track the performance of an index or sector. ETFs are not actively managed and provide investors with lower costs and the ability to buy, sell, and sell short the ETF at any point designed to provide returns and performance characteristics of positions that take on the leverage. Such ETFs are often known as "ultra" or double ETFs. These ETFs may provide returns that are double or more of the return of an index, or double or more the inverse return of an index.

EXCHANGE TRADED NOTES/ETNs

Exchange traded notes, sometimes known as equity linked notes, or index linked notes, are debt securities that base a maturity payment on the performance of an underlying security or group of securities such as an index. ETNs do not make coupon or interest payments to investors during the time the investor owns the ETN. ETNs may be purchased and sold at any time during the trading day and may be purchased on margin and sold short. One very important risk factor to consider when evaluating an ETN is the fact that ETNs are unsecured and carry the credit risk of the issuing bank or broker dealer. Similarly, principal protected notes, or PPNs, which are structured products that guarantee the return of the investor's principal if the note is held until maturity, carry a principal guarantee that is only as good as the issuer's credit rating and therefore are never 100% guaranteed.

ETFs THAT TRACK ALTERNATIVELY WEIGHTED INDEXES

Investing in ETFs that track indexes has become a popular investment strategy. As a result new products have come to market that track the performance of alternative indexes. Equal weight, alternatively weighted, fundamentally weighted, and volatility weighted ETFs offer exposure to other investment styles and may provide enhanced performance. These ETFs present additional risk factors that both registered representatives and investors need to understand. These funds are sometimes marketed as having better performance than other indexes which could be cause for a concern as the ETFs that track these indexes may be complex, thinly traded, and hard to understand for both representatives and retail investors. The lack of liquidity can lead to wider spreads causing the product to be expensive to buy and sell for investors. The portfolios often have high turnovers which can lead to increased transaction costs for the ETF.

ALTERNATIVE FUNDS

Alternative funds, also known as alt funds or liquid alts, invest in nontraditional assets or illiquid assets and may employ alternative investment strategies. There is no standard definition for what constitutes an alt fund, but alt funds are often marketed as a way for retail investors to gain access to hedge funds and actively managed programs that will perform well in a variety of market conditions. These funds claim to reduce volatility, increase diversification, and produce higher returns when compared to long only equity funds and income funds, while providing liquidity. Recommendations for alt funds must be based on the specific strategies employed by the fund, not merely as one overall investment. Retail communication must accurately and fairly detail each fund's operations and objectives in line with the information in the prospectuses. FINRA is concerned that registered representatives and retail investors will not understand how funds will react in certain market conditions or how the fund manager will approach those market conditions. These funds must be reviewed during the new product review process even if the firm has a selling agreement.

FLOATING RATE BANK LOAN FUNDS

These funds invest in bank loans that are traditionally designed for institutional investors. More and more funds and ETFs available to retail investors are investing in these products. The loans are designed to hedge interest rate risk. However, the floating rate loans contain increased liquidity, credit, and call risks to the funds who invest in these products. Floating rate bank loans are also difficult to value and have long settlement times. Funds that invest in these products may have liquidity issues if faced with large redemptions.

STRUCTURED RETAIL PRODUCTS/SRPs

Member firms have been creating their own proprietary products for distribution and sale to retail investors. These SRPs include complex products such as structured notes with complicated payout structures. These SRPs may use proprietary indexes as reference assets that are hard to track, making the products difficult to understand for retail investors. The payout structure may also be based on longer terms and other conditions, adding to the complexity of the products. Firms must ensure that representatives understand the performance characteristics and operational risks prior to recommending these products to investors. All members who create retail communications relating to SRPs must file the communications with FINRA within 10 business days of first use. FINRA is concerned that member firms in an effort to increase revenue will offer complex SRPs through distributors who do not have the knowledge or expertise to properly understand or recommend the products. If the member engages a wholesaler to sell its SRPs, the member must have written supervisory procedures in place to "know your distributor" to ensure that the distribution channels have controls in place regarding the proper training of representatives who sell the products to customers. Additional concerns are created when there are potential conflicts of interest between the creator of the SRP and the wholesale distributor, such as when the two companies are affiliated.

CHAPTER 9

Pretest

INVESTMENT COMPANIES

1. An investor with $20,000 invested in the XYZ growth fund is:
   a. A stockholder in XYZ.
   b. An owner of XYZ.
   c. An owner of an undivided interest in the XYZ growth portfolio.
   d. Both an owner of XYZ and an owner of an undivided interest in the XYZ growth portfolio.

2. All of the following benefit an investor, EXCEPT:
   a. Combination privileges
   b. Emergency withdrawal privileges
   c. Breakpoint sales
   d. Form 1099

3. A mutual fund investor has 500 shares of XYZ growth fund, which has an NAV of 22.30 and a POP of 23.05. The investor wants to invest the money in the biotech fund offered by XYZ, which has an NAV of 17.10 and a POP of 18. If XYZ offers conversion privileges, how many shares will the investor be able to purchase of the biotech fund?
   a. 652
   b. 619
   c. 640
   d. 605

265

4. A mutual fund's custodian bank does which of the following?
   a. It holds customers' securities.
   b. It cancels certificates.
   c. It maintains records for accumulation plans.
   d. It issues certificates.

5. The maximum 12B-1 fee a no-load mutual fund may charge is:
   a. Up to .25 of 1% of the NAV.
   b. Less than .25 of 1% of the NAV.
   c. Up to .25 of 1% of the POP.
   d. Less than .25 of 1% of the POP.

6. The ex-dividend date on a closed-end mutual fund is set by the:
   a. Board of directors.
   b. SEC.
   c. Board of Governors.
   d. FINRA/NYSE.

7. A mutual fund has been seeking to attract new customers to invest in its growth fund. It has been running an advertising campaign that markets the fund as a diversified mutual fund. How much of any one company may the fund own?
   a. 15%
   b. 5%
   c. 10%
   d. 9%

8. An investor wires $10,000 into his mutual fund on Tuesday, March 11, and the money is credited to his account at 3:00 p.m. He will be the owner of record on:
   a. Friday, March 14.
   b. Wednesday, March 12.
   c. Tuesday, March 11.
   d. Tuesday, March 18.

9. As it relates to the bonding of mutual fund employees, which of the following is true?
    a. All fund employees are required to be listed on the bond coverage.
    b. Only key employees are required to be listed on the bond coverage.
    c. All employees must have an individual bond posted for them.
    d. All employees with access to assets must be listed on the bond coverage.

10. A long-term growth fund has a portfolio turnover ratio of 25%. How often does the fund replace its total holdings?
    a. Every 4 years
    b. Once a year
    c. Every 4 months
    d. Every 6 months

CHAPTER 10

Variable Annuities and Retirement Plans

> **INTRODUCTION**
>
> This chapter will cover a variety of important topics relating to annuity products and retirement plans. For most people, saving for retirement has become an important investment objective for at least part of their portfolio. Many investors choose to purchase annuities to help plan for retirement. Over the years a wide range of annuity products have been developed to meet different investment objectives and risk profiles. Candidates will need to fully understand how annuities and retirement plans function in order to successfully complete the exam.

ANNUITIES

An annuity is a contract between an individual and an insurance company. Once the contract is entered into, the individual becomes known as the annuitant. The three basic types of annuities are designed to meet different objectives. The three types of annuities are:

1. Fixed annuities.
2. Variable annuities.
3. Combination annuities.

Although all three types allow the investor's money to grow tax deferred, the type of investments made and how the money is invested varies according to the type of annuity.

FIXED ANNUITIES

A fixed annuity offers investors a guaranteed rate of return regardless of whether the investment portfolio can produce the guaranteed rate. If the performance of the portfolio falls below the rate that was guaranteed, the insurance company owes investors the difference. Because the purchaser of a fixed annuity does not have any investment risk, a fixed annuity is considered an insurance product, not a security. Representatives who sell fixed annuity contracts must have an insurance license. Because fixed annuities offer investors a guaranteed return, the money invested by the insurance company will be used to purchase conservative investments such as mortgages and real estate—investments whose historical performance is predictable enough so that a guaranteed rate can be offered to investors. All of the money invested into fixed annuity contracts is held in the insurance company's general account. Because the rate that the insurance guarantees is not very high, the annuitant may suffer a loss of purchasing power due to inflation risk.

VARIABLE ANNUITIES

An investor seeking to achieve a higher rate of return may elect to purchase a variable annuity. Variable annuities seek to obtain a higher rate of return by investing in stocks, bonds, or mutual fund shares. These securities traditionally offer higher rates of return than more conservative investments. A variable annuity does not offer the investor a guaranteed rate of return, and the investor may lose all or part of the principal. Because the annuitant bears the investment risk associated with a variable annuity, the contract is considered both a security and an insurance product. Representatives who sell variable annuities must have both their securities license and their insurance license. The money and securities contained in a variable annuity contract are held in the insurance company's separate account. The separate account is named as such because the variable annuity's portfolio must be kept "separate" from the insurance company's general funds. The insurance company must have a net worth of $1 million or the separate account must have a net worth of $1 million, in order for the separate account to begin operating. Once the separate account begins operations, it may invest in one of two ways:

1. Directly
2. Indirectly

DIRECT INVESTMENT

If the money in the separate account is invested directly into individual stocks and bonds, the separate account must have an investment adviser to actively manage the portfolio. If the money in the separate account is actively managed and invested directly, then the separate account is considered an open-end investment company under the Investment Company Act of 1940 and must register as such.

INDIRECT INVESTMENT

If the separate account uses the money in the portfolio to purchase mutual fund shares, it is investing in the equity and debt markets indirectly, and an investment adviser is not required to actively manage the portfolio. If the separate account purchases mutual fund shares directly, then the separate account is considered a unit investment trust (UIT) under the Investment Company Act of 1940 and must register as such.

COMBINATION ANNUITIES

For investors who feel that a fixed annuity is too conservative and that a variable annuity is too risky, a combination annuity offers the annuitant features of both a fixed and variable contract. A combination annuity has a fixed portion that offers a guaranteed rate and a variable portion that tries to achieve a higher rate of return. Most combination annuities will allow the investor to move money between the fixed and variable portions of the contract. The money invested in the fixed portion of the contract is invested in the insurance company's general account and is used to purchase conservative investments such as mortgages and real estate. The money invested in the variable side of the contract is invested in the insurance company's separate account and is used to purchase stocks, bonds, or mutual fund shares. Representatives who sell combination annuities must have both their securities license and their insurance license.

BONUS ANNUITIES

An insurance company that issues variable annuity contracts may offer incentives to investors who purchase their annuities. Such incentives are often referred to as bonuses. One type of bonus is known as premium enhancement. Under a premium enhancement option, the insurance company will make an additional contribution to the annuitant's account based on the premium paid by the annuitant. For example, if the annuitant is contributing $1,000 per month, the insurance company may offer to contribute an additional 5% or $50 per month to the account. Another type of bonus offered to annuitants is the ability to withdraw the greater of the account's earnings or up to 15% of the total premiums paid without a penalty. Although the annuitant will not have to pay a penalty to the insurance company, there may be income taxes and a 10% penalty tax owed to the IRS. Bonus annuities often have higher expenses and longer surrender periods than other annuities, and these additional costs and surrender periods need to be clearly disclosed to prospective purchasers. Fixed annuity contracts may not offer bonuses to purchasers.

EQUITY-INDEXED ANNUITIES

Equity-indexed annuities offer investors a return that varies according to the performance of a set index, such as the S&P 500. Equity-indexed annuities will credit additional interest to the investor's account based on the contract's participation rate. If a contract sets the participation rate at 70% of the return for the S&P 500 index, and the index returns 5%, the investor's account will be credited for 70% of the return, or 3.5%. The participation rate may also be shown as a spread rate. If the contract had a spread rate of 3%, and the index returned 10%, the investor's contract would be credited 7%. Equity-indexed annuities may also set a floor rate and a cap rate for the contract. The floor rate is the minimum interest rate that will be credited to the investor's account. The floor rate may be zero or it may be a positive number, depending on the specific contract. The contract's cap rate is the maximum rate that will be credited to the contract. If the return of the index exceeds the cap rate, the investor's account will only be credited up to the cap rate. If the S&P 500 index returns 11% and the cap rate set in the contract is 9%, the investor's account will only be credited 9%.

Feature	Fixed Annuity	Variable Annuity
Payment received	Guaranteed/fixed	May vary in amount
Return	Guaranteed minimum	No guarantee/return may vary in amount
Investment risk	Assumed by insurance company	Assumed by investor
Portfolio	Real estate, mortgages, and fixed-income securities	Stocks, bonds, or mutual fund shares
Portfolio held in	General account	Separate account
Inflation	Subject to inflation risk	Resistant to inflation
Representative registration	Insurance license	Insurance and securities license

RECOMMENDING VARIABLE ANNUITIES

There are a number of factors that will determine if a variable annuity is a suitable recommendation for an investor. Variable annuities are meant to be used as supplements to other retirement accounts such as IRAs and corporate retirement plans. Investors who purchase variable annuities should have income as their investment objective and must be comfortable with the lack of liquidity, costs and tax considerations. Most annuities have initial surrender periods during which the investor will have to pay a substantial penalty to access their funds. Variable annuities should not be recommended to investors who are trying to save for a large purchase or expense such as college tuition or a second home. Variable annuity products are more appropriate for an investor who is looking to create an income stream. A deferred annuity contract would be appropriate for someone seeking retirement income at some point in the future. An immediate annuity contract would be more appropriate for someone seeking to generate current income and who is perhaps already retired. Many annuity contracts have complex features and cost structures which may be difficult for both the representative and investor to understand. The benefits of the contract should outweigh the additional costs of the contract to ensure the contract is suitable for the investor. Illustrations regarding performance of the contract may use a maximum growth rate of 12 percent and all annuity applications must be approved or denied by a principal based on suitability within 7 business days of receipt. A series 24 or series 26 principal may approve or deny a variable annuity application presented by either a series 6 or series 7 registered representative. 1035 exchanges allow investors to move from one annuity contract to another without incurring tax consequences. 1035 exchanges can be a red flag and a cause for concern over abusive sales practices. Because most annuity contracts have surrender charges that may be substantial, 1035 exchanges may result in the investor being worse off and may constitute churning. Prior to executing a 1035 exchange the customer must get a written disclosure and acknowledgement forms comparing the costs and features associated with the exchange. A 1035 exchange should not be considered if the customer has made a 1035 exchange within the last 36 months. FINRA is concerned about firms who employ compensation structures for representatives, which may incentivize the sale of annuities over other investment products with lower costs and which may be more appropriate for investors. Firms should guard against incentivizing agents to sell annuity products over other investments. Members should ensure proper product training for registered representatives and principals for annuities and must have adequate supervision to monitor sales practices and to test their product knowledge.

The focus should be to detect problematic and abusive sales practices. L share annuity contracts are designed with shorter surrender periods but have higher costs to investors. The sales of L share annuity contracts can be a red flag for compliance personnel and may constitute abusive sales practices. All retail communications regarding variable annuities must be filed within 10 days of first use. Contracts which are redeemed by investors within 7 business days will result in the return of all sale commissions.

 TAKENOTE!

The suitability obligation for variable annuities covers the initial purchase and subaccount allocation as well as the exchange of one annuity contract for any other contract. Exempt from suitability determination are any changes made to the allocation of assets among the available subaccounts.

ANNUITY PURCHASE OPTIONS

An investor may purchase an annuity contract in one of three ways:

1. Single payment deferred annuity.
2. Single payment immediate annuity.
3. Periodic payment deferred annuity.

SINGLE PAYMENT DEFERRED ANNUITY

With a single payment deferred annuity, the investor funds the contract completely with one payment and defers receiving payments from the contract until some point in the future, usually after retirement. Money invested in a single payment deferred annuity is used to purchase accumulation units. The number and value of the accumulation units varies as the distributions are reinvested and the value of the separate account's portfolio changes.

SINGLE PAYMENT IMMEDIATE ANNUITY

With a single payment immediate annuity, the investor funds the contract completely with one payment and begins receiving payments from the contract immediately, normally within 60 days. The money that is invested in a single payment immediate annuity is used to purchase annuity units. The number of annuity units remains fixed, and the value changes as the value of the securities in the separate account's portfolio fluctuates.

PERIODIC PAYMENT DEFERRED ANNUITY

With a periodic payment annuity, the investor purchases the annuity by making regularly scheduled payments into the contract. This is known as the accumulation stage. During the accumulation stage, the terms are flexible, and if the investor misses a payment there is no penalty. The money invested in a periodic payment deferred annuity is used to purchase accumulation units. The number and value of the accumulation units fluctuate with the securities in the separate portfolio.

ACCUMULATION UNITS

An accumulation unit represents the investor's proportionate ownership in the separate account's portfolio during the accumulation or deferred stage of the contract. The value of the accumulation unit will fluctuate as the value of the securities in the separate account's portfolio changes. As the investor makes contributions to the account or as distributions are reinvested, the number of accumulation units will vary. An investor will only own accumulation units during the accumulation stage, when money is being paid into the contract or when receipt of payments is being deferred by the investor, such as with a single payment deferred annuity.

 TAKENOTE!

Most annuities allow the investor to designate a beneficiary who will receive the greater of the value of the account or the total premiums paid if the investor dies during the accumulation stage.

ANNUITY UNITS

When an investor changes from the pay-in or deferred stage of the contract to the payout phase, the investor is said to have annuitized the contract. At this point, the investor trades in the accumulation units for annuity units. The number of annuity units is fixed and represents the investor's proportional ownership of the separate account's portfolio during the payout phase. The number of annuity units that the investor receives when the contract is annuitized is based on the payout option selected, the annuitant's age and sex, the value of the account, and the assumed interest rate.

ANNUITY PAYOUT OPTIONS

An investor in an annuity has the choice of taking a lump sum distribution or receiving scheduled payments from the contract. If the investor decides to annuitize the contract and receive scheduled payments, once the payout option is selected, it may not be changed. The following is a list of typical payout options in order from the largest monthly payment to the smallest:

- Life only/straight life
- Life with period certain
- Joint with last survivor

LIFE ONLY/STRAIGHT LIFE

This payout option will give the annuitant the largest periodic payment from the contract, and the investor will receive payments from the contract for his or her entire life. When the investor dies, however, no additional benefits are paid to the estate. If an investor has accumulated a large sum of money in the contract and dies unexpectedly shortly after annuitizing the contract, the insurance company keeps the money in its account.

LIFE WITH PERIOD CERTAIN

A life with period certain payout option will pay out from the contract to the investor or to the investor's estate for the life of the annuitant or for the period certain, whichever is longer. If an investor selects a 10-year period certain when the contract is annuitized and the investor lives for 20 years more, payments will cease on the death of the annuitant. However, if the same investor died only 2 years after annuitizing the contract, payments would go to the investor's estate for another 8 years.

JOINT WITH LAST SURVIVOR

When an investor selects a joint with last survivor option, the annuity is jointly owned by more than one party and payments will continue until the last owner of the contract dies. For example, if a husband and wife are receiving payments from an annuity under a joint with last survivor option and the husband dies, payments will continue to the wife for the rest of her life. The payments received by the wife could be at the same rate as when the husband was alive or at a reduced rate, depending on the contract. The monthly payments will initially be based on the life expectancy of the youngest annuitant.

CHAPTER 10 Variable Annuities and Retirement Plans

FACTORS AFFECTING THE SIZE OF THE ANNUITY PAYMENT

All of the following determine the size of the annuity payments:

- Account value
- Payout option selected
- Age
- Sex
- Account performance vs. the assumed interest rate (AIR)

THE ASSUMED INTEREST RATE (AIR)

When an investor annuitizes a contract, the accumulation units are traded in for annuity units. Once the contract has been annuitized, the insurance company sets a benchmark for the separate account's performance, known as the assumed interest rate (AIR). The AIR is not a guaranteed rate of return; it is only used to adjust the value of the annuity units up or down, based on the actual performance of the separate account. The AIR is an earnings target that the insurance company sets for the separate account. The separate account must meet this earnings target in order to keep the annuitant's payments at the same level. As the value of the annuity unit changes, so does the amount of the payment that is received by the investor. If the separate account outperforms the AIR, an investor would expect payments to increase. If the separate account's performance falls below the AIR, the investor can expect payments to decrease. The performance of the separate account is always measured against the AIR, never against the previous month's performance. An investor's annuity payment is based on the number of annuity units owned by the investor multiplied by the value of the annuity unit. When the performance of the separate account equals the AIR, the value of the annuity unit will remain unchanged, and so will the investor's payment. Selecting an AIR that is realistic is important. If the AIR is too high and the separate account's return cannot equal the assumed rate, the value of the annuity unit will continue to fall, and so will the investor's payment. The opposite is true if the AIR is set too low. As the separate account outperforms the AIR, the value of the annuity unit will continue to rise, and so will the investor's payment. The AIR is only relevant during the payout phase of the contract, when the investor is receiving payments and owns annuity units. The AIR does not concern itself with accumulation units during the accumulation stage or when benefits are being deferred.

TAXATION

Contributions made to an annuity are made with after-tax dollars. The money the investor deposits becomes the cost basis and is allowed to grow tax deferred. When the investor withdraws money from the contract, only the growth is taxed. The cost base is returned to the investor tax free. All money in excess of the investor's cost base is taxed as ordinary income.

SALES CHARGES

There is no maximum sales charge for an annuity contract. The sales charge that is assessed must be reasonable in relation to the total payments over the life of the contract. Most annuity contracts have back-end sales charges or surrender charges similar to a contingent deferred sales charge.

1035 EXCHANGE

If a registered representative suggests that a customer move money from one variable annuity product to another, the representative and the principal of the firm should make sure that the transfer can be done tax free through a 1035 exchange. As a result of the transfer, the investor should not incur any additional taxes or fees and should not lose any accumulated benefits, such as a death benefit. It's important to note that 1035 exchanges are usually frowned upon and can be seen as an abusive sales practice. When an investor moves money from one annuity contract to another the investor will be subject to another sales charge and a new surrender period. Investors who withdraw money from an annuity contract during the surrender period will pay penalties and fees upon making the withdrawal.

Variable Annuity vs. Mutual Fund

Feature	Variable Annuity	Mutual Fund
Maximum sales charge	No max	8.5%
Investment adviser	Yes	Yes
Custodian bank	Yes	Yes
Transfer agent	Yes	Yes
Voting	Yes	Yes
Management	Board of managers	Board of directors
Taxation of growth and reinvestments	Tax-deferred	Currently taxed

RETIREMENT PLANS

For most people, saving for retirement has become an important investment objective for at least part of their portfolio. Investors may participate in retirement plans that have been established by their employers, as well as those they have established for themselves. Both corporate and individual plans may be qualified or nonqualified, and it is important for an investor to understand the difference before deciding to participate. The following is a comparison of the key features of both types of plans:

Feature	Qualified	Nonqualified
Contributions	Pretax	After-tax
Growth	Tax-deferred	Tax-deferred
Participation must be allowed	For everyone	The corporation may choose who gets to participate
IRS approval	Required	Not required
Withdrawals	100% taxed as ordinary income	Growth in excess of cost base is taxed as ordinary income

INDIVIDUAL RETIREMENT PLANS

Individuals may set up a retirement plan that is qualified and allows contributions to the plan to be made with pre-tax dollars. Individuals may also purchase investment products, such as annuities, that allow their money to grow tax deferred. The money used to purchase an annuity has already been taxed, making an annuity a nonqualified product.

All individuals with earned income may establish an individual retirement account (IRA). Contributions to traditional IRAs may or may not be tax deductible, depending on the individual's adjusted gross income and whether the individual is eligible to participate in an employer-sponsored plan. Individuals who do not qualify to participate in an employer-sponsored plan may deduct their IRA contributions regardless of their income level. The level of adjusted gross income that allows an investor to deduct IRA contributions has been increasing since 1998. These tax law changes occur too frequently to make them a practical test question. Our review of IRAs will focus on the four main types, which are:

1. Traditional
2. Roth

3. SEP
4. Educational

TRADITIONAL IRA

Currently, an individual may contribute a maximum of 100% of earned income or $7,000 per year, or up to $14,000 per couple, to a traditional IRA. If only one spouse works, the working spouse may contribute $7,000 to his or her IRA and $7,000 to a separate IRA for the nonworking spouse. Investors over 50 may contribute up to $8,000 of earned income to an IRA. Regardless of whether the IRA contribution was made with pre- or after-tax dollars, the money is allowed to grow tax deferred. All withdrawals from an IRA are taxed as ordinary income regardless of how the growth was generated in the account. Withdrawals from an IRA prior to age 59-1/2 are subject to a 10% penalty tax as well as ordinary income taxes. The 10% penalty will be waived for first-time homebuyers; for educational expenses for the taxpayer's child, grandchildren, or spouse; if the account holder becomes disabled; or if the payments are part of a series of substantially equal payments. Withdrawals from an IRA must begin by April 1 of the year following the year in which the taxpayer reaches 73. If an individual fails to make withdrawals that are sufficient in size and frequency, the individual will be subject to a 25% penalty on the insufficient amount. An individual who makes a contribution to an IRA that exceeds 100% of earned income, or $7,000, whichever is less, will be subject to a penalty of 6% per year on the excess amount for as long as the excess contribution remains in the account.

ROTH IRA

A Roth IRA is a nonqualified account. All deposits that are made to a Roth IRA are made with after-tax dollars. The same contribution limits apply for a Roth IRA. An individual may contribute the lesser of 100% of earned income, to a maximum of $7,000 per person, or $14,000 per couple. Any contribution made to a Roth IRA reduces the amount that may be deposited in a traditional IRA and vice versa. All contributions deposited in a Roth IRA are allowed to grow tax deferred, and all of the growth may be taken out of the account tax-free provided that the individual has reached age 59-1/2 and the assets have been in the account for at least 5 years. A 10% penalty tax will be charged on any withdrawal of earnings prior to age 59-1/2 unless the owner is purchasing a home, has become disabled, or has died. There are no requirements for an individual to take distributions from a Roth IRA by a certain age.

SIMPLIFIED EMPLOYEE PENSION IRA (SEP IRA)

A simplified employee pension (SEP) IRA is used by small corporations and self-employed individuals to plan for retirement. A SEP IRA is attractive to small employers because it allows them to set up a retirement plan for their employees rather quickly and inexpensively. The contribution limit for a SEP IRA far exceeds that of traditional IRAs. The contribution limit is the lesser of 25% of the employee's compensation or $69,000 per year. Should the employees wish to make their annual IRA contributions to their SEP IRAs, they may do so, or they may make their standard contributions to a traditional or Roth IRA.

All eligible employees must open an IRA to receive the employer's contribution to the SEP. If the employee does not open an IRA account, the employer must open one for the employee. The employee must be at least 21 years old, have worked during 3 of the last 5 years for the employer, and have earned at least $550. All eligible employees, as well as the employer, must participate.

The employer may contribute between 0 and 25% of the employee's total compensation, to a maximum of $69,000. Contributions to all SEP IRAs, including the employer's SEP IRA, must be made at the same rate. An employee who is over 73 must also participate and receive a contribution. All eligible employees are immediately vested in the employer's contributions to the plan.

Employer's contributions to a SEP IRA are immediately tax deductible by the employer. Contributions are not taxed at the employee's rate until the employee withdraws the funds. Employees may begin to withdraw money from the plan at age 59-1/2. All withdrawals are taxed as ordinary income, and withdrawals prior to age 59-1/2 are subject to a 10% penalty tax. The employer may contribute up to 25% of the employee's income, up to $69,000.

EDUCATIONAL IRA

An educational IRA allows individuals to contribute up to $2,000 in after-tax dollars to an educational IRA for each student who is under 18 years of age. The money is allowed to grow tax deferred, and the growth may be withdrawn tax free as long as the money is used for educational purposes. If all of the funds have not been used for educational purposes by the time the student reaches 30 years of age, the account must be rolled over to another family member who is under 30 years of age, or distributed to the original student and subject to a 10% penalty tax as well as ordinary income taxes.

529 PLANS

Qualified tuition plans more frequently referred to as 529 plans may be set up either as a prepaid tuition plan or as a college savings plan. With the prepaid tuition plan, the plan locks in a current tuition rate at a specific school. The prepaid tuition plan can be set up as an installment plan or one where the contributor funds the plan with a lump sum deposit. Many states will guarantee the plans but may require that either the contributor or the beneficiary to be a state resident. The plan covers only tuition and mandatory fees. A room and board option is available for some plans. A college cost-savings account may be opened by any adult and the donor does not have to be related to the child. The assets in the college savings plan can be used to cover all costs of qualified higher education including tuition, room and board, books, computers, and mandatory fees. These plans generally have no age limit when assets must be used. College savings accounts are not guaranteed by the state and the value of the account may decline based on the investment results of the account. College savings accounts are not state specific and do not lock in a tuition rate. Contributions to a 529 plan are made with after-tax dollars and are allowed to grow tax deferred. The assets in the account remain under the control of the donor, even after the student reaches the age of majority. The funds may be used to meet the student's educational needs and the growth may be withdrawn federally tax-free. Most states also allow the assets to be withdrawn tax free. Any funds used for non-qualified education expenses will be subject to income tax and a 10% penalty tax. If funds remain or if the student does not attend or complete qualified higher education the funds may be rolled over to another family member within 60 days without incurring taxes and penalties. There are no income limits for the donors and contribution limits vary from state to state. 529 plans have an impact on a student's ability to obtain need based financial aid. However, because the 529 plans are treated as parental assets and not as assets of the student, the plans are assessed at the expected family contribution (EFC) rate of 5.64%. This will have a significantly lower impact than plans and assets that are considered to be assets of the student. Student assets will be assessed at a 20% contribution rate. For your exam, it is important to note that assets in a 529 savings plan may also be used to meet tuition payments for private K–12 schools. The owner of a A 529 plan may rollover the plan once in any consecutive 12 month period without regard to the state of residence. It is important to note that while a 529 plan may be rolled over to another 529 plan, it may not be rolled over to an educational IRA. The donor / owner of 529 plans may contribute the maximum amount to a 529 plan for each child or grandchild. That is to say, the contribution limits are for each plan individually, not collectively. The owner of the plan may select the investments or select from a list of available investment options included in the plan. Prior to investing in a 529 plan, a registered person should disclose the costs and fees associated with the plan. The official statement for the 529 plan will provide further information regarding the costs, fees and risks associated with the plan. Clients should review the tax treatment of the plan in their state prior to investing.

TAKENOTE!

For your exam, it is important to note that assets in a 529 savings plan may also be used to meet tuition payments for private K–12 schools.

LOCAL GOVERNMENT INVESTMENT POOLS (LGIPs)

LGIPs allow states and local governments to manage their cash reserves and to receive money market rates on the funds. LGIPs may also be created to invest the proceeds of a bond offering if the proceeds of the offering are intended to be used to call in an existing bond issue. If the LGIP was created to prerefund an existing issue, additional restrictions will apply as to the type of investments that may be purchased by the pool. LGIPs that are created to manage cash reserves must only invest in securities on the state's legal or approved list. The legal list usually includes investments such as:

- Commercial paper rated in the two highest categories
- U.S. government and agency debt
- Bankers' acceptances
- Repurchase agreements
- Municipal debt issues within the state
- Investment company securities
- Certificates of deposit
- Savings accounts

Each state has an investment advisory board that works with the state treasury office to administer the pools. The main objective of these pools is safety of principal, with liquidity and interest income as secondary objectives. The pools require that the following be detailed in writing:

- Delegation of authority to make investments
- Annual investment activity reports
- Statement of safekeeping of securities

Municipal fund securities are not considered to be investment companies and are not required to register under the Investment Company Act of 1940. Additionally, prepaid tuition plans are not considered to be municipal fund securities. LGIP employees who market the plans directly to investors are exempt from MSRB rules; however, if the LGIP is marketed to investors by employees of a broker dealer, the broker dealer and all of its employees are subject to MSRB rules.

IRA CONTRIBUTIONS

Contributions to IRAs must be made by April 15 of the following calendar year, regardless of whether an extension to file federal income taxes has been filed by the taxpayer. Contributions may be made between January 1 and April 15 for the previous year, the current year, or both. All IRA contributions must be made in cash.

IRA ACCOUNTS

All IRA accounts are held in the name of the custodian for the benefit of the account holder. Traditional custodians include banks, broker dealers, and mutual fund companies.

IRA INVESTMENTS

Individuals who establish IRAs have a wide variety of investments to choose from when deciding how to invest the funds. Investors should always choose investments that fit their investment objectives. The following is a comparison of allowable and nonallowable investments:

Allowable	Nonallowable
Stocks	Margin accounts
Bonds	Short sales
Mutual funds/ETFs	Tangibles/collectibles/art
Annuities	Speculative option trading
UITs	Term life insurance
Limited partnerships	Rare coins
U.S. minted coins	Owner occupied real estate

 TAKENOTE!

It is unwise to put a municipal bond in an IRA. Municipal bonds or municipal bond funds should never be placed in an IRA because the advantage of those investments is that the interest income is free from federal taxes. Because their interest is free from federal taxes, the interest rate that is offered will be less than the rates offered by other alternatives. The advantage of an IRA is that money is allowed to grow tax deferred; therefore, an individual would be better off with a higher yielding taxable bond of the same quality.

ROLLOVER VS. TRANSFER

An individual may want or need to move an IRA from one custodian to another. There are two ways this can be accomplished: a rollover or a transfer.

With an IRA rollover, the individual may take possession of the funds for a maximum of 60 calendar days prior to depositing the funds into another qualified account. An investor may only rollover an IRA once every 12 months. The investor has 60 days from the date of the distribution to deposit 100% of the funds into another qualified account or the investor must pay ordinary income taxes on the distribution and a 10% penalty tax if the investor is younger than 59-1/2.

An investor may transfer an IRA directly from one custodian to another by simply signing an account transfer form. The investor never takes possession of the assets in the account. Investors may directly transfer their IRAs as often as they would like.

THE SECURE ACT OF 2019

The Secure Act of 2019 made substantial changes to retirement planning. Many investors who have other assets saved for retirement or who are still actively working may want to continue to enjoy the tax benefits offered by traditional IRAs. The secure Act increased the age at which investors must take required minimum distributions (RMDs) from IRA accounts. The Secure Act raised the age for RMDs to 73 and removed the age limits for contributions for older workers. The Secure Act also made substantial changes to the rules regarding inherited IRAs. Most individuals who inherit an IRA will be required to withdraw all of the assets within 10 years of the death of the original account owner. Exempt from the 10-year distribution requirement are surviving spouses, disabled or chronically ill individuals, a minor child and individuals who are less than 10 years younger than the decedent. Additionally, The Secure Act modified the rules regarding the use of assets in 529 plans. Individuals who have established 529 plans may withdraw up to $10,000 (lifetime limit) tax free to repay student loans. The Secure Act also had a substantial impact on retirement plans established by both large and small employers. The Secure Act includes the following provisions:

- Increased the contribution limits for small employers who set up 401K plans from 10% to 15% of wages
- Provide small employers with a tax credit of up to $500 per year to create 401K plans or simple IRA plans with automatic enrollment for employees
- Allow employers to offer retirement plans to part-time employees who work either 1,000 hours per year or who have worked at least 500 hours per year for 3 consecutive years
- Allow individuals to withdraw up to $5,000 tax free from their 401k to offset the cost of having or adopting a child
- Require define contribution plans to disclose the lifetime income that could be generated from a lump sum in a retirement account
- Encourage the inclusion of annuities inside retirement plans

KEOGH PLANS (HR-10)

A Keogh plan is a qualified retirement plan set up by self-employed individuals, sole proprietors, and unincorporated businesses. If the business is set up as a corporation, a Keogh may not be used.

CONTRIBUTIONS

Keoghs may only be funded with earned income during a period when the business shows a gross profit. If the business realizes a loss, no Keogh contributions are allowed. A self-employed person may contribute the lesser of 25% of postcontribution income or $69,000. If the business has eligible employees, the employer must make a contribution for the employees at the same rate as the employer's own contribution. Employee contributions are based on the employee's gross income and are limited to $69,000 per year. All money placed in a Keogh plan is allowed to grow tax deferred and is taxed as ordinary income when distributions are made to retiring employees and plan participants. From time to time, a self-employed person may make a nonqualified contribution to a Keogh plan; however, the total of the qualified and nonqualified contributions may not exceed the maximum contribution limit. Any excess contribution may be subject to a 10% penalty tax.

An eligible employee is defined as one that:

- Works full time (at least 1,000 hours per year).
- Is at least 21 years old.
- Has worked at least 1 year for the employer.

WITHDRAWALS

Employees who participate in a Keogh plan must be vested after 5 years. Withdrawals from a Keogh may begin when the participant reaches 59-1/2. Any premature withdrawals are subject to a 10% penalty tax. A Keogh, like an IRA, may be rolled over every 12 months. In the event of a participant's death, the assets will go to the individual's beneficiaries.

TAX-SHELTERED ANNUITIES/TAX-DEFERRED ACCOUNTS

Tax-sheltered annuities (TSAs) and tax-deferred accounts (TDAs) are established as retirement plans for employees of nonprofit and public organizations, such as:

- Public educational institutions (403B)
- Nonprofit organizations (501C3)
- Religious organizations
- Nonprofit hospitals

TSAs/TDAs are qualified plans, and contributions are made with pretax dollars. The money in the plan is allowed to grow tax deferred until it is withdrawn. TSAs/TDAs offer a variety of investment vehicles for participants to choose from, such as:

- Stocks
- Bonds
- Mutual funds
- CDs

PUBLIC EDUCATIONAL INSTITUTIONS (403B)

In order for a school to be considered a public school and qualify to establish a TSA/TDA for its employees, the school must be supported by the state, the local government, or a state agency. State-supported schools include:

- Elementary schools
- High schools
- State colleges and universities
- Medical schools

Any individual who works for a public school, regardless of the position held, may participate in the school's TSA/TDA.

NONPROFIT ORGANIZATIONS/TAX-EXEMPT ORGANIZATIONS (501C3)

Organizations that qualify under the Internal Revenue Code 501C3 as a nonprofit or tax-exempt entity may set up a TSA or TDA for their employees. Examples of nonprofit organizations are:

- Private hospitals
- Charitable organizations
- Trade schools
- Private colleges
- Parochial schools
- Museums
- Scientific foundations
- Zoos

All employees of organizations that qualify under the Internal Revenue Code 501C3 or 403B are eligible to participate as long as they are at least 21 years old and have worked full time for at least 1 year.

CONTRIBUTIONS

In order to participate in a TSA or TDA, employees must enter into a contract with their employer agreeing to make elective deferrals into the plan. The salary-reduction agreement will state the amount and frequency of the elective deferral to be contributed to the TSA. The agreement is binding on both parties and covers only 1 year of contributions. Each year a new salary-reduction agreement must be signed to set forth the contributions for the new year. The employee's elective deferral is limited to a maximum of $23,000 per year. Employer contributions are limited to the lesser of 25% of the employee's earnings or $69,000.

TAX TREATMENT OF DISTRIBUTIONS

All distributions for TSAs/TDAs are taxed as ordinary income in the year in which the distribution is made. Distributions from a TSA/TDA prior to age 59-1/2 are subject to a 10% penalty tax, as well as ordinary income taxes. Distributions from a TSA/TDA must begin by age 73 or be subject to an excess accumulation tax.

CORPORATE PLANS

A corporate retirement plan can be qualified or nonqualified. We first review the nonqualified plans.

NONQUALIFIED CORPORATE RETIREMENT PLANS

Nonqualified corporate plans are funded with after-tax dollars, and the money is allowed to grow tax deferred. If the corporation makes a contribution to the plan, it may not deduct the contribution from its corporate earnings until the plan participant receives the money. Distributions from a nonqualified plan that exceed the investor's cost base are taxed as ordinary income. All nonqualified plans must be in writing, and the employer may discriminate as to who may participate.

PAYROLL DEDUCTIONS

The employee may set up a payroll deduction plan by having the employer make systematic deductions from the employee's paycheck. The money, which has been deducted from the employee's check, may be invested in a variety of ways. Mutual funds, annuities, and savings bonds are all usually available for the employee to choose from. Contributions to a payroll deduction plan are made with after-tax dollars.

DEFERRED COMPENSATION PLANS

A deferred compensation plan is a contract between an employee and an employer. Under the contract, the employee agrees to defer the receipt of money owed to the employee from the employer until after the employee retires. After retirement, the employee will traditionally be in a lower tax bracket and will be able to keep a larger percentage of the money. Deferred compensation plans are traditionally unfunded and, if the corporation goes out of business, the employee becomes a creditor of the corporation and may lose all of the money due under the contract. The employee may only claim the assets if they retire or become disabled; or, in the case of death, the employee's beneficiaries may claim the money owed. Money due under a deferred compensation plan is paid out of the corporation's working funds when the employee or his or her estate claims the assets. Should the employee leave the corporation and go to work for a competing company, the employee may lose the money owed under a noncompete clause. Money owed to the employee under a deferred compensation agreement is traditionally not invested for the benefit of the employee and, as a result, does not increase in value over time. The only product that traditionally is placed in a deferred compensation plan is a term life policy. In the case of the employee's death, the term life policy will pay the employee's estate the money owed under the contract. A 457 plan is a deferred compensation plan established by state and local governments as well as by non profit organizations. These plans are established for the exclusive benefit of higher compensated employees (such as officers and directors only). The contributions into the plan remain the property of the employer and may be subject to claims of creditors. While assets in government sponsored plans may be rolled over tby the employee to an IRA, 401K or 403B plan, assets contained in a non governmental plan may not be rolled over.

QUALIFIED PLANS

All qualified corporate plans must be in writing and established as trusts. A trustee or plan administrator will be appointed for the benefit of all plan holders.

There are two main types of qualified corporate plans: defined benefit plans and defined contribution plans.

DEFINED BENEFIT PLAN

A defined benefit plan is designed to offer the participant a retirement benefit that is known or "defined." Most defined benefit plans are set up to provide employees with a fixed percentage of their salary during their retirement, such as 74% of their average earnings during their five highest-paid years. Other defined benefit plans are structured to pay participants a fixed sum of money for life. Defined benefit plans require the services of an actuary to determine the employer's contribution to the plan based on the participant's life expectancy and benefits promised.

DEFINED CONTRIBUTION PLAN

With a defined contribution plan, only the amount of money that is deposited into the account is known, such as 6% of the employee's salary. Both the employee and the employer may contribute a percentage of the employee's earnings into the plan. The money is allowed to grow tax deferred until the participant withdraws it at retirement. The ultimate benefit under a defined contribution plan is the result of the contributions into the plan as well as the investment results of the plan. The employee's maximum contribution to a defined contribution plan is $23,000 per year. Defined contribution plans include:

- 401K accounts
- Money purchase plans
- Profit-sharing plans
- Thrift plans
- Stock bonus plans

All withdrawals from pension plans are taxed as ordinary income in the year in which the distribution is made.

EMPLOYEE STOCK OWNERSHIP PLANS (ESOPs)

ESOPs are established by employers to provide a way for the employees to benefit from ownership of the company's stock. The plan allows the employer to take a tax deduction based on the market value of the stock.

PROFIT-SHARING PLANS

Profit-sharing plans let the employer reward the employees by letting them "share" in a percentage of the corporation's profits. Profit-sharing plans are based on a preset formula, and the money may be paid directly to the employee or placed in a retirement account. In order for a profit-sharing plan to be qualified, the corporation must have substantial and recurring profits. The maximum contribution to a profit-sharing plan is the lesser of 100% of the employee's compensation or $69,000.

401K AND THRIFT PLANS

401K and thrift plans allow employees to contribute a fixed percentage of their salary to their retirement account and have the employer match some or all of the contribution. The employer's contributions provide a current tax deduction to the employer; the employee is not taxed on the contributions until they are withdrawn.

ROLLING OVER A PENSION PLAN

An employee who leaves an employer may move a pension plan to another company's plan or to another qualified account. This may be accomplished by a direct transfer or by rolling over the plan. With a direct transfer, the assets in the plan go directly to another plan administrator, and the employee never has physical possession of the assets. With a rollover, the employee takes physical possession of the assets. The plan administrator is required to withhold 20% of the total amount to be distributed, and the employee has 60 calendar days to deposit 100% of the assets into another qualified plan. The employee must file with the federal government at tax time to receive a return of the 20% of the assets that were withheld by the plan administrator.

EMPLOYEE RETIREMENT INCOME SECURITY ACT OF 1974 (ERISA)

The Employee Retirement Income Security Act of 1974 (ERISA) is a federal law that establishes legal and operational guidelines for private pension and employee benefit plans. Not all decisions directly involving a plan, even when made by a fiduciary, are subject to ERISA's fiduciary rules. These decisions are business judgment–type decisions and are commonly called "settlor" functions. This caveat is sometimes referred to as the "business decision" exception to ERISA's fiduciary rules. Under this concept, even though the employer is the plan sponsor and administrator, it will not be considered as acting in a fiduciary capacity when creating, amending, or terminating a plan. Among the decisions that would be considered settlor functions are:

- Choosing the type of plan or options in the plan.
- Amending a plan, including changing or eliminating plan options.
- Requiring employee contributions or changing the level of employee contributions.
- Terminating a plan, or part of a plan, including terminating or amending the plan as part of a bankruptcy process.

ERISA also regulates all of the following:

- Pension plan participation
- Funding
- Vesting
- Communication
- Beneficiaries

PLAN PARTICIPATION

All plans governed by ERISA may not discriminate among who may participate in the plan. All employees must be allowed to participate if:

- They are at least 21 years old.
- They have worked at least 1 year full time (1,000 hours).

FUNDING

Plan funding requirements set forth guidelines on how the money is deposited into the plan and how the employer and employee may contribute to the plan.

VESTING

Vesting refers to the process of how the employer's contribution becomes the property of the employee. An employer may be as generous as it likes, but it may not be more restrictive than either one of the following vesting schedules:

- 3- to 6-year gradual vesting schedule.
- 3-year cliff: the employee is not vested at all until 3 years, at which point the employee becomes 100% vested.

COMMUNICATION

All corporate plans must be in writing at inception, and the employee must be given annual updates.

BENEFICIARIES

All plan participants must be allowed to select a beneficiary who may claim the assets in case of the plan participant's death.

ERISA 404C SAFE HARBOR

All individuals and entities acting in a fiduciary capacity must act solely in the interest of the plan participants. Investment advisers, trustees and all individuals who exercise discretion over the plan including those who select the administrative personnel or committee are considered to be fiduciaries. ERISA Rule 404C provides an exemption from liability or a "safe harbor" for plan fiduciaries and protects them from liabilities that may arise from investment losses that result from the participant's own actions. This safe harbor is available so long as:

- The participant exercises control over the assets in their account.
- Participants have ample opportunity to enter orders for their account and to provide instructions regarding their account.
- A broad range of investment options is available for the participant to choose from and the options offer suitable investments for a variety or investment objectives and risk profiles.
- Information regarding the risks and objective of the investment options is readily available to plan participants.

DEPARTMENT OF LABOR FIDUCIARY RULES

The Department of Labor has enacted significant legislation for financial professionals who service and maintain retirement accounts for clients. These new rules subject financial professionals to higher fiduciary standards. These standards require financial professionals to place the interest of the client ahead of the interest of the broker dealer or investment advisory firm. Professionals who service retirement accounts are still permitted to earn commissions and/or a fee based on the assets in the account and may still offer proprietary products to investors. However, the rule requires that the client receive significant disclosures relating to the fees and costs associated with the servicing of the account. Simply charging the lowest fee will not ensure compliance with the fiduciary standard. Both the firm and the individual servicing the account must put the interests of the client ahead of their own.

CHAPTER 10 Variable Annuities and Retirement Plans

Broker dealers and advisory firms must establish written supervisory procedures and training programs designed to supervise and educate their personnel on the new requirements for retirement accounts. Many representatives will now be required to obtain the Series 65 or Series 66 license to comply with the new Department of Labor rules.

DEPARTMENT OF LABOR PROHIBITED TRANSACTIONS

In order to protect retirement plan participants the Department of Labor has identified a number of prohibited transactions. A prohibited transaction is a transaction between a plan and a disqualified person and is prohibited by law. A disqualified person is any of the following:

- A plan fiduciary
- A plan service provider
- Employer whose employees are covered by the plan
- Employee organization (unions) whose members are covered by the plan
- Officers, Directors, 10 percent stockholders and highly compensated employees earning more than 10 percent of the employer's annual compensation
- Family members of persons named above including spouses, children and spouses of children

Prohibited transactions generally include the following transactions:

- A transfer of plan income or assets to, or use of them by or for the benefit of, a disqualified person
- Any act of a fiduciary by which plan income or assets are used for his or her own interest
- The receipt of consideration by a fiduciary for his or her own account from any party dealing with the plan in a transaction that involves plan income or assets
- The sale, exchange, or lease of property between a plan and a disqualified person

- Lending money or extending credit between a plan and a disqualified person
- Furnishing goods, services, or facilities between a plan and a disqualified person.

The two possible penalties that can be levied for prohibited transactions in retirement accounts are taxes determined by the IRS and/or civil penalties determined by the Department of Labor. The initial tax (IRS penalty) on a prohibited transaction is 15% of the amount involved for each year (or part of a year) in the tax period. If the transaction isn't corrected within the tax period, an additional tax of 100% of the amount involved is imposed. If the prohibited transaction isn't corrected during the tax period, The IRS (usually) will grant a 90 day extension to correct the transaction. The date of extension is based on the day the IRS mails a notice of deficiency for the 100% tax. This correction period (the tax period plus the 90 days) can be extended if the IRS grants a reasonable amount of time needed to correct the transaction or based upon a petition to the Tax Court. The potential penalties assessed by the department of labor are based on a two tier system. Tier one can be no more than 5% of the amount involved and tier two can be no more than 100% of the amount involved. Tier two is imposed if the transaction is not corrected within 90 days. Note that the IRS penalties and the DOL penalties for prohibited transactions in retirement accounts differ, as do the time frames given to correct the transactions. Certain transactions are exempt from being treated as prohibited transactions. For example, a prohibited transaction does not take place if a disqualified person receives a benefit to which he or she is entitled as a plan participant or beneficiary. However, the benefit must be figured and paid under the same terms as for all other participants and beneficiaries. For transactions done in retirement accounts the Department of Labor can grant four types of prohibited transaction exemptions (PTEs); Statutory, Administrative, Class and Individual. The latter two, class and individual, are sub-types of administrative exemptions. A statutory exemption is an act passed into law by a legislative body such as Congress. In general most statutory exemptions are not allowed for anyone vested in the plan. These would include IRA owners (individuals), partners with more than 10% capital in the plan sponsor, sole proprietorships, officers, or employees of S Corps who own more than 5% of the corporation's stock, or employers who have established IRA programs for their employees. The Department of Labor (DOL) has granted class exemptions for certain types of investments under conditions that protect the safety and security of the plan assets. In addition, a plan sponsor may request that the DOL grant an administrative exemption for a proposed transaction or series of transactions that would otherwise be a prohibited transaction. Applications to exempt prohibited transactions are decided by the Department of Labor. In order to have an application considered by the DOL it must first be submitted to the Employee Benefits Security Administration (EBSA) office of exemption determinations. When an application is submitted to the Employee Benefits Security Administration (EBSA), amending the application, adding additional information to it, or withdrawing it is allowed. If the application is ultimately denied by the Department of Labor (DOL), the applicant will receive a denial letter, at which time they can submit a request for the application to be reconsidered or submit a new application.

HEALTH SAVINGS ACCOUNTS

A tax advantaged health savings account may be established to help offset the potential impact of medical expenses incurred by individuals who maintain a high deductible health insurance plan. Many individuals select a health insurance plan with a high deductible to lower the monthly premium expenses. A high deductible health plan is often used to insure against catastrophic illness. Individuals covered by these plans may elect to establish a health savings account. The individual, their employer or both may make contributions to the health savings account. The contribution limit varies and is based on the person's age and the type of health insurance coverage. If a person is eligible on the first day of the last month of the year, the person may make a full contribution for that year. This is known as the "last month rule." Contributions to the health savings account may be made with pretax dollars. The money in the account grows tax free and be used tax free for qualified medical expenses. The individual may use the money to pay the expense directly to the health care provider to reimburse themselves for payments they have made for qualified medical expenses incurred for themselves, their spouse or any dependent claimed on their tax return. Prescription drugs are considered to be qualified medical expenses. If the person requires a nonprescription drug to be covered the person still must get a prescription from their doctor. If money is used for non-qualified medical expenses the money will be subject to income taxes and could be subject to a 20% penalty tax. The money is allowed to accumulate over time and any unused amounts may be carried over to future years. If the owner of an HSA dies the account will pass to the owner's spouse and will be treated as the spouse's HSA. If the beneficiary is not the spouse the account will cease to be an HAS and the amount will be taxable to the beneficiary in the year in which the owner dies.

CHAPTER 10

Pretest

VARIABLE ANNUITIES AND RETIREMENT PLANS

1. A doctor makes the maximum contribution to his Keogh plan while earning $300,000 per year. How much can he contribute to an IRA?
   a. $69,000
   b. $18,000
   c. $8,500
   d. $7,000

2. An individual owns a variable annuity with an assumed interest rate of 5%. If the separate account earns 4%, the individual would expect which of the following?
   I. The value of the annuity unit to go up
   II. The amount of the payment to go down
   III. The amount of the payment to go up
   IV. The value of the annuity unit to go down
   a. II and IV
   b. I and III
   c. I and II
   d. II and III

3. A school principal has deposited $15,000 in a tax-deferred annuity through a payroll deduction plan. The account has grown in value to $22,000. The principal plans to retire and take a lump sum distribution. On what amount does he pay taxes?
   a. $22,000
   b. $15,000
   c. $7,000
   d. $0

4. The maximum amount that a couple may contribute to their IRAs at any one time is:
   a. $2,000.
   b. $7,000.
   c. $14,000.
   d. 400% of the annual limit.

5. An investor has deposited $100,000 into a qualified retirement account over a 10-year period. The value of the account has grown to $175,000, and the investor plans to retire and take a lump sum withdrawal. The investor will pay:
   a. Capital gains tax on $75,000 only.
   b. Ordinary income taxes on the $75,000 only.
   c. Ordinary income taxes on the whole $175,000.
   d. Ordinary income taxes on the $100,000 and capital gains on the $75,000.

6. A 42-year-old investor wants to put $20,000 into a plan to help meet the educational expenses of his 12-year-old son. He wants to make a lump sum deposit. Which of the following would you recommend?
   a. A 529 plan
   b. A Coverdell IRA
   c. A Roth IRA
   d. A growth mutual fund

7. A client who is 65 years old has invested $10,000 in a Roth IRA. It has now grown to $14,000. He plans to retire and take a lump sum distribution. He will pay taxes on:
    a. $0.
    b. $14,000.
    c. $4,000.
    d. $10,000.

8. A fixed annuity guarantees all of the following, EXCEPT:
    a. Income for life
    b. Protection from inflation
    c. Rate of return
    d. Protection from investment risk

9. A self-employed individual may open a SEP IRA to plan for his retirement. The maximum contribution to the plan is:
    a. $7,000.
    b. $14,000.
    c. $28,000.
    d. The lesser of 25% of the postcontribution income, up to $69,000.

CHAPTER 11

Securities Industry Rules and Regulations

> **INTRODUCTION**
>
> Federal and state securities laws, as well as industry regulations, have been enacted to ensure that all industry participants adhere to a high standard of just and equitable trade practices. In this chapter, we will review the rules and regulations, as well as the registration requirements, for firms, agents, and securities.

THE SECURITIES EXCHANGE ACT OF 1934

The Securities Exchange Act of 1934 was the second major piece of legislation that resulted from the market crash of 1929. The Securities Exchange Act regulates the secondary market that consists of investor-to-investor transactions. All transactions between two investors that are executed on any of the exchanges or in the OTC market are secondary market transactions. In a secondary market transaction, the selling security holder receives the money, not the issuing corporation. The Securities Exchange Act of 1934 also regulates all individuals and firms that conduct business in the securities industry. The Securities Exchange Act of 1934:

- Created the SEC.
- Requires registration of broker dealers and agents.
- Regulates the exchanges and FINRA.

- Requires net capital for broker dealers.
- Regulates short sales.
- Regulates insider transactions.
- Requires public companies to solicit proxies.
- Requires segregation of customer and firm assets.
- Authorized the Federal Reserve Board to regulate the extension of credit for securities purchases under Regulation T.
- Regulates the handling of client accounts.
- Regulates interstate securities transactions.

THE SECURITIES AND EXCHANGE COMMISSION (SEC)

One of the biggest components of the Securities Exchange Act of 1934 was the creation of the SEC. The SEC is the ultimate securities industry authority and is a direct government body. Five commissioners are appointed to 5-year terms by the president, and each must be approved by the Senate. No more than three members may be from any one political party. During their term, commissioners may not engage in any outside employment. The SEC is not a self-regulatory organization (SRO) or a designated examining authority (DEA). An SRO is an organization that regulates its own members, such as the NYSE or FINRA. A DEA inspects a broker dealer's books and records, and can also be the NYSE or FINRA. All broker dealers, exchanges, agents, and securities must register with the SEC. All exchanges are required to file a registration statement with the SEC that includes its articles of incorporation, bylaws, and constitution. All new rules and regulations adopted by an exchange must be disclosed to the SEC as soon as they are enacted. Issuers of securities with more than 500 shareholders and with assets exceeding $10,000,000, or issuers whose securities are traded on an exchange or Nasdaq must register with the SEC, file quarterly (10-Q) and annual (10-K) reports, and follow certain rules relating to the solicitation of proxies from stockholders. The issuer must file the proxy with the SEC, and the proxy must be in the required form and be accompanied by certain information. A broker dealer that conducts business with the public must register with the SEC and maintain a certain level of financial solvency, known as net capital. All broker dealers are required to forward a financial statement to all customers of the firm. Additionally, all employees of the broker dealer who are involved in securities sales, have access to cash and securities, or who supervise employees must be fingerprinted.

EXTENSION OF CREDIT

The Securities Act of 1934 gave the authority to the Federal Reserve Board (FRB) to regulate the extension of credit by broker dealers for the purchase of securities by their customers. The following is a list of the regulations of the different lenders and the regulation that gave the Federal Reserve Board the authority to govern their activities:

- Regulation T: Broker dealers
- Regulation U: Banks
- Regulation G: All other financial institutions

TAKENOTE!

Exempt securities issued by the U.S. government and municipal governments are exempt from most of the conditions of the Securities Exchange Act of 1934, including Regulation T, antimanipulation rules, proxy requirements, and insider reporting.

FINRA

The Maloney Act of 1938 was an amendment to the Securities Exchange Act of 1934 that allowed the creation of the National Association of Securities Dealers (NASD), which is now part of FINRA. The NASD became the SRO for the OTC market, and its purpose was to regulate the broker dealers who conduct business in the OTC market. The NASD, now part of FINRA, was organized into four major bylaws:

1. Rules of Fair Practice
2. Uniform Practice Code
3. Code of Procedure
4. Code of Arbitration

THE RULES OF FAIR PRACTICE/RULES OF CONDUCT

The Rules of Fair Practice are designed to ensure just and equitable trade practices among members in their dealings with the public. In short, the Rules of Fair Practice require members to deal fairly with the public. The Rules of

Fair Practice may also be called the Conduct Rules or the Rules of Conduct. They govern, among other things:

- Commissions and markups.
- Communications with the public.
- Customer recommendations.
- Claims made by representatives.

THE UNIFORM PRACTICE CODE

The Uniform Practice Code sets forth guidelines for how FINRA members transact business with other members. The Uniform Practice Code sets standards of business practices among its members and regulates:

- Settlement dates.
- Ex-dividend dates.
- Rules of good delivery.
- Confirmations.
- Don't know (DK) procedures.

THE CODE OF PROCEDURE

The Code of Procedure regulates how the FINRA investigates complaints and violations. The Code of Procedure regulates the discovery phase of alleged violations of Rules of Fair Practice. The Code of Procedure is not concerned with money; it is only concerned with rule violations.

THE CODE OF ARBITRATION

The Code of Arbitration provides a forum to resolve disputes. Arbitration provides a final and binding resolution to disputes involving a member and:

- Another member.
- A registered agent.
- A bank.
- A customer.

FINRA is divided into districts based on geography. Each district elects a committee to administer the association's rules. The committee is composed of up to 12 members who serve up to a 3-year term. The committee appoints the Department of Enforcement to handle all trade practice complaints within the district and has the power to assess penalties against members who have violated one or more of the association's rules. The FINRA executive committee consists of the Board of Governors, which oversees the national business of FINRA.

BECOMING A MEMBER OF FINRA

FINRA sets strict qualification standards that all prospective members must meet prior to being granted membership. Each firm will appoint an executive representative who is authorized to deal with the association with regard to the member's business. The firm must review the appointment of the executive quarterly and must notify FINRA if the executive changes within 17 business days of the end of the quarter. Any firm that engages in interstate securities transactions with public customers is required to become a member of FINRA. Additionally, any broker dealer that wishes to participate as a selling group member in the distribution of mutual fund shares must also be a member of FINRA.

In order to become a member of FINRA, a firm must:

- Meet net capital requirements (solvency).
- Have at least two principals to supervise the firm.
- Have an acceptable business plan detailing its proposed business activities.
- Attend a premembership interview.

Members must also agree to:

- Abide by all of FINRA's rules.
- Abide by all federal and state laws.
- Pay dues, fees, and membership assessments as required by the association.

The FINRA member must pay the following fees:

- A basic membership fee
- A fee for each representative and principal
- A fee based on the firm's gross income
- A fee for all branch offices

A member failing to pays fees may be suspended or have its membership canceled upon 15 days written notice from FINRA.

The following are not eligible for membership with FINRA:

- Firms that have been expelled, barred, or suspended by a national securities association or exchange.
- Firms that are subject to a court injunction barring them from engaging in the securities business.
- Firms deemed nonqualified or unsuitable by the Board of Governors.
- Firms that have been barred from association with members of a national securities association or exchange.

All members must deal with nonmembers as members of the general public and may not offer nonmembers selling concessions. All suspended or expelled members must also be treated as members of the general public. The following are exempt from this rule:

- Transactions in government securities
- Transactions in municipal securities
- Transactions executed on an exchange
- Foreign broker dealers ineligible for registration with FINRA who have a correspondent relationship with a member or have agreed to treat non-members in the United States as members of the general public

REGISTRATION OF AGENTS/ASSOCIATED PERSONS

All individuals who engage in securities transactions with the public are required to be registered as an associated person. Failure to register people who engage in securities transactions can result in disciplinary charges being brought against the member. Prior to becoming registered as an associated person, all individuals must be sponsored by a member firm. All sponsoring firms are required to ascertain the applicant's:

- Business character.
- Educational background.
- Professional background.

Once a member has certified the above information regarding the applicant, it may formally submit the individual's application for becoming an associated person, which is known as Form U-4. The employee must fill out the form completely and submit the form with a set of fingerprints. A principal of the member firm must sign the application and certify that he or she has reviewed the applicant's background. All employees of the broker dealer who engage in any of the following activities must be fingerprinted:

- Sale of securities
- Have access to or contact with cash or securities
- Have access to or prepare records of original entry
- Supervise individuals engaged in any of the activities listed

STATE REGISTRATION

In addition to registering with FINRA, all broker dealers and agents must register in their home state as well as in any state in which they transact business.

RETAIL COMMUNICATIONS/ COMMUNICATIONS WITH THE PUBLIC

Member firms will seek to increase their business and exposure through the use of both retail and institutional communications. Strict regulations are in place to ensure that all communications with the public adhere to industry guidelines. Some communications with the public are available to a general audience and include:

- Television/radio
- Publicly accessible websites
- Motion pictures
- Newspapers/magazine
- Telephone directory listings
- Signs/billboards
- Computer/Internet postings
- Videotape displays
- Other public media
- Recorded telemarketing messages

Other types of communications are offered to a targeted audience. These communications include:

- Market reports
- Password-protected websites
- Telemarketing scripts

- Form letters or e-mails (sent to more than 25 people)
- Circulars
- Research reports
- Printed materials for seminars
- Option worksheets
- Performance reports
- Prepared scripts for TV or radio
- Reprints of ads or sales literature

FINRA RULE 2210

FINRA Rule 2210 replaces the advertising and sales literature rules previously used to regulate member communications with the public. FINRA Rule 2210 streamlines member communication rules and reduces the number of communication categories from six to three. The three categories of member communication are:

1. Retail communication
2. Institutional communication
3. Correspondence

RETAIL COMMUNICATION

Retail communication is defined as any written communication distributed or made available to 25 or more retail investors in a 30-day period. The communication may be distributed in hard copy or in electronic formats. The definition of a retail investor is any investor who does not meet the definition of an institutional investor. Retail communication now contains all components of advertising and sales literature. All retail communications must be approved by a registered principal prior to first use. The publication of a post in a chat room or other online forum will not require the prior approval of a principal so long as such post does not promote the business of the member firm and does not provide investment advice. Additionally, generic advertising will also be exempt from the prior approval requirements. All retail communication must be maintained by the member for 3 years. If the member firm is a new member firm that has been in existence for fewer than 12 months based on the firm's approval date in the Central Registration Depository (CRD), the member must file all retail communications with FINRA 10 days prior to its first use unless the communication has been previously filed and contains no material changes or has been filed by another member, such as an investment company or ETF sponsor. Member firms that have been established for more than 12 months may file retail communications with FINRA 10 days after the communication is first used. Investment companies, ETF sponsors, and retail communications regarding variable annuities must be filed 10 days prior to first use. Should FINRA determine that a member firm is making false or misleading statements in its retail communications with the public, FINRA may require the member to file all of its retail communication with the public with the association 10 days prior to its first use.

TAKENOTE!

Research reports covering only securities listed on a national securities exchange and exclude from Rule 2210's filing requirements additionally a free writing prospectus is exempt from filing with the SEC and is not subject to Rule 2210's filing or content standards.

INSTITUTIONAL COMMUNICATIONS

Intuitional communication is defined as any written communication distributed or made available exclusively to institutional investors. The communication may be distributed in hard copy or in electronic formats. Institutional communications do not have to be approved by a principal prior to first use so long as the member has established policies and procedures regarding the use of institutional communications and has trained its employees on the proper use of institutional communication. Institutional communication is also exempt from FINRA's filing requirement, but like retail communications it must be maintained by a member for 3 years. If the member believes that the institutional communication or any part thereof may be seen by even a single retail investor, the communication must be handled as all other retail communication and is subject to the approval and filing requirements as if it was retail communication. An institutional investor is a person or firm that trades securities for his or her own account or for the accounts of others. Institutional investors are generally limited to large financial companies. Because of their size and sophistication, fewer protective laws cover institutional investors. It is important to note that there is no minimum size for an institutional account. Institutional investors include:

- Broker dealers
- Investment advisers

- Investment companies
- Insurance companies
- Banks
- Trusts
- Savings and loans
- Government agencies
- Employment benefit plans with more than 100 participants
- Any non-natural person with more than $50,000,000 in assets

CORRESPONDENCE

Correspondence consists of electronic and written communications between the member and up to 25 retail investors in a 30-day period. With the increase in acceptance of e-mail as business communication, it would be impractical for a member to review all correspondence between the member and a customer. The member instead may set up procedures to review a sample of all correspondence, both electronic and hard copy. If the member reviews only a sample of the correspondence, the member must train its associated people on their firm's procedures relating to correspondence and must document the training and ensure that the procedures are followed. Even though the member is not required to review all correspondence, the member must still retain all correspondence. The member should, where practical, review all incoming hard copy correspondence. Letters received by the firm could contain cash, checks, securities, or complaints.

BROKER DEALER WEBSITES

A broker dealer will not be deemed to have a place of business in a state where it does not maintain an office simply by virtue of the fact that the publicly available website established by the firm or one of its agents is accessible from that state so long as the following conditions are met:

- The website clearly states that the firm may only conduct business in states where it is properly registered to do so.
- The website only provides general information about the firm and does not provide specific investment advice.
- The firm or its agent may not respond to Internet inquiries with the intent to solicit business without first meeting the registration requirements in the state of the prospective customer.

The content of any website must be reviewed and approved by a principal prior to its first use and must be filed with FINRA within 10 days of use. If the firm or its agent updates the website and the update materially changes the information contained on the website, the update must be reapproved by a principal and refiled with FINRA. The website may (but is not required to) use the FINRA logo so long as the use is only to demonstrate that the firm is a FINRA member and a hyperlink to the FINRA website is included in close proximity to the logo.

GENERIC ADVERTISING

Generic advertising is generally designed to promote firm awareness and to advertise the products and services generally offered through the firm. Generic ads will generally include:

- Securities products offered (i.e., stocks, bonds, mutual funds)
- Contact name, number, and address
- Types of accounts offered (i.e., individual, IRA, 401K).

TOMBSTONE ADS

A tombstone ad is an announcement of a new security offering coming to market. Tombstone ads may be run while the securities are still in registration with the SEC and may only include:

- A description of the securities
- A description of the business
- A description of the transaction
- Required disclaimers
- The time and place of any stockholders meetings regarding the sale of the securities

Tombstone ads must include the following:

- A statement that the securities registration has not yet become effective
- A statement that responding to the ad does not obligate the prospect
- A statement as to where a prospectus may be obtained
- A statement that the ad does not constitute an offer to sell the securities and that an offer may only be made by the prospectus

All retail communication is required to be approved by a principal of the firm prior to its first use. A general security principal (Series 24) may approve most advertising and sales literature. Any retail communication relating to options must be approved by a registered options principal or the compliance registered options principal. Research reports must be approved by a supervisory analyst.

TESTIMONIALS

From time to time, firms will use testimonials made by people of national or local recognition in an effort to generate new business for the firm. If the individual giving the testimonial is quoting past performance relating to the firm's recommendations, it must be accompanied by a disclaimer that past performance is not indicative of future performance. If the individual giving the testimony was compensated in any way, the fact that the person received compensation must also be disclosed. Should the individual's testimony imply that the person making the testimony is an expert, a statement regarding that person's qualifications as an expert must also be contained in the ad or sales literature. Research prepared by outside parties must disclose the name of the preparer.

FREE SERVICES

If a member firm advertises free services to customers or to people who respond to an ad, the services must actually be free to everyone, with no strings attached.

MISLEADING COMMUNICATIONS

The following are some examples of misleading statements which are not allowed to appear in advertising or sales literature:

- Excessive use of hedge clauses
- Implying an endorsement by FINRA, the NYSE, or the SEC
- Printing the FINRA logo in type that is larger than the type used for the member's name
- Implying that the member has larger research facilities than it actually has
- Implying that an individual has higher qualifications than he or she actually has

SECURITIES INVESTOR PROTECTION CORPORATION ACT OF 1970

The Securities Investor Protection Corporation (SIPC) is a government-sponsored corporation that provides protection to customers in the event of a broker dealer's failure. All broker dealers that are registered with the SEC are required to be SIPC members. All broker dealers are required to pay annual dues to SIPC's insurance fund to cover losses due to broker dealer failure. If a broker dealer fails to pay its SIPC assessment, it may not transact business until it is paid. Should a firm fall below its net capital requirement, it is deemed to be insolvent, and SIPC will petition in court to have a trustee appointed to liquidate the firm and protect the customers. The trustee must be a disinterested party and, once the trustee is appointed, the firm may not conduct business or try to conceal any assets.

CUSTOMER COVERAGE

SIPC protects customers of a brokerage firm in much the same way that the FDIC protects customers of banks. SIPC covers customer losses that result from broker dealer failure, not from market losses. SIPC covers up to $500,000 per separate customer. Of the $500,000, up to $250,000 may be in cash. Most broker dealers carry additional private insurance to cover larger accounts, but SIPC is the industry-funded insurance and is required by all broker dealers. The following are examples of separate customers:

Customer	Securities Market Value	Cash	SIPC Coverage
Mr. Jones	$320,000	$75,000	All
Mr. & Mrs. Jones	$290,000	$90,000	All
Mrs. Jones	$397,000	$82,000	All

All of the accounts shown would be considered separate customers, and SIPC would cover the entire value of all of the accounts. If an account has in excess of $250,000 in cash, the individual would not be covered for any amount exceeding $250,000 in cash and would become a general creditor for the rest. SIPC does not consider a margin account and cash account as separate customers, and the customer would be covered for the maximum of $500,000. SIPC does not offer coverage for commodities contracts, and all member firms must display the SIPC sign in their lobby. If a broker dealer purchases additional insurance over and above the required SIPC insurance all customers must be notified 30 days prior to any reduction or cancelation of the coverage.

THE SECURITIES ACTS AMENDMENTS OF 1975

The Securities Acts Amendments of 1975 gave the authority to the MSRB to regulate the issuance and trading of municipal bonds. The MSRB has no enforcement division. Its rules are enforced by other regulators.

THE INSIDER TRADING AND SECURITIES FRAUD ENFORCEMENT ACT OF 1988

The Insider Trading and Securities Fraud Enforcement Act of 1988 set forth guidelines and controls for the use and dissemination of nonpublic material information. Nonpublic information is information that is not known by people outside of the company. Material information is information regarding a situation or development that will materially affect the company in the present or in the future. It is not only just for insiders to have this type of information, but it is required in order for them to do their jobs effectively. It is, however, unlawful for an insider to use this information to profit from a forthcoming move in the stock price. An insider is defined as any officer, director, 10% stockholder, or anyone who is in possession of nonpublic material information, as well as the spouse of any such person. Additionally, it is unlawful for the insider to divulge any of this information to any outside party. Trading on inside information has always been a violation of the Securities Exchange Act of 1934, but the Insider Trading and Securities Fraud Enforcement Act prescribed stricter penalties for violators, which include:

- A fine of the greater of 300% of the amount of the gain or 300% of the amount of the loss avoided or $1,000,000 for the person who acts on the information
- A fine of up to $1,000,000 for the person who divulges the information
- Insider traders may be sued by the affected parties
- Criminal prosecutions and fines up to $5,000,000 for individuals and fines of up to $25,000,000 for corporations

Information becomes public information once it has been disseminated over public media. The SEC will pay a reward of up to 10% to informants who turn in individuals who trade on inside information. In addition to the insiders already listed, the following are also considered insiders:

- Accountants
- Attorneys
- Investment bankers

FIREWALLS

Broker dealers that act as underwriters and investment bankers for corporate clients must have access to information regarding the company in order to advise the company properly. The broker dealer must ensure that no inside information is passed between its investment banking department and its retail trading departments. The broker dealer is required to physically separate these divisions by a firewall. The broker dealer must maintain written supervisory procedures to adequately guard against the wrongful use or dissemination of inside information.

TELEMARKETING RULES

FINRA Rule 3230 regulates how telemarketing calls are made by businesses. On your exam you may see the telemarketing rule tested under the telephone Consumer Protection Act of 1991, FINRA Rule 3230, or as telemarketing rules. Telemarketing calls that are designed to have consumers invest in or purchase goods, services, or property must adhere to the strict guidelines. All firms must:

- Call only between the hours of 8:00 a.m. and 9:00 p.m. in the potential customer's time zone.
- Maintain a "Do Not Call" list. Individuals placed on the Do Not Call list may not be contacted by anyone at the firm for 5 years.
- Give the prospect the firm's name, address, and phone number. Caller ID must display firm name and phone number caller ID blocking may not be used.
- Have adequate policies and procedures to maintain a Do Not Call list.
- Train representatives on calling policies and use of the Do Not Call list.
- Ensure that any fax solicitations have the firm's name, address, and phone number and prohibit the use of unsolicited faxes.

 TAKENOTE!

An interesting situation can arise when a customer of the firm who maintains an account with the firm is on the firm-specific Do Not Call list. In these cases representatives may not contact the customer unless it is to verify account information such as mailing address. The customer may not be contacted to discuss holdings in the account or to make a recommendation.

DO NOT CALL LIST EXEMPTIONS

The following are exempt from the prohibited calls listed above:

- Calls to existing customers who have executed a transaction or who have had an account containing cash or securities on deposit within the last 18 months or to a person who has contacted the member within the last 3 months
- Calls to a person where the caller has a personal relationship with the recipient
- Calls to a person who has given written permission to be contacted by the firm and the number where the person may be contacted
- Inadvertent calls to a number that now appears on the national Do Not Call list but were not included on the Do Not Call list used by the member, as long as that list was not more than 31 days old.

THE PENNY STOCK COLD CALL RULE

SEC Rules 15g-2 through 15g-9, collectively known as the penny stock cold call rule, were enacted in order to ensure that investors do not purchase penny stocks without knowing the risks. A penny stock is an unlisted security that trades below $5 per share and whose issuer does not meet the minimum financial listing requirements for an exchange or Nasdaq. Prior to purchasing a penny stock:

- The agent must make sure that the purchase is suitable for the customer.
- The customer must sign a suitability statement.
- The firm must supply a current quote.
- The firm must disclose the amount of commission earned by the firm and the agent.

Established customers are exempt from the penny stock cold call rule. An established customer is one who has made three transactions in three different penny stocks on three different days. An established customer is also one who has had cash or securities on deposit with the firm during the previous 12 months. Also exempt from the rule are:

- Transactions executed by broker dealers whose commissions or markups from penny stock transactions do not exceed 5% of their total commissions or markups.
- Transactions with institutional investors.
- Private placements.

- Unsolicited transactions.
- Transactions with officers, directors, or 5% stockholders.

If a customer has an account containing a penny stock, the broker dealer carrying the customer's account must send the customer an account statement detailing the name and amount of each penny stock held in the customer's account and the value of the securities to the extent the value can be determined.

VIOLATIONS AND COMPLAINTS

FINRA's Code of Procedure sets forth guidelines for the investigation of alleged violations and complaints against a member firm or a registered representative. FINRA staff originates many complaints against member firms and associated persons during their routine examinations of member firms. Complaints and allegations of wrongdoing may also originate from a customer of the member firm or from another member. If a FINRA staff member has received a complaint that alleges a violation of securities regulations, it is up to FINRA to determine if the complaint is meritorious. FINRA will begin an investigation of the complaint by notifying the member and/or the associated person that a complaint has been received and will request that the member or an associated person respond in writing. All requests for information must be met within 25 days from the day that the request was made. If the member fails to provide the requested information within the 25-day timeframe, FINRA will send out a second request for the information. The second request will give the firm or the representative an additional 14 days to provide the information requested. If the information is not provided by the end of the 14 days, FINRA may choose to take action against the firm or the representative for failing to respond.

RESOLUTION OF ALLEGATIONS

Should FINRA find that the allegation is baseless, the association may dismiss it without action. However, if FINRA finds that the allegation has merit, it may be resolved through minor rule violation (MRV) procedure or through a formal hearing process. If the firm or the representative does not contest the allegations, it may sign an acceptance waiver and consent (AWAC) to resolve the issue. By signing the AWAC, the firm or representative does not contest the allegations, accepts whatever penalty is being prescribed, and waives its right to appeal. Additionally, by signing the AWAC, the firm or the representative does not admit to any wrongdoing; it simply does not contest it.

MINOR RULE VIOLATION

A minor rule violation letter is traditionally used in cases that involve only small violations. FINRA has outlined a number of rule violations that qualify to be resolved using MRV procedure. It is offered to respondents in an effort to avoid a costly hearing. Under MRV procedure, the maximum penalty is a censure and a $2,500 fine. If MRV procedure is offered, the member or associated person has 10 business days to accept it. By signing the MRV letter, the respondent does not admit or deny the allegations and gives up its right to appeal the decision. Should the offer of MRV procedure not be accepted, the Department of Enforcement will proceed with a formal hearing to determine if a violation has occurred. Possible penalties, after having been found to have violated one or more of the association's rules, are:

- Censure
- Suspension for up to 1 year
- Expulsion for up to 10 years
- Barred for life
- Fined any amount
- Any other penalty deemed appropriate, such as restitution

Decisions of the Department of Enforcement may be appealed within 15 days to the National Adjudicatory Counsel (NAC). If no action is taken, the decision of the Department of Enforcement becomes final in 45 days. Should the NAC determine that the appeal is meritorious, it must start a review within a 45-day period. The decision of the NAC may be appealed to the SEC and finally to the court system. Upon final determination, all fines, penalties, and costs must be paid promptly.

MEDIATION

Mediation is an informal attempt by two parties to try to resolve a dispute prior to entering into the formal arbitration process. During the mediation process, the two parties meet to discuss the contested issue, and the dialog is monitored by a mediator. The mediator is a neutral person with industry knowledge suggested by FINRA, who tries to help the parties reach an agreement. If the mediator is not acceptable, the parties may select another mediator from a list of approved mediators or their own independent mediator. Prior to entering into the mediation process, both parties must agree to try to resolve the issue in mediation and must split the mediator's fee. The mediation process begins with an initial joint meeting where both parties lay out their claims for the mediator and the other party. During the second phase of the process, each side meets with the mediator individually in meetings known as caucuses. The mediator is a neutral party and will not disclose information provided during the caucus sessions to the opposing side. The mediation process will continue until an agreement is reached, the mediator declares an impasse with no possible resolution, or one of the parties or the mediator withdraws from the process in writing. The mediation process may provide a resolution for all or some of the contested issues. Issues that are not resolved in mediation may be resolved through formal arbitration. A person who served as a mediator in a dispute that ultimately ends up in arbitration may not serve on the arbitration panel.

CODE OF ARBITRATION

FINRA's Code of Arbitration procedure provides parties with a forum to resolve disputes. Most claims submitted to arbitration are financial in nature, although other claims may be submitted. Sexual harassment and discrimination claims are not required to be resolved in arbitration unless both parties specifically agree to arbitrate. Class action claims are also not resolved in arbitration. Class action status is awarded by the court system. Arbitration provides a cost-effective alternative to dispute resolution, and many disputes will be resolved much sooner than they otherwise may have been in court. All industry members are required to settle all disputes through arbitration. A public customer, however, must agree in writing to settle any dispute through arbitration. When a customer opens an account with a broker dealer, the broker dealer will often have the customer sign a customer agreement, although this is not required by industry standards. The customer agreement usually contains a predispute arbitration clause where the customer agrees to settle any dispute that may arise in arbitration rather than in court. Should the customer request a copy of the pre-dispute arbitration clause the member has 10 business days to provide it to the customer.

THE ARBITRATION PROCESS

Arbitration begins when an aggrieved party, known as the claimant, files a statement of claim, along with a submission agreement and payment for the arbitration fee with FINRA. The party alleged to have caused the claimant harm must respond to the statement of claim within 45 calendar days and is known as the respondent. The response is sent to both the arbitration director and the claimant. The claimant then has 10 calendar days to reply to both the arbitration director and respondent. Dispute resolution through arbitration is available for matters involving:

- Member vs. member
- Bank vs. member
- Member vs. bank
- Member vs. registered representative
- Registered representative vs. member
- Customer vs. member
- Member vs. customer

SIMPLIFIED ARBITRATION

Simplified arbitration is available for disputes involving amounts of $50,000 or less. Traditionally, simplified arbitration provides no opportunity for a hearing. Parties submit their case in writing only. One arbitrator reviews the case and renders a decision. If a public customer is involved, the customer may request a hearing for disputes up to $50,000. For amounts that exceed $50,000, a hearing must be held.

LARGER DISPUTES

Larger disputes will be submitted to a panel of up to three arbitrators to render a decision on the matter. A hearing will take place, and evidence and testimony will be presented to the panel. The number of arbitrators must always be odd, so the panel will be made up of one or three arbitrators from both the public and the industry. An arbitrator will be deemed to be a nonpublic or industry arbitrator if the person is or was in the securities industry at any point during the last 5 years. Included in this definition are persons associated with hedge funds and accountants and attorneys whose practice within the last 2 years has been dedicated to industry clients at least 20 percent of the time. An accountant or attorney will be deemed to be a public arbitrator if in the last 2 years 10% or less of the business of such professional is dedicated to industry clients and the revenue received was less than $50,000.

AWARDS UNDER ARBITRATION

Awards under arbitration are final and binding; there is no appeal. If a monetary payment has been awarded, the party required to pay has 30 days to comply with the decision. A member or a registered representative who fails to pay an award under arbitration is subject to suspension. All pending arbitrations, arbitrations settled prior to final judgment, and arbitrations settled in favor of the customer will be disclosed on BrokerCheck. If an arbitration is settled in favor of the firm or representative, it will be removed from BrokerCheck. Any sanction by a regulator that carries a penalty of $15,000 or more will also be disclosed on BrokerCheck.

POLITICAL CONTRIBUTIONS

FINRA enforces the rules enacted by the MSRB for its members that engage in municipal securities business. MSRB Rule G-38 puts strict limits on political contributions that may be made by a municipal finance professional (MFP). An MFP is an agent who is primarily engaged in any of the following:

- Soliciting municipal underwriting
- Acting as a financial adviser or consultant
- Trading or selling municipal securities
- Providing investment advice or issuing research reports relating to municipal securities to the public
- Direct supervision of any agent acting in the above capacity
- Executives who oversee municipal dealers or departments

MFPs may only make political contributions to a candidate in an election where they are eligible to vote. The maximum amount of their contribution is limited to $250 per candidate per election. If an MFP donates more than $250 or makes a contribution to a candidate in an election where he or she is not able to vote, a violation has occurred, and the employing firm will be banned from engaging in municipal securities business with the issuer for 2 years. The 2-year ban will follow the MFP should the MFP change firms. Both the new firm and the previous employer will be subject to the amount of time that remains on the 2-year ban. Should an MFP make a political contribution to an incumbent that would subject the employing firm to a ban, that ban will expire if the incumbent loses the election. This political contribution does not apply to federal elections such as for Senators.

EXAMPLE   If an MFP donated $200 to a mayoral candidate in a district where the MFP does not live and, as a result, could not vote in the election, the employing firm could not underwrite that municipality's debt for 2 years.

If an MFP contributes more than $250 or contributes to a candidate that he or she is not entitled to vote for, the employing firm must notify the issuer by filing Forms G37 and G38 by the last day of the month following the end of each calendar quarter. These forms will tell the issuer:

- The amount of the contribution and the contributor category.
- The name and title of the political official and his or her political party.
- A list of the municipal issuers the firm engages in business with.

If the contribution is in line with MSRB Rule 37, the employing firm is not required to file Forms G37 and G38. If an executive officer gives more than $250, the donation must be reported, but would not ban the firm from engaging in municipal securities business with the issuer. Additionally, if the firm employs consultants to help the firm obtain municipal securities business from issuers, the firm must send Forms G37 and G38 to the MSRB at the end of each calendar quarter, listing:

- The name of the consultant or company.
- The role in which the consultant is acting and the amount of compensation.
- A list of municipal securities business obtained by using the consultant.
- A copy of all consulting agreements.
- Termination dates for consulting agreements.

The dealer also must disclose information relating to the use of consultants to the issuers. The dealer may disclose the information on an issue-specific basis or on an issuer-specific basis. If the dealer notifies issuers on an issuer basis, the dealer must send issuers updated information annually, even if there have been no changes. It is important to note that FINRA rules differ from MSRB rules. FINRA allows associated persons to make political contributions of up to $350 per candidate. This limit is in effect for candidates the associated person may vote for. If the associated person cannot vote for the candidate, the contribution limit is $150.

INVESTMENT ADVISER REGISTRATION

It is unlawful for an investment adviser to conduct securities business without being duly registered or exempt from registration. State registration exemptions are provided for investment advisers who:

- Are federally registered.
- Manage portfolios for investment companies.
- Manage portfolios in excess of $110,000,000.
- Have no office in the state and conduct business exclusively with financial institutions.
- Have no office in the state and offer advice to fewer than five clients in any 12-month period. This is known as the de minimis exemption.

THE NATIONAL SECURITIES MARKET IMPROVEMENT ACT OF 1996/ THE COORDINATION ACT

The National Securities Markets Improvement Act of 1996 eliminated regulatory duplication of effort and established registration requirements for investment advisers. A federally covered investment adviser must register with the SEC and is any investment adviser that:

- Manages at least $110,000,000.
- Manages investment company portfolios.
- Is not registered under state laws.

All federally registered investment advisers must pay state filing fees and notify the administrator in the states in which they conduct business. The state securities administrator may not audit a federally covered investment adviser unless that adviser's principal office is located in that administrator's state. An investment adviser is required to register with the state if it manages less than $100 million. Once the investment adviser reaches $100 million in assets under management (AUM), the adviser becomes eligible for federal registration. An investment adviser who manages between $100 million and $110 million may choose to register either with the state or with the SEC. If the investment adviser thinks that its asset base will exceed $110 milion, it should register with the SEC. An investment adviser that manages $110 million or more must register with the SEC. If a federally covered investment adviser's AUM falls below $90 million, the adviser must withdraw its federal registration by filling

Form ADV-W and is required to required to register with the appropriate states within 180 days. Like most regulations, there are rare exceptions to the rule of when an investment adviser may register with the SEC. The Dodd Frank Wall Street Reform Act of 2010 increased the AUM for federal registration to its current levels and defined three categories of investment advisers:

1. Small adviser: Advisers with less than $25,000,000 AUM.
2. Midsize advisers: Advisers with $25,000,000–$100,000,000 AUM.
3. Large advisers: Advisers with more than $100,000,000 AUM.

Pension consultants must have at least $200,000,000 AUM to be eligible to become federally registered

INVESTMENT ADVISER REGISTRATION REQUIREMENTS

An investment adviser must file the following with the state securities administrator before becoming registered:

- Application Form ADV.
- Filing fees.
- Audited balance sheet within 90 days of year end.

INVESTMENT ADVISER CAPITAL REQUIREMENTS

An investment adviser must maintain a minimal level of financial solvency. Advisers with custody of customers' cash and securities must maintain minimum net capital of $35,000. If the adviser is unable to meet this requirement, it may post a surety bond. Deposits of cash and securities will alleviate the surety bond requirement. An adviser is considered to have custody if it has its customers' cash and securities held at the firm or if it has full discretion over customers' accounts. Full discretion allows the adviser to withdraw cash and securities from the customer's account without consulting the customer. Advisers that have only limited discretionary authority over customers' accounts need to maintain a minimum of $10,000 in net capital. An adviser with limited discretionary authority may only buy and sell securities for the customer's benefit without consulting the customer. Advisers may not withdraw or deposit cash or securities without the customer's consent. Investment adviser representatives are not required to maintain a minimum level of liquidity.

INVESTMENT ADVISER REPRESENTATIVES

All investment adviser representatives who maintain an office within the state must register with the state. An investment adviser representative is an individual who:

- Gives advice on the value of the securities.
- Gives advice on the advisability of buying or selling securities.
- Solicits new advisory clients.
- Is an officer, director, or partner of the investment adviser.

An investment adviser may not employ any representative who is not duly registered. Clerical and administrative employees are not considered representatives and do not need to register.

EXAMS FOR INVESTMENT ADVISER REPRESENTATIVES

The state securities administrator may require investment adviser representatives as well as the officers and directors of the firm to take an exam, which may be oral, written, or both. All registration become effective at noon 30 days after the application has been filed. The administrator may require that an announcement of the investment adviser's intended registration be published in the newspaper.

INVESTMENT ADVISER ADVERTISING AND SALES LITERATURE

All advertising and sales literature for an investment adviser must be filed with the state securities administrator. The administrator may require prior approval of:

- Form letters.
- Prospectuses.
- Pamphlets.

> **TAKENOTE!**
>
> An investment adviser may not use any type of testimonial from clients in their advertising or sales literature. The adviser is also prohibited from having clients cite return information relating to their account with the adviser.

The following records must be kept for a minimum of 5 years for investment advisors:

- Advertising and sales literature
- Account statements
- Order tickets/order memorandum

All investment advisers must keep accurate records relating to the following:

- Cash receipts and disbursements
- Income and expense ledgers
- Order tickets, including customer's name
- Adviser's name, including executing broker and discretionary information
- Ledgers and confirmations for all customers for whom the adviser has custody
- Financial statements and trial balance
- All written recommendations to customers
- Copies of advertisements, circulars, and articles sent to more than 10 people
- Copies of calculations sent to more than 10 people

All books and records must be kept for 5 years readily accessible and for 2 years at the adviser's office. Records may be kept on a computer or microfiche as long as the data may be viewed and printed.

INVESTMENT ADVISER BROCHURE DELIVERY

An investment adviser is required to provide all prospective clients with a brochure or with Form ADV Part II at least 48 hours prior to the signing of the contract, or at least at the time of the signing of the contract if the client is given a 5-day grace period to withdraw without penalty. The brochure or Form ADV Part II will state:

- How and when fees are charged.
- The types of securities the adviser does business in.
- How recommendations are made.
- The type of clients the adviser has.
- The qualifications of officers and directors.

SOFT DOLLARS

Brokerage firms will often provide investment advisers with services that go beyond execution and research to assist the investment adviser in its business. These services are provided in exchange for commission business and are known as soft dollars. The services received should normally be research related. However, in some instances the services received are used for other purposes and benefit the adviser. In order for the soft dollar arrangement to be included in the safe harbor provisions, investment advisers must ensure that the services received are for the benefit of the client and pay careful attention to the disclosure requirements relating to all soft dollar arrangements. If an adviser receives soft dollar compensation from a broker dealer to whom the adviser directs customer transactions (known as directed transactions) the adviser must disclose any arrangement to clients. The fees charged to execute the transactions should be fair and reasonable, in line with what is available in the marketplace, and in line with the value of the services offered to the adviser and its clients. The execution fees are not required to be the lowest and simply using a broker dealer whose services are more expensive will not constitute a breach of the adviser's fiduciary duty. If the adviser directs transactions to a broker dealer in exchange services that benefit the adviser, the adviser must disclose all facts relating to the arrangement and receive the client's written consent to enter into the arrangement, even if such arrangement does not increase the costs to the client. If the adviser selects broker dealers to execute client orders based on the research or other services provided, it must be disclosed on form ADV.

The SEC has divided soft dollar considerations into the following categories:

- Goods/services
- Accounting fees

- Association membership fees
- Cable television
- Commission rebates
- Computer hardware
- Computer software
- Conferences/seminars
- Consulting services
- Courier/postage/express mail
- Custodial fees
- Electronic databases
- Employee salary/benefits
- Execution assistance
- Industry publications
- Legal fees
- Management fees
- Miscellaneous expenses
- Office equipment/supplies
- Online quotation and news services
- Portfolio management software
- Rent
- Research/analysis reports
- Telephone expenses
- Travel expenses
- Tuition/training costs
- Utilities expenses

 TAKENOTE!

Only the items that can truly be deemed to be for the benefit of the client are within the safe harbor. Valuation software and other research-related items are within the safe harbor, while paying for a laptop or rent for the adviser would not be within the safe harbor.

THE UNIFORM SECURITIES ACT

In the early half of the twentieth century, state securities regulators developed their state's rules and regulations for transacting securities business within their state. The result was regulations that varied widely from state to state. The Uniform Securities Act (USA) laid out model legislation for all states in an effort to make each state's rules and regulations more uniform and easier to address. The USA, also known as "The Act," sets minimum qualification standards for each state securities administrator. The state securities administrator is the top securities regulator within the state. The state securities administrator may be the attorney general of that state or an individual appointed specifically to that post. The USA also:

- Prohibits the state securities administrator from using the post for personal benefit or from disclosing information.
- Gives the state securities administrator authority to enforce the rules of the USA within that state.
- Gives the administrator the ability to set certain registration requirements for broker dealers, agents, and investment advisers.
- Allows state securities administrators to set fee and testing requirements.
- Allows state securities administrators the authority to suspend or revoke the state registration of a broker dealer, agent, investment adviser, or a security or a security's exemption from registration.
- Sets civil and criminal penalties for violators.

The state-based laws set forth by the USA are also known as blue-sky laws.

CHAPTER 11

Pretest

SECURITIES INDUSTRY RULES AND REGULATIONS

1. Your firm is looking to increase its book of business and is planning to step up its marketing efforts. Which of the following would not be considered retail communication?

    a. A research report

    b. A prospecting script

    c. An invitation to a seminar

    d. A letter to a customer requesting a meeting to discuss her portfolio

2. You have an account with a brokerage firm that has filed for bankruptcy. There is $370,000 in market value in the account and $75,000 in cash. Your spouse also has an account with $300,000 in market value and $90,000 in cash. What will the SIPC cover?

    a. A total of $500,000 for both accounts

    b. Everything

    c. The cash only

    d. The securities only

3. Which of the following acts concerns itself with the registration of broker dealers and their required net capital?

    a. SIPC Act of 1970

    b. Securities Exchange Act of 1934

    c. Broker Dealer Fiscal Responsibility Act of 1937

    d. Securities Act of 1933

4. Under the Insider Trading and Securities Fraud Enforcement Act of 1988, the maximum fine for violators is:
   a. Three times the amount of money made.
   b. Three times the amount of money the investor avoided losing.
   c. Unlimited.
   d. Treble damages.

5. A brokerage firm wants to appeal a decision of the Department of Enforcement. The appeal will first go to the:
   a. SEC.
   b. Court of Appeals.
   c. National Appeal Board.
   d. National Adjudicatory Council.

6. An MFP donates $2,500 to a candidate in an election in which he is not able to vote. The candidate running for municipal office is an old college friend of the MFP. Which of the following is true?
   a. The employing firm has no restrictions due to the relationship between the MFP and the candidate.
   b. If the employing firm wants to bid on an offering in that municipality, it must get prior permission from FINRA.
   c. The firm is restricted from bidding on offerings in that municipality for 2 years.
   d. The firm is restricted from bidding on offerings in that municipality for 270 days.

7. Sanctions imposed by FINRA are effective within how many days of a written decision?
   a. 15 days
   b. 30 days
   c. 60 days
   d. 45 days

8. A registered broker dealer must do which of the following?

    I. Pay SIPC dues

    II. Display the SIPC sign

    III. Post a fidelity bond

    IV. Obtain fingerprint records for associated persons

    a. I and II
    b. I and III
    c. I, II, and III
    d. I, II, III, and IV

9. A registered representative who does not contest the accusations of FINRA may sign which of the following to resolve the issue?

    a. An AWAC
    b. A no-contest letter
    c. An offer of settlement
    d. A submission agreement

10. Which of the following is considered retail communication?

    I. An e-mail to a representative's client list

    II. The firm's website

    III. Invitations to a seminar

    IV. Flyers handed out during a presentation

    a. III and IV
    b. I and II
    c. I, III, and IV
    d. I, II, III, and IV

11. All of the following are exempt from the Do Not Call policies, EXCEPT:

    a. A call from a religious organization.
    b. A call from a nonprofit organization seeking to raise money.
    c. A call to an existing client.
    d. A call to another state.

12. An investor has filed a complaint with FINRA alleging that his firm has violated industry rules. Which of the following bylaws govern the resolution of such matters?
    a. Rules of Fair Practice
    b. Uniform Practice Code
    c. Code of Procedure
    d. Code of Arbitration

13. A new member firm that has not filed with FINRA is required to:
    a. File its advertisements 10 days after first use.
    b. File its advertisements 10 days prior to first use.
    c. Receive FINRA approval to begin advertising.
    d. File its advertisements 5 days prior to first use.

14. A syndicate has published a tombstone ad prior to the issue becoming effective. Which of the following must appear in the tombstone ad?
    I. A statement that the registration has not yet become effective
    II. A statement that the tombstone ad is not an offer to sell the securities
    III. Contact information
    IV. A no commitment statement
    a. I and III
    b. II and IV
    c. III and IV
    d. I, II, III, and IV

Answer Keys

CHAPTER 1: EQUITY AND DEBT SECURITIES

1. (B) A stockholder does not get to vote directly for executive compensation.
2. (B) Each ADR represents from 1 to 10 shares of the foreign company. ADR holders do have the right to vote and receive dividends. Foreign governments put restrictions on the foreign ownership of stock from time to time.
3. (B) The shareholders may vote to approve an increase in the number of authorized shares. All of the other choices are correct.
4. (B) The Options Clearing Corporation (OCC) issues all standardized options.
5. (D) Common stockholders do not have voting power in the matter of bankruptcy.
6. (D) Bonds registered as to principal only will still require the investor to clip coupons and present them for payment.
7. (D) Bearer bonds are issued without a name on them, meaning that whoever has possession of the bond may clip the coupons and claim the interest.
8. (D) Raw land may never be depreciated because its useful life does not decline over time. The value or useful life of the other choices does decline over time and may be depreciated.
9. (A) Choice I is incorrect in that an option is a contract between two parties, which determines the time and price at which a security may be bought or sold.
10. (C) Call sellers and put buyers are both bearish. Both investors want the value of the stock to fall.

CHAPTER 2: BROKERAGE OFFICE PROCEDURES AND BACK-OFFICE OPERATIONS

1. (B) A principal is not required to obtain a copy of the employee's U5 directly from the employee. The principal may obtain it from FINRA as well.

2. (C) All gifts given to the employee of another member firm must be given to the member for distribution to the employee, and a record must be kept of the gift.

3. (D) The sales assistant who accepts orders would have to register.

4. (C) Shareholders who attend the meeting will not be able to vote by the proxy they received, they will vote at the meeting. Shareholders must return their proxies 10 days prior to the annual meeting.

5. (A) Firms that do not self-clear are required to do all of the choices listed except clear on an omnibus basis.

6. (B) A customer who purchases a security and decides that it is unsuitable is not a reason to reject delivery.

7. (D) The seller will not keep the dividend.

8. (D) A customer must receive a statement whenever there is activity in the account. The investor purchased the shares 2 months ago and must have received a statement that month. Because the shares were purchased on margin, interest is being charged on the loan. The debiting of interest to the customer's account is considered activity, and the customer must receive a statement for those months as well.

9. (D) A firm may charge a fee for all of the services listed but must charge the fee to all customers.

10. (A) A firm may ignore a call for cash for up to $1,000.

CHAPTER 3: RECORD KEEPING, FINANCIAL REQUIREMENTS, AND CLEARING

1. (C) Broker dealers must post trades to the blotter by the end of the following business day, or T + 1.

2. (B) General ledgers must be maintained for 6 years. All of the other records must be maintained for 3 years.

3. (D) Trial balances must be prepared no later than by the 10th business day following the month's end.

4. (B) A broker dealer that executes mutual fund orders on a wire basis must have net capital of $25,000.

5. (B) FOCUS Part I reports are filed electronically and are required to be filed by carrying firms within 10 days of the month's end.

6. (B) The firm's minimum net capital is $50,000 because it is receiving customers' cash and securities.

7. (A) A broker dealer must deposit 105% of customer credit balances in a special reserve account.

8. (D) The Depository Trust Company (DTC) holds securities registered in street name in journal entry form and broker dealer free-credit balances. The DTC does not hold physical securities, customer securities, or customer free-credit balances.

9. (D) Broker dealer bank records only need to be kept for 3 years. All of the other records listed are required to be kept for 6 years.

10. (C) The minutes from board of director's meetings must be kept for the life of the firm and for 2 years readily accessible.

CHAPTER 4: ISSUING CORPORATE SECURITIES

1. (D) All of the items listed must appear in the tombstone ad.

2. (D) All of the parties listed may be held liable to the purchasers of the new issue.

3. (A) A corporation must issue common stock before it issues any preferred stock.

4. (C) The number of nonaccredited investors is limited to 35 in any 12-month period.

5. (B) Rule 145 covers mergers involving a stock swap or offer of another company's securities in exchange for its current stock.

6. (C) Anytime the SEC wants more information regarding a new issue it will issue a deficiency letter.

7. (B) Purchasers of stock in a company that has just gone public for the first time that will be listed and reporting financials must get a prospectus for 25 days.

8. (A) All of the answers listed will appear in the preliminary prospectus, except the offering price and the proceeds to the company.

9. (C) An insider may sell securities under Rule 144 for 90 days. Form 144 must be filed at or prior to the time the order is placed with a broker to sell the securities.

CHAPTER 5: TRADING SECURITIES

1. (C) A firm that makes markets in Nasdaq securities is trying to make the spread, which is the difference between the bid and ask. Spreads have narrowed significantly, making it more difficult for market makers to earn a profit on the spread.

2. (D) Mini-maxi and best efforts are types of underwriting commitments, not types of orders.

3. (A) The inside market is the highest bid and the lowest offer.

4. (A) Specialists/DMMs on the NYSE work for themselves or for a specialist firm.

5. (D) All of the choices listed would be firm except quotes for direct participation programs (DPP). Two-sided pink OTC quotes are firm.

6. (D) All of the answers are correct with regard to a market on close order except that it must be executed on the closing price or as close to the closing trade as possible. Four minutes is too far away from the close to be reasonable.

7. (B) The order has been elected because the stock has traded though the stop price. The order has now become a limit order to sell the stock at 160.

8. (D) An investor would not be considered long for the purposes of entering a sell order if the investor was long an in-the-money call option. For the investor to be considered long the security, the investor would have to exercise the in the money call option.

CHAPTER 6: GENERAL SUPERVISION

1. (A) A branch office may advertise and may conduct the member's business at the branch office. It may not do the other choices listed.

2. (C) The firm is required to record all international transfers in excess of $3,000.

3. (D) An OSJ may do all of the activities listed.

4. (B) A satellite office may conduct business with the public.

5. **(B)** All branch offices are required to be supervised by an OSJ, and a registered representative may act as the manager of the branch.
6. **(A)** Branch offices are not required to be directly inspected by the firm. By inspecting the OSJ, the firm is inspecting the branch as well.
7. **(C)** A member carrying customer accounts must do choices I, II, and III, but must only inform customers of the information once per year.
8. **(B)** A Suspicious Activity Report (SAR) must be filed for questionable transactions of $5,000 or more.
9. **(D)** A firm's anti-money-laundering program must be approved by senior management.

CHAPTER 7: CUSTOMER ACCOUNTS

1. **(A)** The custodian is the nominal owner of the securities in a UGMA account. The securities are registered in the name of the custodian for the benefit of the minor, who is the beneficial owner.
2. **(B)** The assets of the decedent will be distributed according to the will.
3. **(A)** Although the minor's Social Security number is listed on the account, it does not appear in the account title.
4. **(C)** Transactions in discretionary accounts do not need to be approved prior to execution. The transactions need to be approved promptly.
5. **(C)** A UTMA account allows the assets to remain in the account until the beneficial owner reaches the age of 25.
6. **(D)** An adult may never have a joint account with a minor.
7. **(D)** A firm receiving ACAT instructions must send a report of the positions to be transferred to the new firm upon validation.
8. **(D)** All orders must be marked as to whether discretion was used.
9. **(C)** It is not the responsibility of the agent to inform the IRS.
10. **(D)** A firm may only pledge customers' securities as joint collateral if all parties agree in writing.

CHAPTER 8: MARGIN ACCOUNTS

1. **(C)** The NYSE/FINRA set the minimum maintenance for a new margin account.

2. (B) The initial minimum for a new margin account is the greater of $2,000 or 50% of the purchase price.

3. (C) The customer must sign the hypothecation agreement to pledge the securities as collateral for the margin loan.

4. (B) To find the minimum equity given a long market value, simply multiply the market value by .25. In this case, $48,000 × .25 = $14,000.

5. (A) Municipal bonds are exempt from Regulation T; the margin requirement is set by the SROs.

6. (A) To find the minimum maintenance, multiply the long market value by .25. In this case, 96,500 × .25 = $24,125.

7. (D) When buying a municipal bond in a margin account, investors must deposit the greater of 7% of par value or 15% of the market value. In this case, 15% × $54,000 = $8,100.

8. (B) The $2,000 minimum equity requirement is only for the initial deposit.

9. (A) The market value could fall to $72,000. This is found by dividing the debit balance by .75. In this case, 54,000/.75 = 72,000.

10. (C) If an investor uses the SMA to withdraw cash, the SMA is reduced and the debit balance is increased by an equal amount.

CHAPTER 9: INVESTMENT COMPANIES

1. (C) An investor in a mutual fund portfolio has an undivided interest in that portfolio and is not an investor or stockholder in the fund company itself.

2. (C) A breakpoint sale is a violation committed by a representative who is trying to earn a larger commission by not informing the investor that a breakpoint sales charge reduction is available at a slightly higher dollar level.

3. (A) The investor will redeem the shares of the growth portfolio at the NAV and will purchase the shares of the biotech portfolio at the NAV because XYZ offers conversion privileges. The investor will sell 500 shares of the growth fund at 22.30 for a total of $11,150. The investor will then purchase the shares of the biotech fund at 17.10. In this case, 11,150/17.10 = 652.

4. (C) A mutual fund's custodian maintains books and records for accumulation plans.

5. (A) A 12B-1 fee may be up to 1/4 of 1% of the NAV.

6. (D) The ex date is set by the NYSE/FINRA for a closed-end fund, just like for a stock.

7. (C) A mutual fund that calls itself a diversified fund is limited to owning no more than 10% of any one company.

8. (C) New shares will be created for the investor as soon as the mutual fund company receives the money. The investor becomes an owner of record on that day.

9. (D) Employees with access to cash and securities must be bonded.

10. (A) A fund with a portfolio turnover ratio of 25% replaces its portfolio every 4 years.

CHAPTER 10: VARIABLE ANNUITIES AND RETIREMENT PLANS

1. (D) Investors may always make a contribution to their IRA as long as they have earned income. The maximum allowable contribution is 100% of earned income up to $7,000.

2. (A) The individual would expect both the amount of the payment and the value of the annuity unit to go down. The performance of the separate account underperformed the AIR.

3. (C) This is a nonqualified plan, meaning that the money is deposited after taxes. The retiree will only pay taxes on the growth.

4. (D) The maximum amount that a couple may contribute to their IRAs at any one time is $28,000. Between January 1 and April 15, a contribution may be made for the prior year, the current year, or both: $7,000 × 2 × 2 = $28,000.

5. (C) The retirement account is qualified, which means the investor has deposited the money pre-tax. Therefore, all of the money is taxed as ordinary income when it is withdrawn.

6. (A) A 529 plan would allow the investor to make a lump sum deposit.

7. (A) The money has been deposited in a Roth IRA after taxes. It is allowed to grow tax deferred. If you are over 59-1/2 and the money has been in the IRA for at least 5 years, then it may all be withdrawn without paying taxes on the growth.

8. (B) A fixed annuity does not provide protection from inflation. If inflation rises, the holder of a fixed annuity may end up worse off due to the loss of value of the dollar.

9. (D) The maximum contribution for a SEP IRA is the lesser of 25% of income or $69,000.

CHAPTER 11: SECURITIES INDUSTRY RULES AND REGULATIONS

1. (D) The letter to a particular customer would not be considered retail communication it would be considered correspondence.
2. (B) Everything is covered. SIPC covers $500,000 per separate customer, of which up to $250,000 may be cash, so both accounts are fully covered.
3. (B) The Securities Exchange Act of 1934 regulates the activities of broker dealers and their required capital.
4. (C) The maximum fine for someone found to have acted on inside information is unlimited.
5. (D) All appeals will first be heard by the National Adjudicatory Council.
6. (C) The firm is restricted from bidding on offerings in that municipality for 2 years, because the donation was greater than $250.
7. (B) The decision of FINRA is effective in 30 days.
8. (D) A registered broker dealer is required to perform all of the items listed.
9. (A) The registered representative may sign an Acceptance Waiver and Consent (AWAC) to resolve the issue.
10. (D) All of the choices listed are considered retail communication including the firm's website.
11. (D) A call to another state is not exempt from the Do Not Call requirements.
12. (C) The Code of Procedure handles the resolution of complaints.
13. (B) A new member firm is required to file its ads as part of retail communication 10 days prior to its first use.
14. (D) All of the choices listed must appear in the tombstone ad.

Glossary of Exam Terms

A

AAA/Aaa	The highest investment-grade rating for bond issuers awarded by Standard & Poor's and Moody's ratings agencies.
acceptance waiver and consent (AWAC)	A process used when a respondent does not contest an allegation made by FINRA. The respondent accepts the findings without admitting any wrongdoing and agrees to accept any penalty for the violation.
account executive (AE)	An individual who is duly licensed to represent a broker dealer in securities transactions or investment banking business. Also known as a registered representative.
accredited investor	Any individual or institution that meets one or more of the following: (1) a net worth exceeding $1 million, excluding the primary residence, or (2) is single and has an annual income of $200,000 or more or $300,000 jointly with a spouse.
accretion	An accounting method used to step up an investor's cost base for a bond purchased at a discount.
accrued interest	The portion of a debt securities future interest payment that has been earned by the seller of the security. The purchaser must pay this amount of accrued interest to the seller at the time of the transaction's settlement. Interest accrues from the date of the last interest payment date up to, but not including, the transaction's settlement date.
accumulation stage	The period during which an annuitant is making contributions to an annuity contract.
accumulation unit	A measure used to determine the annuitant's proportional ownership interest in the insurance company's separate account during the accumulation stage. During the accumulation stage, the number of accumulation units owned by the annuitant changes and their value varies.
acid-test ratio	A measure of corporate liquidity found by subtracting inventory from current assets and dividing the result by the current liabilities.
ACT	*See* Automated Comparison Transaction (ACT) service.
ad valorem tax	A tax based on the value of the subject property.

adjusted basis	The value assigned to an asset after all deductions or additions for improvements have been taken into consideration.
adjusted gross income (AGI)	An accounting measure employed by the IRS to help determine tax liability. AGI = earned income + investment income (portfolio income) + capital gains + net passive income.
administrator	(1) An individual authorized to oversee the liquidation of an intestate decedent's estate. (2) An individual or agency that administers securities' laws within a state.
ADR/ADS	See American depositary receipt (ADR).
advance/decline line	Measures the health of the overall market by calculating advancing issues and subtracting the number of declining issues.
advance refunding	The early refinancing of municipal securities. A new issue of bonds is sold to retire the old issue at its first available call date or maturity.
advertisement	Any material that is distributed by a broker dealer or issuer for the purpose of increasing business or public awareness for the firm or issuer. The broker dealer or issuer must distribute advertisements to an audience that is not controlled. Advertisements are distributed through any of the following: newspapers/magazines, radio, TV, billboards, telephone.
affiliate	An individual who owns 10% or more of the company's voting stock. In the case of a direct participation program (DPP), this is anyone who controls the partnership or is controlled by the partnership.
agency issue	A debt security issued by any authorized entity of the U.S. government. The debt security is an obligation of the issuing entity, not an obligation of the U.S. government (with the exception of Ginnie Mae and the Federal Import Export Bank issues).
agency transaction	A transaction made by a firm for the benefit of a customer. The firm merely executes a customer's order and charges a fee for the service, which is known as a commission.
agent	A firm or an individual who executes securities transactions for customers and charges a service fee known as a commission. Also known as a broker.
aggregate indebtedness	The total amount of the firm's customer-related debts.
allied member	An owner-director or 5% owner of an NYSE member firm. Allied members may not trade on the floor.
all-or-none (AON) order	A non-time-sensitive order that stipulates that the customer wants to buy or sell all of the securities in the order.
all-or-none underwriting	A type of underwriting that states that the issuer wants to sell all of the securities being offered or none of the securities being offered. The proceeds from the issue will be held in escrow until all securities are sold.
alpha	A measure of the projected change in the security's price as a result of fundamental factors relating only to that company.
alternative minimum tax (AMT)	A method used to calculate the tax liability for some high-income earners that adds back the deductions taken for certain tax preference items.

Glossary of Exam Terms

AMBAC Indemnity Corporation	Insures the interest and principal payments for municipal bonds.
American depositary receipt (ADR)/American depositary security (ADS)	A receipt representing the beneficial ownership of foreign securities being held in trust overseas by a foreign branch of a U.S. bank. ADRs/ADSs facilitate the trading and ownership of foreign securities and trade in the United States on an exchange or in the over-the-counter markets.
American Stock Exchange (AMEX)	An exchange located in New York using the dual-auction method and specialist system to facilitate trading in stocks, options, exchange-traded funds, and portfolios. AMEX was acquired by the NYSE Euronext and is now part of NYSE Alternext.
amortization	An accounting method that reduces the value of an asset over its projected useful life. Also the way that loan principal is systematically paid off over the life of a loan.
annual compliance review	All firms must hold at least one compliance meeting per year with all of its agents.
annuitant	An individual who receives scheduled payments from an annuity contract.
annuitize	A process by which an individual converts from the accumulation stage to the payout stage of an annuity contract. This is accomplished by exchanging accumulation units for annuity units. Once a payout option is selected, it cannot be changed.
annuity	A contract between an individual and an insurance company that is designed to provide the annuitant with lifetime income in exchange for either a lump sum or periodic deposits into the contract.
annuity unit	An accounting measure used to determine an individual's proportionate ownership of the separate account during the payout stage of the contract. The number of annuity units owned by an individual remains constant, and their value, which may vary, is used to determine the amount of the individual's annuity payment.
appreciation	An asset's increase in value over time.
arbitrage	An investment strategy used to profit from market inefficiencies.
arbitration	A forum provided by both the NYSE and FINRA to resolve disputes between two parties. Only a public customer may not be forced to settle a dispute through arbitration. The public customer must agree to arbitration in writing. All industry participants must settle disputes through arbitration.
ask	See offer.
assessed value	A base value assigned to property for the purpose of determining tax liability.
assessment	An additional amount of taxes due as a result of a municipal project that the homeowner benefits from. Also an additional call for capital by a direct participation program.
asset	Anything of value owned by an individual or a corporation.
asset allocation fund	A mutual fund that spreads its investments among different asset classes (i.e., stocks, bonds, and other investments) based on a predetermined formula.
assignee	A person to whom the ownership of an asset is being transferred.

assignment	(1) The transfer of ownership or rights through a signature. (2) The notification given to investors who are short an option that the option holder has exercised its right and they must now meet their obligations as detailed in the option contract.
associated person	Any individual under the control of a broker dealer, issuer, or bank, including employees, officers, and directors, as well as those individuals who control or have common control of a broker dealer, issuer, or bank.
assumed interest rate (AIR)	(1) A benchmark used to determine the minimum rate of return that must be realized by a variable annuity's separate account during the payout phase in order to keep the annuitant's payments consistent. (2) In the case of a variable life insurance policy, the minimum rate of return that must be achieved in order to maintain the policy's variable death benefit.
at-the-close order	An order that stipulates that the security is to be bought or sold only at the close of the market, or as close to the close as is reasonable, or not at all.
at the money	A term used to describe an option when the underlying security price is equal to the exercise price of the option.
at-the-opening order	An order that stipulates that the security is to be bought or sold only at the opening of the market, or as close to the opening as is reasonable, or not at all.
auction market	The method of trading employed by stock exchanges that allows buyers and sellers to compete with one another in a centralized location.
authorized stock	The maximum number of shares that a corporation can sell in an effort to raise capital. The number of authorized shares may only be changed by a vote of the shareholders.
Automated Comparison Transaction (ACT) service	ACT is the service that clears and locks Nasdaq trades.
average cost	A method used to determine the cost of an investment for an investor who has made multiple purchases of the same security at different times and prices. An investor's average cost may be used to determine a cost base for tax purposes or to evaluate the profitability of an investment program, such as dollar-cost averaging. Average cost is determined by dividing the total dollars invested by the number of shares purchased.
average price	A method used to determine the average price paid by an investor for a security that has been purchased at different times and prices, such as through dollar-cost averaging. An investor's average price is determined by dividing the total of the purchase prices by the number of purchases.

B

BBB/Baa	The lowest ratings assigned by Standard & Poor's and Moody's for debt in the investment-grade category.
back-end load	A mutual fund sales charge that is assessed upon the redemption of the shares. The amount of the sales charge to be assessed upon redemption decreases the longer the shares are held. Also known as a contingent deferred sales charge.

backing away	The failure of an over-the-counter market maker to honor firm quotes. It is a violation of FINRA rules.
balanced fund	A mutual fund whose investment policy requires that the portfolio's holdings are diversified among asset classes and invested in common and preferred stock, bonds, and other debt instruments. The exact asset distribution among the asset classes will be predetermined by a set formula that is designed to balance out the investment return of the fund.
balance of payments	The net balance of all international transactions for a country in a given time.
balance of trade	The net flow of goods into or out of a country for a given period. Net exports result in a surplus or credit; net exports result in a deficit or net debit.
balance sheet	A corporate report that shows a company's financial condition at the time the balance sheet was created.
balance sheet equation	Assets = liabilities + shareholders equity.
balloon maturity	A bond maturity schedule that requires the largest portion of the principal to be repaid on the last maturity date.
bankers' acceptance (BA)	A letter of credit that facilitates foreign trade. BAs are traded in the money market and have a maximum maturity of 270 days.
basis	The cost that is assigned to an asset.
basis book	A table used to calculate bond prices for bonds quoted on a yield basis and to calculate yields for bonds quoted on a price basis.
basis point	Measures a bond's yield; 1 basis point is equal to 1/100 of 1%.
basis quote	A bond quote based on the bond's yield.
bearer bond	A bond that is issued without the owner's name being registered on the bond certificate or the books of the issuer. Whoever has possession of (bears) the certificate is deemed to be the rightful owner.
bearish	An investor's belief that prices will decline.
bear market	A market condition that is characterized by continuing falling prices and a series of lower lows in overall prices.
best efforts underwriting	A type of underwriting that does not guarantee the issuer that any of its securities will be sold.
beta	A measure of a security's or portfolio's volatility relative to the market as a whole. A security or portfolio whose beta is greater than 1 will experience a greater change in price than overall market prices. A security or portfolio with a beta of less than 1 will experience a price change that is less than the price changes realized by the market as a whole.
bid	A price that an investor or broker dealer is willing to pay for a security. It is also a price at which an investor may sell a security immediately and the price at which a market maker will buy a security.
blind pool	A type of direct participation program where less than 75% of the assets to be acquired have been identified.
block trade	A trade involving 10,000 shares or market value of over $200,000.

blotter	A daily record of broker dealer transactions.
blue chip stock	Stock of a company whose earnings and dividends are stable regardless of the economy.
blue sky	A term used to describe the state registration process for a security offering.
blue-sky laws	Term used to describe the state-based laws enacted under the Uniform Securities Act.
board broker	*See* order book official.
board of directors	A group of directors elected by the stockholders of a corporation to appoint and oversee corporate management.
Board of Governors	The governing body of FINRA. The board is made up of 27 members elected by FINRA's membership and the board itself.
bona fide quote	*See* firm quote.
bond	The legal obligation of a corporation or government to repay the principal amount of debt along with interest at a predetermined schedule.
bond anticipation note	Short-term municipal financing sold in anticipation of long-term financing.
bond buyer indexes	A group of yield-based municipal bond indexes published daily in the *Daily Bond Buyer*.
bond counsel	An attorney for the issuer of municipal securities who renders the legal opinion.
bond fund	A fund whose portfolio is made up of debt instruments issued by corporations, governments, and/or their agencies. The fund's investment objective is usually current income.
bond interest coverage ratio	A measure of the issuer's liquidity. It demonstrates how many times the issuer's earnings will cover its bond interest expense.
bond quotes	Corporate and government bond quotes are based on a percentage of par. Municipal bonds are usually quoted on a yield-to-maturity basis.
bond rating	A rating that assesses the financial soundness of issuers and their ability to make interest and principal payments in a timely manner. Standard & Poor's and Moody's are the two largest ratings agencies. Issuers must request and pay for the service to rate their bonds.
bond ratio	A measure used to determine how much of the corporation's capitalization was obtained through the issuance of bonds.
bond swap	The sale and purchase of two different bonds to allow the investor to claim a loss on the bond being sold without violating wash sale rules.
book entry	Securities that are issued in book entry form do not offer any physical certificates as evidence of ownership. The owner's name is registered on the books of the issuer, and the only evidence of ownership is the trade confirmation.
book value	A corporation's book value is the theoretical liquidation value of the company. Book value is in theory what someone would be willing to pay for the entire company.
book value per bond	A measure used to determine the amount of the corporation's tangible value for each bond issued.

book value per share	Used to determine the tangible value of each common share. It is found by subtracting intangible assets and the par value of preferred stock from the corporation's total net worth and dividing that figure by the number of common shares outstanding.
branch office	A branch office of a member firm is required to display the name of the member firm and is any office in which the member conducts securities business outside of its main office.
breadth	A measure of the broad market's health. It measures how many stocks are increasing and how many are declining.
breakdown	A technical term used to describe the price action of a security when it falls below support to a lower level and into a new trading range.
breakeven point	The point at which the value of a security or portfolio is exactly equal to the investor's cost for that security or portfolio.
breakout	A technical term used to describe the price action of a security when it increases past resistance to a higher level and into a new trading range.
breakpoint sale	The practice of selling mutual fund shares in dollar amounts that are just below the point where an investor would be entitled to a sales charge reduction. A breakpoint sale is designed for the purpose of trying to earn a larger commission. This is a violation of the Rules of Fair Practice and should never be done.
breakpoint schedule	A breakpoint schedule offers mutual fund investors reduced sales charges for larger dollar investments.
broad-based index	An index that represents a large cross-section of the market as a whole. The price movement of the index reflects the price movement of a large portion of the market, such as the S&P 500 or the Wilshire 5000.
broker	*See* agent.
broker dealer	A person or firm who buys and sells securities for its own account and for the accounts of others. When acting as a broker or agent for a customer, the broker dealer is merely executing the customer's orders and charging the customer a fee known as a commission. When acting as a dealer or principal, the broker dealer is trading for its own account and participating in the customer's transaction by taking the other side of the trade and charging the customer a markup or markdown. A firm also is acting as a principal or dealer when it is trading for its own account and making markets in OTC securities.
broker's broker	(1) A municipal bond dealer who specializes in executing orders for other dealers who are not active in the municipal bond market. (2) A specialist on the exchange executing orders for other members or an OTC market.
bullish	An investor who believes that the price of a security or prices as a whole will rise is said to be bullish.
bull market	A market condition that is characterized by rising prices and a series of higher highs.
business cycle	The normal economic pattern that is characterized by four stages: expansion, peak, contraction, and trough. The business cycle constantly repeats itself and the economy is always in flux.
business day	The business day in the securities industry is defined as the time when the financial markets are open for trading.

buyer's option	A settlement option that allows the buyer to determine when the transaction will settle.
buy in	An order executed in the event of a customer's or firm's failure to deliver the securities it sold. The buyer repurchases the securities in the open market and charges the seller for any loss.
buying power	The amount of money available to buy securities.
buy stop order	A buy stop order is used to protect against a loss or to protect a profit on a short sale of stock.

C

call	(1) A type of option that gives the holder the right to purchase a specified amount of the underlying security at a stated price for a specified period of time. (2) The act of exercising a call option.
callable bond	A bond that may be called in or retired by the issuer prior to its maturity date.
callable preferred	A preferred share issued with a feature allowing the issuing corporation to retire it under certain conditions.
call date	A specific date after which the securities in question become callable by the issuer.
call feature	A condition attached to some bonds and preferred stocks that allows the issuer to call in or redeem the securities prior to their maturity date and according to certain conditions.
call price	The price that will be paid by the issuer to retire the callable securities in question. The call price is usually set at a price above the par value of the bond or preferred stock, which is the subject of the call.
call protection	A period of time, usually right after the securities' issuance, when the securities may not be called by the issuer. Call protection usually ranges from 5 to 10 years.
call provision	*See* call feature.
call risk	The risk borne by the owner of callable securities that may require that the investor accept a lower rate of return once the securities have been called. Callable bonds and preferred stock are more likely to be called when interest rates are low or are falling.
call spread	An option position consisting of one long and one short call on the same underlying security with different strike prices, expirations, or both.
call writer	An investor who has sold a call.
capital	Money and assets available to use in an attempt to earn more money or to accumulate more assets.
capital appreciation	An increase in an asset's value over time.
capital assets	Tangible assets, including securities, real estate, equipment, and other assets, owned for the long term.
capital gain	A profit realized on the sale of an asset at a price that exceeds its cost.

capitalization	The composition of a company's financial structure. It is the sum of paid-in capital + paid-in surplus + long-term debt + retained earnings.
capital loss	A loss realized on the sale of an asset at a price that is lower than its cost.
capital market	The securities markets that deal in equity and debt securities with more than 1 year to maturity.
capital risk	The risk that the value of an asset will decline and cause an investor to lose all or part of the invested capital.
capital stock	The sum of the par value of all of a corporation's outstanding common and preferred stock.
capital structure	*See* capitalization.
capital surplus	The amount of money received by an issuer in excess of the par value of the stock at the time of its initial sale to the public.
capped index option	An index option that trades like a spread and is automatically exercised if it goes 30 points in the money.
capping	A manipulative practice of selling stock to depress the price.
carried interest	A sharing arrangement for an oil and gas direct participation program where the general partner shares in the tangible drilling costs with the limited partners.
cash account	An account in which the investor must deposit the full purchase price of the securities by the fourth business day after the trade date. The investor is not required by industry regulations to sign anything to open a cash account.
cash assets ratio	The most liquid measure of a company's solvency. The cash asset ratio is found by dividing cash and equivalents by current liabilities.
cash dividend	The distribution of corporate profits to shareholders of record. Cash dividends must be declared by the company's board of directors.
cash equivalent	Short-term liquid securities that can quickly be converted into cash. Money market instruments and funds are the most common examples.
cash flow	A company's cash flow equals net income plus depreciation.
cashiering department	The department in a brokerage firm that is responsible for the receipt and delivery of cash and securities.
cash management bill	Short-term federal financing issued in minimum denominations of $10 million.
cash settlement	A transaction that settles for cash requires the delivery of the securities from the seller as well as the delivery of cash from the buyer on the same day of the trade. A trade done for cash settles the same day.
catastrophe call	The redemption of a bond by an issuer due to the destruction of the facility that was financed by the issue. Issuers will carry insurance to cover such events and to pay off the bondholders.
certificate of deposit (CD)	An unsecured promissory note issued as evidence of ownership of a time deposit that has been guaranteed by the issuing bank.
certificates of accrual on Treasury securities	Zero-coupon bonds issued by brokerage firms and collateralized by Treasury securities.
change	The difference between the current price and the previous day's closing price.

Chicago Board of Trade (CBOT)	A commodity exchange that provides a marketplace for agricultural and financial futures.
Chicago Board Options Exchange (CBOE)	The premier option exchange in the United States for listed options.
Chinese wall	The physical separation that is required between investment banking and trading and retail divisions of a brokerage firm. Now known as a firewall.
churning	Executing transactions that are excessive in their frequency or size in light of the resources of the account for the purpose of generating commissions. Churning is a violation of the Rules of Fair Practice.
class A share	A mutual fund share that charges a front-end load.
class B share	A mutual fund share that charges a back-end load.
class C share	A mutual fund share that charges a level load.
class D share	A mutual fund share that charges a level load and a back-end load.
classical economics	A theory stating that the economy will do the best when the government does not interfere.
clearing firm	A firm that carries its customers' cash and securities and/or provides the service to customers of other firms.
clearinghouse	An agency that guarantees and settles futures and option transactions.
close	The last price at which a security traded for the day.
closed-end indenture	A bond indenture that will not allow additional bonds to be issued with the same claim on the issuer's assets.
closed-end investment company	A management company that issues a fixed number of shares to investors in a managed portfolio and whose shares are traded in the secondary market.
closing date	The date when sales of interest in a direct participation plan will cease.
closing purchase	An order executed to close out a short option position.
Code of Arbitration Procedure	The FINRA bylaw that provides for a forum for dispute resolution relating to industry matters. All industry participants must arbitrate in public and the customer must agree to arbitration in writing.
Code of Procedure	The FINRA bylaw that sets guidelines for the investigation of trade practice complaints and alleged rule violations.
coincident indicator	An economic indicator that moves simultaneously with the movement of the underlying economy.
collateral	Assets pledged to a lender. If the borrower defaults, the lender will take possession of the collateral.
collateral trust certificate	A bond backed by the pledge of securities the issuer owns in another entity.
collateralized mortgage obligation (CMO)	A corporate debt security that is secured by an underlying pool of mortgages.

collection ratio	A measure of a municipality's ability to collect the taxes it has assessed.
collect on delivery (COD)	A method of trade settlement that requires the physical delivery of the securities to receive payment.
combination	An option position with a call and put on the same underlying security with different strike prices and expiration months on both.
combination fund	A mutual fund that tries to achieve growth and current income by combining portfolios of common stock with portfolios of high-yielding equities.
combination preferred stock	A preferred share with multiple features, such as cumulative and participating.
combination privileges	A feature offered by a mutual fund family that allows an investor to combine two simultaneous purchases of different portfolios in order to receive a reduced sales charge on the total amount invested.
combined account	A margin account that contains both long and short positions.
commercial paper	Short-term unsecured promissory notes issued by large financially stable corporations to obtain short-term financing. Commercial paper does not pay interest and is issued at a discount from its face value. All commercial paper matures in 270 days or less and matures at its face value.
commingling	A FINRA violation resulting from the mixing of customer and firm assets in the same account.
commission	A fee charged by a broker or agent for executing a securities transaction.
commission house broker	A floor broker who executes orders for the firm's account and for the accounts of the firm's customers on an exchange.
common stock	A security that represents the ownership of a corporation. Common stockholders vote to elect the board of directors and to institute major corporate policies.
common stock ratio	A measure of how much of a company's capitalization was obtained through the sale of common stock. The ratio is found by summing the par value of the common stock, excess paid in capital, and retained earnings, and then dividing that number by the total capitalization.
competitive bid underwriting	A method of underwriter selection that solicits bids from multiple underwriters. The underwriter submitting the best terms will be awarded the issue.
compliance department	The department of a broker dealer that ensures that the firm adheres to industry rules and regulations.
concession	The amount of an underwriting discount that is allocated to a syndicate member or a selling group member for selling new securities.
conduct rules	The Rules of Fair Practice.
conduit theory	The IRS classification that allows a regulated investment company to avoid paying taxes on investment income it distributes to its shareholders.
confirmation	The receipt for a securities transaction that must be sent to all customers either on or before the completion of a transaction. The confirmation must show the trade date, settlement date, and total amount due to or from the customer. A transaction is considered to be complete on settlement date.

consolidated tape	The consolidated tape A displays transactions for NYSE securities that take place on the NYSE, all regional exchanges, and the third markets. The consolidated tape B reports transactions for AMEX stocks that take place on the American Stock Exchange, all regional exchanges, and in the third market.
consolidation	A chart pattern that results from a narrowing of a security's trading range.
constant dollar plan	An investment plan designed to keep a specific amount of money invested in the market regardless of the market's condition. An investor will sell when the value of the account rises and buy when the value of the account falls.
constant ratio plan	An investment plan designed to keep the investor's portfolio invested at a constant ratio of equity and debt securities.
construction loan note	A short-term municipal note designed to provide financing for construction projects.
constructive receipt	The time when the IRS determines that the taxpayer has effectively received payment.
consumer price index (CPI)	A price-based index made up of a basket of goods and services that are used by consumers in their daily lives. An increase in the CPI indicates a rise in overall prices, while a decline in the index represents a fall in overall prices.
consumption	A term used to describe the purchase of newly produced household goods.
contemporaneous trader	A trader who enters an order on the other side of the market at the same time as a trader with inside information enters an order. Contemporaneous traders can sue traders who act on inside information to recover losses.
contingent deferred sales charge	See back-end load.
contraction	A period of declining economic output. Also known as a recession.
contractual plan	A mutual fund accumulation plan under which the investor agrees to contribute a fixed sum of money over time. If the investor does not complete or terminates the contract early, the investor may be subject to penalties.
control	The ability to influence the actions of an organization or individual.
control person	A director or officer of an issuer or broker dealer or a 10% stockholder of a corporation.
control stock	Stock that is acquired or owned by an officer, director, or person owning 10% or more of the outstanding stock of a company.
conversion price	The set price at which a convertible security may be exchanged for another security.
conversion privilege	The right offered to a mutual fund investor that allows the investor to move money between different portfolios offered by the same mutual fund family without paying another sales charge.
conversion ratio	The number of shares that can be received by the holder of a convertible security if it were converted into the underlying common stock.
convertible bond	A bond that may be converted or exchanged for common shares of the corporation at a predetermined price.
convertible preferred stock	A preferred stock that may be converted or exchanged for common shares of the corporation at a predetermined price.

cooling-off period	The period of time between the filing of a registration statement and its effective date. During this time, the SEC is reviewing the registration statement and no sales may take place. The cooling-off period is at least 20 days.
coordination	A method of securities registration during which a new issue is registered simultaneously at both the federal and state levels.
corporate account	An investment account for the benefit of a company that requires a corporate resolution listing the names of individuals who may transact business in the company's name.
corporate bond	A legally binding obligation of a corporation to repay a principal amount of debt along with interest at a predetermined rate and schedule.
corporation	A perpetual entity that survives after the death of its officers, directors, and stockholders. It is the most common form of business entity.
correspondent broker dealer	A broker dealer who introduces customer accounts to a clearing broker dealer.
cost basis	The cost of an asset, including any acquisition costs. It is used to determine capital gains and losses.
cost depletion	A method used to determine the tax deductions for investors in oil and gas programs.
cost of carry	All costs incurred by an investor for maintaining a position in a security, including margin interest and opportunity costs.
coterminous	Municipalities that share the same borders and have overlapping debt.
coupon bond	*See* bearer bond.
coupon yield	*See* nominal yield.
covenant	A promise made by an issuer of debt that describes the issuer's obligations and the bondholders' rights.
covered call	The sale of a call against a long position in the underlying security.
covered put	The sale of a put against a short position in the underlying security or against cash that will allow the person to purchase the security if the put is exercised.
CPI	*See* consumer price index (CPI).
credit agreement	The portion of the margin agreement that describes the terms and conditions under which credit will be extended to the customer.
credit balance	The cash balance in a customer's account.
credit department	*See* margin department.
credit risk	The risk that the issuer of debt securities will default on its obligation to pay interest or principal on a timely basis.
credit spread	An option position that results in a net premium or credit received by the investor from the simultaneous purchase and sale of two calls or two puts on the same security.
crossed market	A market condition that results when a broker enters a bid for a stock that exceeds the offering price for that stock. Also a condition that may result when a broker enters an offer that is lower than the bid price for that stock.

crossing stock	The pairing off of two offsetting customer orders by the same floor broker. The floor broker executing the cross must first show the order to the crowd for possible price improvement before crossing the orders.
crossover point	The point at which all tax credits have been used up by a limited partnership; results in a tax liability for the partners.
cum rights	A stock that is the subject of a rights offering and is trading with the rights attached to the common stock.
cumulative preferred stock	A preferred stock that entitles the holder to receive unpaid dividends prior to the payment of any dividends to common stockholders. Dividends that accumulate in arrears on cumulative issues are always the first dividends to be paid by a corporation.
cumulative voting	A method of voting that allows stockholders to cast all of their votes for one director or to distribute them among the candidates they wish to vote for. Cumulative voting favors smaller investors by allowing them to have a larger say in the election of the board of directors.
current assets	Cash, securities, accounts receivable, and other assets that can be converted into cash within 12 months.
current liabilities	Corporate obligations, including accounts payable, that must be paid within 12 months.
current market value (CMV)/current market price (CMP)	The present value of a marketable security or of a portfolio of marketable securities.
current ratio	A measure of a corporation's short-term liquidity found by dividing its current assets by its current liabilities.
current yield	A relationship between a securities annual income relative to its current market price. Determined by dividing annual income by the current market price.
CUSIP (Committee on Uniform Securities Identification Procedures)	A committee that assigns identification numbers to securities to help identify them.
custodial account	An account operated by a custodian for the benefit of a minor.
custodian	A party responsible for managing an account for another party. In acting as a custodian, the individual or corporation must adhere to the prudent man rule and only take such actions as a prudent person would do for him- or herself.
customer	Any individual or entity that maintains an account with a broker dealer.
customer agreement	An agreement signed by a customer at the time the account is opened, detailing the conditions of the customer's relationship with the firm. The customer agreement usually contains a predispute arbitration clause.
customer ledger	A ledger that lists all customer cash and margin accounts.
customer protection rule	Rule 15C3-3 requires that customer assets be kept segregated from the firm assets.
cyclical industry	An industry whose prospects fluctuate with the business cycle.

D

Daily Bond Buyer	A daily publication for the municipal securities industry that publishes information related to the municipal bond market and official notices of sales.
dated date	The day when interest starts to accrue for bonds.
dealer	(1) A person or firm who transacts securities business for its own account. (2) A brokerage firm acting as a principal when executing a customer's transaction or making markets over the counter.
dealer paper	Commercial paper sold to the public by a dealer, rather than placed with investors directly by the issuer.
debenture	An unsecured promissory note issued by a corporation backed only by the issuer's credit and promise to pay.
debit balance	The amount of money a customer owes a broker dealer.
debit spread	An option position that results in a net premium paid by the investor from the simultaneous purchase and sale of two calls or two puts on the same security.
debt securities	A security that represents a loan to the issuer. The owner of a debt security is a creditor of the issuing entity, be it a corporation or a government.
debt service	The scheduled interest payments and repayment of principal for debt securities.
debt service account	An account set up by a municipal issuer to pay the debt service of municipal revenue bonds.
debt service ratio	Indicates the issuer's ability to pay its interest and principal payments.
debt-to-equity ratio	A ratio that shows how highly leveraged the company is. It is found by dividing total long-term debt by total shareholder equity.
declaration date	The day chosen by the board of directors of a corporation to pay a dividend to shareholders.
deduction	An adjustment taken from gross income to reduce tax liability.
default	The failure of an issuer of debt securities to make interest and principal payments when they are due.
default risk	*See* credit risk.
defeasance	Results in the elimination of the issuer's debt obligations by issuing a new debt instrument to pay off the outstanding issue. The old issue is removed from the issuer's balance sheet and the proceeds of the new issue are placed in an escrow account to pay off the now-defeased issue.
defensive industry	A term used to describe a business whose economic prospects are independent from the business cycle. Pharmaceutical companies, utilities, and food producers are examples of defensive industries.
deferred annuity	A contract between an individual and an insurance company that delays payments to the annuitant until some future date.

deferred compensation plan	A contractual agreement between an employer and an employee under which the employee elects to defer receiving money owed until after retirement. Deferred compensation plans are typically unfunded, and the employee could lose all the money due under the agreement if the company goes out of business.
deficiency letter	A letter sent to a corporate issuer by the SEC, requesting additional information regarding the issuer's registration statement.
defined benefit plan	A qualified retirement plan established to provide a specific amount of retirement income for the plan participants. Unlike a defined contribution plan, the individual's retirement benefits are known prior to reaching retirement.
defined contribution plan	A qualified retirement plan that details the amount of money that the employer will contribute to the plan for the benefit of the employee. This amount is usually expressed as a percentage of the employee's gross annual income. The actual retirement benefits are not known until the employee reaches retirement, and the amount of the retirement benefit is a result of the contributions to the plan, along with the investment experience of the plan.
deflation	The economic condition that is characterized by a persistent decline in overall prices.
delivery	As used in the settlement process, results in the change of ownership of cash or securities.
delivery vs. payment	A type of settlement option that requires that the securities be physically received at the time payment is made.
delta	A measure of an option's price change in relation to a price change in the underlying security.
demand deposit	A deposit that a customer has with a bank or other financial institution that will allow the customer to withdraw the money at any time or on demand.
Department of Enforcement	The FINRA committee that has original jurisdiction over complaints and violations.
depletion	A tax deduction taken for the reduction in the amount of natural resources (e.g., gas, gold, oil) available to a business or partnership.
depreciation	A tax deduction taken for the reduction of value in a capital asset.
depreciation expense	A noncash expense that results in a reduction in taxable income.
depression	An economic condition that is characterized by a protracted decline in economic output and a rising level of unemployment.
derivative	A security that derives its value in whole or in part based on the price of another security. Options and futures are examples of derivative securities.
designated order	An order entered by an institution for a new issue of municipal bonds that states what firm and what agent is going to get the sales credit for the order.
devaluation	A significant fall in the value of a country's currency relative to other currencies. Devaluation could be the result of poor economic prospects in the home country. In extreme circumstances, it can be the result of government intervention.
developmental drilling program	An oil or gas program that drills for wells in areas of proven reserves.

developmental fee	A fee paid to organizers of a direct participation plan for the development of plans, obtaining financing or zoning authorizations, and other services.
diagonal spread	A spread that is created through the simultaneous purchase and sale of two calls or two puts on the same underlying security that differ in both strike price and expiration months.
dilution	A reduction in a stockholder's proportional ownership of a corporation as a result of the issuance of more shares. Earnings per share may also be diluted as a result of the issuance of additional shares.
direct debt	The total amount of a municipality's debt that has been issued by the municipality for its own benefit and for which the municipality is responsible to repay.
direct paper	Commercial paper sold to investors directly from the issuer without the use of a dealer.
direct participation program (DPP)	An entity that allows all taxable events to be passed through to investors, including limited partnerships and subchapter S corporations.
discount	The amount by which the price of a security is lower than its par value.
discount bond	A bond that is selling for a price that is lower than its par value.
discount rate	The rate that is charged to Federal Reserve member banks on loans directly from the Federal Reserve. This rate is largely symbolic, and member banks only borrow directly from the Federal Reserve as a last resort.
discretion	Authorization given to a firm or a representative to determine which securities are to be purchased and sold for the benefit of the customer without the customer's prior knowledge or approval.
discretionary account	An account where the owner has given the firm or the representative authority to transact business without the customer's prior knowledge or approval. All discretionary accounts must be approved and monitored closely by a principal of the firm.
disintermediation	The flow of money from traditional bank accounts to alternative higher yielding investments. This is more likely to occur as the Federal Reserve tightens monetary policy and interest rates rise.
disposable income	The sum of money an individual has left after paying taxes and required expenditures.
disproportional allocation	A method used by FINRA to determine if a free-riding violation has occurred with respect to a hot issuer. A firm is only allowed to sell up to 10% of a new issue to conditionally approved purchasers.
disproportionate sharing	An oil and gas sharing arrangement where the general partner pays a portion of the cost but receives a larger portion of the program's revenues.
distribution	Cash or property sent to shareholders or partners.
distribution stage	The period of time during which an annuitant is receiving payments from an annuity contract.
diversification	The distribution of investment capital among different investment choices. By purchasing several different investments, investors may be able to reduce their overall risk by minimizing the impact of any one security's adverse performance.

diversified fund/diversified management company	A mutual fund that distributes its investment capital among a wide variety of investments. In order for a mutual fund to market itself as a diversified mutual fund it must meet the 75-5-10 rule: 75% of the fund's assets must be invested in securities issued by other entities, no more than 5% of the fund's assets may be invested in any one issuer, and the fund may own no more than 10% of any one company's outstanding securities.
dividend	A distribution of corporate assets to shareholders. A dividend may be paid in cash, stock, or property or product.
dividend department	The department in a brokerage firm that is responsible for the collecting of dividends and crediting them to customer accounts.
dividend disbursement agent	An agent of the issuer who pays out the dividends to shareholders of record.
dividend payout ratio	The amount of a company's earnings that were paid out to shareholders relative to the total earnings that were available to be paid out to shareholders. It can be calculated by dividing dividends per share by earnings per share.
dividend yield	Also known as a stock's current yield. It is a relationship between the annual dividends paid to shareholders relative to the stock's current market price. To determine a stock's dividend yield, divide annual dividends by the current market price.
DJIA	See Dow Jones Industrial Average.
doctrine of mutual reciprocity	An agreement that the federal government would not tax interest income received by investors in municipal bonds and that reciprocally the states would not tax interest income received by investors in federal debt obligations.
dollar bonds	A term issue of municipal bonds that are quoted as a percentage of par rather than on a yield basis.
dollar-cost averaging	A strategy of investing a fixed sum of money on a regular basis into a fluctuating market price. Over time an investor should be able to achieve an average cost per share that is below the average price per share. Dollar-cost averaging is a popular investment strategy with mutual fund investors.
donor	A person who gives a gift of cash or securities to another person. Once the gift has been made, the donor no longer has any rights or claim to the security. All gifts to a minor are irrevocable.
do not reduce (DNR)	An order qualifier for an order placed under the market that stipulates that the price of the order is not to be reduced for the distribution of ordinary dividends.
don't know (DK)	A term used to describe a dealer's response to a confirmation for a trade they "don't know" doing.
Dow Jones Composite Average	A price weighted index composed of 65 stocks that is used as an indicator of market performance.
Dow Jones Industrial Average (DJIA)	A price weighted index composed of 30 industrial companies. The Dow Jones is the most widely quoted market index.
Dow Jones Transportation Average	A price weighted index composed of 20 transportation stocks.

Dow Jones Utility Average	An index composed of 15 utility stocks.
Dow theory	A theory that believes that the health of the market and the economy may be predicted by the performance of the Dow Jones Industrial Average.
dry hole	A term used to describe a nonproducing well.
dual-purpose fund	A mutual fund that offers two classes of shares to investors. One class is sold to investors seeking income and the other class is sold to investors seeking capital appreciation.

E

early withdrawal penalty	A penalty tax charged to an investor for withdrawing money from a qualified retirement plan prior to age 59-1/2, usually 10% on top of ordinary income taxes.
earned income	Money received by an individual in return for performing services.
earnings per share	The net amount of a corporation's earnings available to common shareholders divided by the number of common shares outstanding.
earnings per share fully diluted	The net amount of a corporation's earnings available to common shareholders after taking into consideration the potential conversion of all convertible securities.
eastern account	A type of syndicate account that requires all members to be responsible for their own allocation as well as for their proportional share of any member's unsold securities.
economic risk	The risk of loss of principal associated with the purchase of securities.
EE savings bonds	Nonmarketable U.S. government zero-coupon bonds that must be purchased from the government and redeemed to the government.
effective date	The day when a new issue's registration with the SEC becomes effective. Once the issue's registration statement has become effective, the securities may then be sold to investors.
efficient market theory	A theory that states that the market operates and processes information efficiently and prices in all information as soon as it becomes known.
Employee Retirement Income Security Act of 1974 (ERISA)	The legislation that governs the operation of private-sector pension plans. Corporate pension plans organized under ERISA guidelines qualify for beneficial tax treatment by the IRS.
endorsement	The signature on the back of a security that allows its ownership to be transferred.
EPS	*See* earnings per share.
equipment leasing limited partnership	A limited partnership that is organized to purchase equipment and lease it to corporations to earn lease income and to shelter passive income for investors.
equipment trust certificate	A bond backed by a pledge of large equipment, such as airplanes, railroad cars, and ships.

equity	A security that represents the ownership in a corporation. Both preferred and common equity holders have an ownership interest in the corporation.
equity financing	The sale of common or preferred equity by a corporation in an effort to raise capital.
equity option	An option to purchase or sell common stock.
ERISA	See Employee Retirement Income Security Act of 1974.
erroneous report	A report of an execution given in error to a client. The report is not binding on the firm or on the agent.
escrow agreement	Evidence of ownership of a security provided to a broker dealer as proof of ownership of the underlying security for covered call writers.
Eurobond	A bond issued in domestic currency of the issuer but sold outside of the issuer's country.
Eurodollar	A deposit held outside of the United States denominated in U.S. dollars.
Eurodollar bonds	A bond issued by a foreign issuer denominated in U.S. dollars.
Euroyen bonds	Bonds issued outside of Japan but denominated in yen.
excess equity (EE)	The value of an account's equity in excess of Regulation T.
exchange	A market, whether physical or electronic, that provides a forum for trading securities through a dual-auction process.
exchange distribution	A distribution of a large block of stock on the floor of the exchange that is crossed with offsetting orders.
exchange privilege	The right offered by many mutual funds that allows an investor to transfer or move money between different portfolios offered through the same fund company. An investor may redeem shares of the fund, which is being sold at the NAV, and purchase shares of the new portfolio at the NAV without paying another sales charge.
ex date/ex-dividend date	The first day when purchasers of a security will no longer be entitled to receive a previously declared dividend.
executor/executrix	An individual with the authority to manage the affairs of a decedent's estate.
exempt security	A security that is exempt from the registration requirements of the Securities Act of 1933.
exempt transaction	A transaction that is not subject to state registration.
exercise	An investor's election to take advantage of the rights offered through the terms of an option, a right, or a warrant.
exercise price	The price at which an option investor may purchase or sell a security. Also the price at which an investor may purchase a security through a warrant or right.
existing property program	A type of real estate direct participation program that purchases existing property for the established rental income.
expansion	A period marked by a general increase in business activity and an increase in gross domestic product.
expansionary policy	A monetary policy enacted through the Federal Reserve Board that in-creases money supply and reduces interest rates in an effort to stimulate the economy.

expense ratio	The amount of a mutual fund's expenses relative to its assets. The higher the expense ratio, the lower the investor's return. A mutual fund's expense ratio tells an investor how efficiently a mutual fund operates, not how profitable the mutual fund is.
expiration cycle	A 4-month cycle for option expiration: January, April, July, and October; February, May, August, and November; or March, June, September, and December.
expiration date	The date on which an option ceases to exist.
exploratory drilling program	A direct participation program that engages in the drilling for oil or gas in new areas seeking to find new wells.
exploratory well	Also known as wildcatting. The drilling for oil or gas in new areas in an effort to find new wells.
ex rights	The common stock subject to a rights offering trade without the rights attached.
ex rights date	The first day when the common stock is subject to a rights offering trade without the rights attached.
ex warrants	Common trading without the warrants attached.

F

face-amount certificate company (FAC)	A type of investment company that requires an investor to make fixed payments over time or to deposit a lump sum, and that will return to the investor a stated sum known as the face amount on a specific date.
face amount/face value	*See* par.
fail to deliver	An event where the broker on the sell side of the transaction fails to deliver the security.
fail to receive	An event where the broker on the buy side of the transaction fails to receive the security from the broker on the sell side.
Fannie Mae	*See* Federal National Mortgage Association.
Farm Credit Administrator	The agency that oversees all of the activities of the banks in the Federal Farm Credit System.
Federal Deposit Insurance Corporation (FDIC)	The government insurance agency that provides insurance for bank depositors in case of bank failure.
Federal Farm Credit System	An organization of banks that is designed to provide financing to farmers for mortgages, feed and grain, and equipment.
federal funds rate	The rate banks charge each other on overnight loans.
Federal Home Loan Mortgage Corporation (FHLMC; Freddie Mac)	A publicly traded for-profit corporation that provides liquidity to the secondary mortgage market by purchasing pools of mortgages from lenders and, in turn, issues mortgage-backed securities.

Federal Intermediate Credit Bank	Provides short-term financing to farmers for equipment.
Federal National Mortgage Association (FNMA; Fannie Mae)	A publicly traded for-profit corporation that provides liquidity to the secondary mortgage market by purchasing pools of mortgages and issuing mortgage-backed securities.
Federal Open Market Committee (FOMC)	The committee of the Federal Reserve Board that makes policy decisions relating to the nation's money supply.
Federal Reserve Board	A seven-member board that directs the policies of the Federal Reserve System. The members are appointed by the President and approved by Congress.
Federal Reserve System	The nation's central banking system, the purpose of which is to regulate money supply and the extension of credit. The Federal Reserve System is composed of 12 central banks and 24 regional banks, along with hundreds of national and state chartered banks.
fictitious quote	A quote that is not representative of an actual bid or offer for a security.
fidelity bond	A bond that must be posted by all broker dealers to ensure the public against employee dishonesty.
fill or kill (FK)	A type of order that requires that all of the securities in the order be purchased or sold immediately or not at all.
final prospectus	The official offering document for a security that contains the security's final offering price along with all information required by law for an investor to make an informed decision.
firm commitment underwriting	Guarantees the issuer all of the money right away. The underwriters purchase all of the securities from the issuer regardless of whether they can sell the securities to their customers.
firm quote	A quote displayed at which the dealer is obligated to buy or sell at least one round lot at the quoted price.
fiscal policy	Government policy designed to influence the economy through government tax and spending programs. The President and Congress control fiscal policy.
5% markup policy	FINRA's guideline that requires all prices paid by customers to be reasonably related to a security's market price. The 5% policy is a guideline, not a rule, and it does not apply to securities sold through a prospectus.
fixed annuity	An insurance contract where the insurance company guarantees fixed payments to the annuitant, usually until the annuitant's death.
fixed assets	Assets used by a corporation to conduct its business, such as plant and equipment.
flat	A term used to describe a bond that trades without accrued interest, such as a zero-coupon bond or a bond that is in default.
floor broker	An individual member of an exchange who may execute orders on the floor.
floor trader	Members of the exchange who trade for their own accounts. Members of the NYSE may not trade from the floor for their own accounts.
flow of funds	A schedule of expenses and interested parties that prioritizes how payments will be made from the revenue generated by a facility financed by a municipal revenue bond.

forced conversion	The calling in of convertible bonds at a price that is less than the market value of the underlying common stock into which the bonds may be converted.
foreign currency	Currency of another country.
foreign currency option	An option to purchase or sell a specified amount of another country's currency.
Form 10-K	An annual report filed by a corporation detailing its financial performance for the year.
Form 10-Q	A quarterly report filed by a corporation detailing its financial performance for the quarter.
form letter	A letter sent out by a brokerage firm or a registered representative to more than 25 people in a 90-day period. Form letters are subject to approval and recordkeeping requirements.
forward pricing	The way in which open-end mutual funds are valued for investors who wish to purchase or redeem shares of the fund. Mutual funds usually price their shares at the end of the business day. The price to be paid or received by the investor will be the price that is next calculated after the fund receives the order.
401K	A qualified retirement plan offered by an employer.
403B	A qualified retirement plan offered to teachers and employees of nonprofit organizations.
fourth market	A transaction between two large institutions without the use of a broker dealer.
fractional share	A portion of a whole share that represents ownership of an open-end mutual fund.
fraud	Any attempt to gain an unfair advantage over another party through the use of deception, concealment, or misrepresentation.
free credit balance	Cash reserves in a customer's account that have not been invested. Customers must be notified of their free credit balances at least quarterly.
free look	A privilege offered to purchasers of contractual plans and insurance policies that will allow the individual to cancel the contract within the free-look period, usually 45 days.
freeriding	The purchase and sale of a security without depositing the money required to cover the purchase price as required by Regulation T.
freeriding and withholding	The withholding of new issue securities offered by a broker dealer for the benefit of the brokerage firm or an employee.
front-end load	(1) A sales charge paid by investors in open-end mutual funds that is paid at the time of purchase. (2) A contractual plan that seeks to assess sales charges in the first years of the plan and may charge up to 50% of the first year's payments as sales charges.
frozen account	An account where the owner is required to deposit cash or securities up front, prior to any purchase or sale taking place. An account is usually frozen as a result of a customer's failure to pay or deliver securities.
full power of attorney	A type of discretionary authority that allows a third party to purchase and sell securities as well as to withdraw cash and securities without the owner's prior consent or knowledge. This type of authority is usually reserved to trustees and attorneys.

fully registered bonds	A type of bond issuance where the issuer has a complete record of the owners of the bonds and who is entitled to receive interest and principal payments. The owners of fully registered bonds are not required to clip coupons.
functional allocation	An arrangement for oil and gas programs where the general partner pays the tangible drilling costs and the limited partner absorbs the intangible drilling costs.
fundamental analyst	A method of valuing the company that takes into consideration the financial performance of the corporation, the value of its assets, and the quality of its management.
funded debt	Long-term debt obligations of corporations or municipalities.
fungible	Easily exchangeable items with the same conditions.

G

general account	An insurance company's account that holds the money and investments for fixed contracts and traditional life insurance policies.
general obligation bond	A municipal bond that is backed by the taxing power of the state or municipality.
general partner	The partner in a general partnership who manages the business and is responsible for any debt of the program.
general securities principal	An individual who has passed the Series 24 exam and may supervise the activities of the firm and its agents.
generic advertising	Advertising designed to promote name recognition for a firm and securities as investments, but does not recommend specific securities.
good 'til cancel (GTC)	An order that remains on the books until it is executed or canceled.
goodwill	An intangible asset of a corporation, such as its name recognition and reputation, that adds to its value.
Government National Mortgage Association (GNMA; Ginnie Mae)	A government corporation that provides liquidity to the mortgage markets by purchasing pools of mortgages that have been insured by the Federal Housing Administration and the Veterans Administration. Ginnie Mae issues pass-through certificates to investors backed by the pools of mortgages.
government security	A security that is an obligation of the U.S. government and that is backed by the full faith and credit of the U.S. government, such as Treasury bills, notes, and bonds.
grant anticipation note (GAN)	Short-term municipal financing issued in anticipation of receiving a grant from the federal government or one of its agencies.
greenshoe option	An option given to an underwriter of common stock that will allow it to purchase up to an additional 15% of the offering from the issuer at the original offering price to cover over-allotments for securities that are in high demand.
gross domestic product (GDP)	The value of all goods and services produced by a country within a period of time. GDP includes government purchases, investments, and exports minus imports.
gross income	All income received by a taxpayer before deductions for taxes.
gross revenue pledge	A flow-of-funds pledge for a municipal revenue bond that states that debt service will be paid first.

growth fund	A fund whose objective is capital appreciation. Growth funds invest in common stocks to achieve their objective.
growth stock	The stock of a company whose earnings grow at a rate that is faster than the growth rate of the economy as a whole. Growth stocks are characterized by increased opportunities for appreciation and little or no dividends.
guardian	An individual who has a fiduciary responsibility for another, usually a minor.

H

halt	A temporary stop in the trading of a security. If a common stock is halted, all derivatives and convertibles will be halted as well.
head and shoulders	A chart pattern that indicates a reversal of a trend. A head-and-shoulders top indicates a reversal of an uptrend and is considered bearish. A head-and-shoulders bottom is the reversal of a downtrend and is considered bullish.
hedge	A position taken in a security to offset or reduce the risk associated with the risk of another security.
HH bond	A nonmarketable government security that pays semiannual interest. Series HH bonds are issued with a $500 minimum value and may only be purchased by trading matured Series EE bonds; they may not be purchased with cash.
high	The highest price paid for a security during a trading session or during a 52-week period.
holder	An individual or corporation that owns a security. The holder of a security is also known as being long the security.
holding period	The length of time during which an investor owns a security. The holding period is important for calculating tax liability.
hold in street name	The registration of customer securities in the name of the broker dealer. Most customers register securities in the name of the broker dealer to make the transfer of ownership easier.
horizontal spread	Also known as a calendar spread. The simultaneous purchase and sale of two calls or two puts on the same underlying security with the same exercise price but with different expiration months.
hot issue	A new issue of securities that trades at an immediate premium to its offering price in the secondary market.
HR 10 plan	*See* Keogh plan.
hypothecation	The customer's pledge of securities as collateral for a margin loan.

I

immediate annuity	An annuity contract purchased with a single payment that entitles the holder to receive immediate payments from the contract. The annuitant purchases annuity units and usually begins receiving payments within 60 days.
immediate family	An individual's immediate family includes parents, parents-in-law, children, spouse, and any relative financially dependent upon the individual.
immediate or cancel (IOC)	An order that is to be executed as fully as possible immediately and whatever is not executed will be canceled.
income bond	A highly speculative bond that is issued at a discount from par and only pays interest if the issuer has enough income to do so. The issuer of the income bond only promises to pay principal at maturity. Income bonds trade flat without accrued interest.
income fund	A mutual fund whose investment objective is to achieve current income for its shareholders by investing in bonds and preferred stocks.
income program	A type of oil and gas program that purchases producing wells to receive the income received from the sale of the proven reserves.
income statement	A financial statement that shows a corporation's revenue and expenses for the time period in question.
indefeasible title	A record of ownership that cannot be challenged.
index	A representation of the price action of a given group of securities. Indexes are used to measure the condition of the market as a whole, such as with the S&P 500, or can be used to measure the condition of an industry group, such as with the Biotech index.
index option	An option on an underlying financial index. Index options settle in cash.
indication of interest	An investor's expression of a willingness to purchase a new issue of securities after receiving a preliminary prospectus. The investor's indication of interest is not binding on either the investor or the firm.
Individual Retirement Account (IRA)	A self-directed retirement account that allows individuals with earned income to contribute the lesser of 100% of earned income or the annual maximum per year. The contributions may be made with pre- or after-tax dollars, depending on the individual's level of income and whether he or she is eligible to participate in an employer's sponsored plan.
industrial development bond	A private-purpose municipal bond whose proceeds are used to build a facility that is leased to a corporation. The debt service on the bonds is supported by the lease payments.
inflation	The persistent upward pressure on the price of goods and services over time.
initial margin requirement	The initial amount of equity that a customer must deposit to establish a position. The initial margin requirement is set by the Federal Reserve Board under Regulation T.
initial public offering (IPO)	The first offering of common stock to the general investing public.
in part call	A partial call of a bond issue for redemption.

inside information	Information that is not known to people outside of the corporation. Information becomes public only after it is released by the corporation through a recognized media source. Inside information may be both material and immaterial. It is only illegal to trade on inside material information.
inside market	The highest bid and the lowest offer for a security.
insider	A company's officers, directors, large stockholders of 10% or more of the company, and anyone who is in possession of nonpublic material information, along with the immediate family members of the same.
Insider Trading and Securities Fraud Enforcement Act of 1988	Federal legislation that made the penalties for people trading on material nonpublic information more severe. Penalties for insider traders are up to the greater of 300% of the amount of money made or the loss avoided or $1 million and up to 5 years in prison. People who disseminate inside information may be imprisoned and fined up to $1 million.
INSTINET	A computer network that facilitates trading of large blocks of stocks between institutions without the use of a broker dealer.
institutional account	An account in the name of an institution but operated for the benefit of others (i.e., banks and mutual funds). There is no minimum size for an institutional account.
institutional communication	Any communication that is distributed exclusively to institutional investors. Institutional communication does not require the preapproval of a principal but must be maintained for 3 years by the firm.
institutional investor	An investor who trades for its own account or for the accounts of others in large quantities and is covered by fewer protective laws.
insurance covenant	The promise of an issuer of revenue bonds to maintain insurance on the financed project.
intangible asset	Nonphysical property of a corporation, such as trademarks and copyrights.
intangible drilling cost (IDC)	Costs for an oil and gas program that are expensed in the year in which they are incurred for such things as wages, surveys, and well casings.
interbank market	An international currency market.
interest	The cost for borrowing money, usually charged at an annual percentage rate.
interest rate option	An option based on U.S. government securities. The options are either rate-based or priced-based options.
interest rate risk	The risk borne by investors in interest-bearing securities, which subjects the holder to a loss of principal should interest rates rise.
interlocking directorate	Corporate boards that share one or more directors.
Internal Revenue Code (IRC)	The codes that define tax liabilities for U.S. taxpayers.
interpositioning	The placing of another broker dealer in between the customer and the best market. Interpositioning is prohibited unless it can be demonstrated that the customer received a better price because of it.

interstate offering	A multistate offering of securities that requires that the issuer register with the SEC as well as with the states in which the securities will be sold.
in the money	A relationship between the strike price of an option and the underlying security's price. A call is in the money when the strike price is lower than the security's price. A put is in the money when the strike price is higher than the security's price.
intrastate offering	*See* Rule 147.
intrinsic value	The amount by which an option is in the money.
introducing broker	*See* correspondent broker dealer.
inverted yield curve	A yield curve where the cost of short-term financing exceeds the cost of long-term financing.
investment adviser	Anyone who charges a fee for investment advice or who holds himself out to the public as being in the business of giving investment advice for a fee.
Investment Advisers Act of 1940	The federal legislation that sets forth guidelines for business requirements and activities of investment advisers.
investment banker	A financial institution that is in the business of raising capital for companies and municipalities by underwriting securities.
investment company	A company that sells undivided interests in a pool of securities and manages the portfolio for the benefit of the investors. Investment companies include management companies, unit investment trusts, and face-amount companies.
Investment Company Act of 1940	Federal legislation that regulates the operation and registration of investment companies.
investment-grade security	A security that has been assigned a rating in the highest rating tier by a recognized ratings agency.
investment objective	An investor's set of goals as to how he or she is seeking to make money, such as capital appreciation or current income.
investor	The purchaser of a security who seeks to realize a profit.
IRA rollover	The temporary distribution of assets from an IRA and the subsequent reinvestment of the assets into another IRA within 60 days. An IRA may be rolled over only once per year and is subject to a 10% penalty and ordinary income taxes if the investor is under 59-1/2 and if the assets are not deposited in another qualified account within 60 days.
IRA transfer	The movement of assets from one qualified account to another without the account holder taking possession of the assets. Investors may transfer an IRA as often as they like.
issued stock	Stock that has actually been sold to the investing public.
issuer	Any entity that issues or proposes to issue securities.

J

joint account	An account that is owned by two or more parties. Joint accounts allow either party to enter transactions for the account. Both parties must sign a joint account agreement. All joint accounts must be designated as joint tenants in common or with rights of survivorship.
joint tenants in common (JTIC)	A joint account where the assets of a party who has died transfer to the decedent's estate, not the other tenant.
joint tenants with rights of survivorship (JTWROS)	A joint account where the assets of a party who has died transfer to the surviving party, not the decedent's estate.
joint venture	An interest in an operation shared by two or more parties. The parties have no other relationship beyond the joint venture.
junk bond	A bond with a high degree of default risk that has been assigned a speculative rating by the ratings agencies.
junk bond fund	A speculative bond fund that invests in high-yield bonds in order to achieve a high degree of current income.

K

Keogh plan	A qualified retirement account for self-employed individuals. Contributions are limited to the lesser of 20% of their gross income or up to the annual limit.
Keynesian economics	An economic theory that states that government intervention in the marketplace helps sustain economic growth.
know-your-customer rule	Industry regulation that requires a registered representative to be familiar with the customer's financial objectives and needs prior to making a recommendation; also known as Rule 405.

L

lagging indicator	A measurement of economic activity that changes after a change has taken place in economic activity. Lagging indicators are useful confirmation tools when determining the strength of an economic trend. Lagging indicators include corporate profits, average duration of unemployment, and labor costs.
last in, first out (LIFO)	An accounting method used that states that the last item that was produced is the first item sold.
leading indicator	A measurement of economic activity that changes prior to a change in economic activity. Leading economic indicators are useful in predicting a coming trend in economic activity. Leading economic indicators include housing permits, new orders for durable goods, and the S&P 500.

LEAPS (long-term equity anticipation securities)	A long-term option on a security that has an expiration of up to 39 months.
lease rental bonds	A municipal bond that is issued to finance the building of a facility that will be rented out. The lease payments on the facility will support the bond's debt service.
legal list	A list of securities that have been approved by certain state securities regulators for purchase by fiduciaries.
legal opinion	An opinion issued by a bond attorney stating that the issue is a legally binding obligation of the state or municipality. The legal opinion also contains a statement regarding the tax status of the interest payments received by investors.
legislative risk	The risk that the government may do something that adversely affects an investment.
letter of intent (LOI)	A letter signed by the purchaser of mutual fund shares that states the investor's intention to invest a certain amount of money over a 13-month period. By agreeing to invest this sum, the investor is entitled to receive a lower sales charge on all purchases covered by the letter of intent. The letter of intent may be backdated up to 90 days from an initial purchase. Should the investor fail to invest the stated sum, a sales charge adjustment will be charged.
level load	A mutual fund share that charges a flat annual fee, such as a 12B-1 fee.
level one	A Nasdaq workstation service that allows the agent to see the inside market only.
level two	A Nasdaq workstation service that allows the order-entry firm to see the inside market, to view the quotes entered by all market makers, and to execute orders.
level three	A Nasdaq workstation service that allows market-making firms to see the inside market, to view the quotes entered by all market makers, to execute orders, and to enter their own quotes for the security. This is the highest level of Nasdaq service.
leverage	The use of borrowed funds to try to obtain a rate of return that exceeds the cost of the funds.
liability	A legal obligation to pay a debt either incurred through borrowing or through the normal course of business.
life annuity/straight life	An annuity payout option that provides payments over the life of the annuitant.
life annuity with period certain	An annuity payout option that provides payments to the annuitant for life or to the annuitant's estate for the period certain, whichever is longer.
life contingency	An annuity payout option that provides a death benefit in case the annuitant dies during the accumulation stage.
limit order	An order that sets a maximum price that the investor will pay in the case of a buy order or the minimum price the investor will accept in the case of a sell order.
limited liability	A protection afforded to investors in securities that limits their liability to the amount of money invested in the securities.
limited partner	A passive investor in a direct participation program who has no role in the project's management.

limited partnership (LP)	An association of two or more partners with at least one partner being the general partner who is responsible for the management of the partnership.
limited partnership agreement	The foundation of all limited partnerships. The agreement is the contract between all partners, and it spells out the authority of the general partner and the rights of all limited partners.
limited power of attorney/limited trading authorization	Legal authorization for a representative or a firm to affect purchases and sales for a customer's account without the customer's prior knowledge. The authorization is limited to buying and selling securities and may not be given to another party.
limited principal	An individual who has passed the Series 26 exam and may supervise Series 6 limited representatives.
limited representative	An individual who has passed the Series 6 exam and may represent a broker dealer in the sale of mutual fund shares and variable contracts.
limited tax bond	A type of general obligation bond that is issued by a municipality that may not increase its tax rate to pay the debt service of the issue.
liquidity	The ability of an investment to be readily converted into cash.
liquidity risk	The risk that an investor may not be able to sell a security when needed or that selling a security when needed will adversely affect the price.
listed option	A standardized option contract that is traded on an exchange.
listed security	A security that trades on one of the exchanges. Only securities that trade on an exchange are known as listed securities.
loan consent agreement	A portion of the margin agreement that allows the broker dealer to loan out the customer's securities to another customer who wishes to borrow them to sell the security short.
locked market	A market condition that results when the bid and the offer for a security are equal.
LOI	*See* letter of intent.
London Interbank Offered Rate (LIBOR)	The interbank rates for dollar-denominated deposits in England.
long	A term used to describe an investor who owns a security.
long market value	The total long market value of a customer's account.
long-term gain	A profit realized through the sale of a security at a price that is higher than its purchase price after being held for more than 12 months.
long-term loss	A loss realized through the sale of a security at a price that is lower than its purchase price after being held for more than 12 months.
loss carry forward	A capital loss realized on the sale of an asset in 1 year that is carried forward in whole or part to subsequent tax years.
low	The lowest price at which a security has traded in any given period, usually measured during a trading day or for 52 weeks.

M

M1	The most liquid measure of the money supply. It includes all currency and demand and NOW deposits (checking accounts).
M2	A measure of the money supply that includes M1 plus all time deposits, savings accounts, and noninstitutional money market accounts.
M3	A measure of the money supply that includes M2 and large time deposits, institutional money market funds, short-term repurchase agreements, and other large liquid assets.
maintenance call	A demand for additional cash or collateral made by a broker dealer when a margin customer's account equity has fallen below the minimum requirement of the NYSE or that is set by the broker dealer.
maintenance covenant	A promise made by an issuer of a municipal revenue bond to maintain the facility in good repair.
Major Market Index (XMI)	An index created by the Amex to AMEX 15 of the 30 largest stocks in the Dow Jones Industrial Average.
Maloney Act of 1938	An amendment to the Securities Exchange Act of 1934 that gave the NASD (now part of FINRA) the authority to regulate the over-the-counter market.
managed underwriting	An underwriting conducted by a syndicate led by the managing underwriter.
management company	A type of investment company that actively manages a portfolio of securities in order to meet a stated investment objective. Management companies are also known as mutual funds.
management fee	(1) The fee received by the lead or managing underwriter of a syndicate. (2) The fee received by a sponsor of a direct participation program.
managing partner	The general partner in a direct participation program.
managing underwriter	The lead underwriter in a syndicate who is responsible for negotiating with the issuer, forming the syndicate, and settling the syndicate account.
margin	The amount of customer equity that is required to hold a position in a security.
margin account	An account that allows the customer to borrow money from the brokerage firm to buy securities.
margin call	A demand for cash or collateral mandated by the Federal Reserve Board under Regulation T.
margin department	The department in a broker dealer that calculates money owed by the customer or money due the customer.
margin maintenance call	*See* maintenance call.
mark to the market	The monitoring of the current value of a position relative to the price at which the trade was executed for securities purchased on margin or on a when-issued basis.
markdown	The profit earned by a dealer on a transaction when purchasing securities for its own account from a customer.

marketability	The ability of an investment to be exchanged between two investors. A security with an active secondary market has a higher level of marketability than one whose market is not as active.
market arbitrage	A type of arbitrage that consists of purchasing a security in one marketplace and selling it in another to take advantage of price inefficiencies.
market letter	A regular publication, usually issued by an investment adviser, that offers information and/or advice regarding securities, market conditions, or the economy as a whole.
market maker	A Nasdaq firm that is required to quote a continuous two-sided market for the securities in which it trades.
market not held	A type of order that gives the floor broker discretion over the time and price of execution.
market on close	An order that will be executed at whatever price the market is at, either on the closing print or just prior to the closing print.
market on open	An order that will be executed at whatever price the market is at, either on the opening print or just after the opening print.
market order	A type of order that will be executed immediately at the best available price once it is presented to the market.
market-out clause	A clause in an underwriting agreement that gives the syndicate the ability to cancel the underwriting if it finds a material problem with the information or condition of the issuer.
market risk/ systematic risk	The risk inherent in any investment in the market that states an investor may lose money simply because the market is going down.
market value	The value of a security that is determined in the marketplace by the investors who enter bids and offers for a security.
markup	The compensation paid to a securities dealer for selling a security to a customer from its inventory.
markup policy	FINRA's guideline that states that the price that is paid or received by an investor must be reasonably related to the market price for that security. FINRA offers 5% as a guideline for what is reasonable to charge investors when they purchase or sell securities.
material information	Information that would affect a company's current or future prospects or an investor's decision to invest in the company.
maturity date	The date on which a bond's principal amount becomes payable to its holders.
member	A member of FINRA or one of the 1,366 members of the NYSE.
member firm	A firm that is a member of the NYSE, FINRA, or another self-regulatory organization.
member order	A retail order entered by a member of a municipal bond syndicate for which the member will receive all of the sales credit.
mini maxi underwriting	A type of best efforts underwriting that states that the offering will not become effective until a minimum amount is sold and sets a maximum amount that may be sold.

minimum death benefit	The minimum guaranteed death benefit that will be paid to the beneficiaries if the holder of a variable life insurance policy dies.
minus tick	A trade in an exchange-listed security that is at a price that is lower than the previous trade.
modern portfolio theory	An investing approach that looks at the overall return and risk of a portfolio as a whole, not as a collection of single investments.
modified accelerated cost recovery system (MACRS)	An accounting method that allows the owner to recover a larger portion of the asset's value in the early years of its life.
monetarist theory	A theory that states that the money supply is the driving force in the economy and that a well-managed money supply will benefit the economy.
monetary policy	Economic policy that is controlled by the Federal Reserve Board and controls the amount of money in circulation and the level of interest rates.
money market	The secondary market where short-term highly liquid securities are traded. Securities traded in the money market include T-bills, negotiable CDs, bankers' acceptances, commercial paper, and other short-term securities with less than 12 months to maturity.
money market mutual fund	A mutual fund that invests in money market instruments to generate monthly interest for its shareholders. Money market mutual funds have a stable NAV that is equal to $1, but it is not guaranteed.
money supply	The total amount of currency, loans, and credit in the economy. The money supply is measured by M1, M2, M3, and L.
moral obligation bond	A type of municipal revenue bond that will allow the state or municipality to vote to cover a shortfall in the debt service.
multiplier effect	The ability of the money supply to grow simply through the normal course of banking. When banks and other financial institutions accept deposits and subsequently loan out those deposits to earn interest, the amount of money in the system grows.
municipal bond	A bond issued by a state or political subdivision of a state in an effort to finance its operations. Interest earned by investors in municipal bonds is almost always free from federal income taxes.
municipal bond fund	A mutual fund that invests in a portfolio of municipal debt in an effort to produce income that is free from federal income taxes for its investors.
Municipal Bond Investors Assurance Corp. (MBIA)	An independent insurance company that will, for a fee received from the issuer, insure the interest and principal payments on a municipal bond.
municipal note	A short-term municipal issue sold to manage the issuer's cash flow, usually in anticipation of the offering of long-term financing.
Municipal Securities Rulemaking Board (MSRB)	The self-regulatory organization that oversees the issuance and trading of municipal bonds. The MSRB's rules are enforced by other industry SROs.

Munifacts	A service that provides real-time secondary market quotes. Munifacts is now known as Thomson Muni Market Monitor.
mutual fund	An investment company that invests in and manages a portfolio of securities for its shareholders. Open-end mutual funds sell their shares to investors on a continuous basis and must stand ready to redeem their shares upon the shareholder's request.
mutual fund custodian	A qualified financial institution that maintains physical custody of a mutual fund's cash and securities. Custodians are usually banks, trust companies, or exchange member firms.

N

naked	The sale of a call option without owning the underlying security or the sale of a put option without being short the stock or having cash on deposit that is sufficient to purchase the underlying security.
narrow-based index	An index that is based on a market sector or a limited number of securities.
National Securities Clearing Corporation (NSCC)	The clearing intermediary through which clearing member firms reconcile their securities accounts.
NAV (net asset value)	The net value of a mutual fund after deducting all its liabilities. A mutual fund must calculate its NAV at least once per business day. To determine NAV per share, simply divide the mutual fund's NAV by the total number of shares outstanding.
negotiability	The ability of an investment to be freely exchanged between noninterested parties.
negotiable certificate of deposit	A certificate issued by a bank for a time deposit in excess of $100,000 that can be exchanged between parties prior to its maturity date. FDIC insurance only covers the first $250,000 of the principal amount should the bank fail.
NOW (negotiable order of withdrawal) Account	A type of demand deposit that allows the holder to write checks against an interest-bearing account.
net change	The difference between the previous day's closing price and the price of the most recently reported trade for a security.
net current assets per share	A calculation of the value per share that excludes fixed assets and intangibles.
net debt per capita	A measure of a municipal issuer's ability to meet its obligations. It measures the debt level of the issuer in relation to the population.
net debt to assessed valuation	A measure of the issuer's ability to meet its obligations and to raise additional revenue through property taxes.
net direct debt	The total amount of general obligation debt, including notes and short-term financing, issued by a municipality or state.

net interest cost (NIC)	A calculation that measures the interest cost of a municipal issue over the life of all bonds. Most competitive underwritings for municipal securities are awarded to the syndicate that submits the bid with the lowest NIC.
net investment income	The total sum of investment income derived from dividend and interest income after subtracting expenses.
net revenue pledge	A pledge from a revenue bond that pays maintenance and operation expenses first, then debt service.
net total debt	The total of a municipality's direct debt plus its overlapping debt.
net worth	The value of a corporation after subtracting all of its liabilities. A corporation's net worth is also equal to shareholder's equity.
new account form	Paperwork that must be filled out and signed by the representative and a principal of the firm prior to the opening of any account being opened for a customer.
new construction program	A real estate program that seeks to achieve capital appreciation by building new properties.
new housing authority (NHA)	A municipal bond issued to build low-income housing. NHA bonds are guaranteed by the U.S. government and are considered the safest type of municipal bonds. NHA bonds are not considered to be double-barreled bonds.
new issue	See initial public offering (IPO).
New York Stock Exchange (NYSE)	A membership organization that provides a marketplace for securities to be exchanged in one centralized location through a dual-auction process.
no-load fund	A fund that does not charge the investor a sales charge to invest in the fund. Shares of no-load mutual funds are sold directly from the fund company to the investor.
nominal owner	An individual or entity registered as the owner of record of securities for the benefit of another party.
nominal quote	A quote given for informational purposes only. A trader who identifies a quote as being nominal cannot be held to trading at the prices that were clearly identified as being nominal.
nominal yield	The yield that is stated or named on the security. The nominal yield, once it has been set, never changes, regardless of the market price of the security.
noncompetitive bid	A bid submitted for Treasury bills where the purchaser agrees to accept the average of all yields accepted at the auction. Noncompetitive tenders are always the first orders filled at the auction.
noncumulative preferred	A type of preferred stock whose dividends do not accumulate in arrears if the issuer misses the payment.
nondiscrimination	A clause that states that all eligible individuals must be allowed to participate in a qualified retirement plan.
nondiversification	An investment strategy that concentrates its investments among a small group of securities or issuers.
nondiversified management company	An investment company that concentrates its investments among a few issuers or securities and does not meet the diversification requirements of the Investment Company Act of 1940.

nonfixed UIT	A type of UIT that allows changes in the portfolio and traditionally invests in mutual fund shares.
nonqualified retirement plan	A retirement plan that does not allow contributions to be made with pre-tax dollars; that is, the retirement plan does not qualify for beneficial tax treatment from the IRS for its contributions.
nonsystematic risk	A risk that is specific to an issuer or an industry.
note	An intermediate-term interest-bearing security that represents an obligation of its issuer.
not-held (NH) order	An order that gives the floor broker discretion as to the time and price of execution.
numbered account	An account that has been designated a number for identification purposes in order to maintain anonymity for its owner. The owner must sign a statement acknowledging ownership.

O

odd lot	A transaction that is for less than 100 shares of stock or for less than 5 bonds.
odd lot differential	An additional fee that may be charged to an investor for the handling of odd lot transactions (usually waived).
odd lot theory	A contrarian theory that states that small investors will invariably buy and sell at the wrong time.
offer	A price published at which an investor or broker dealer is willing to sell a security.
offering circular	The offering document that is prepared by a corporation selling securities under a Regulation A offering.
office of supervisory jurisdiction (OSJ)	An office identified by the broker dealer as having supervisory responsibilities for agents. It has final approval of new accounts, makes markets, and structures offerings.
Office of the Comptroller of the Currency	An office of the U.S. Treasury that is responsible for regulating the practices of national banks.
official notice of sale	The notice of sale published in the *Daily Bond Buyer* by a municipal issuer that is used to obtain an underwriter for municipal bonds.
official statement	The offering document for a municipal issuer that must be provided to every purchaser if the issuer prepares one.
oil and gas direct participation program	A type of direct participation program designed to invest in oil and gas production or exploration.
oil depletion allowance	An accounting method used to reduce the amount of reserves available from a producing well.
omnibus account	An account used by an introducing member to execute and clear all of its customers' trades.
open-end covenant	A type of bond indenture that allows for the issuance of additional bonds with the same claim on the collateral as the original issue.

open-end investment company	*See* mutual fund.
option	A contract between two investors to purchase or sell a security at a given price for a certain period of time.
option agreement	A form that must be signed and returned by an option investor within 15 days of the account's approval to trade options.
option disclosure document	A document that must be furnished to all option investors at the time the account is approved for options trading. It is published by the Options Clearing Corporation (OCC), and it details the risks and features of standardized options.
Options Clearing Corporation (OCC)	The organization that issues and guarantees the performance of standardized options.
order book official (OBO)	Employees of the CBOE who are responsible for maintaining a fair and orderly market in the options assigned to them and for executing orders that have been left with them.
order department	The department of a broker dealer that is responsible for routing orders to the markets for execution.
order memorandum/ order ticket	The written document filled out by a registered representative that identifies, among other things, the security, the amount, the customer, and the account number for which the order is being entered.
original issue discount (OID)	A bond that has been issued to the public at a discount to its par value. The OID on a corporate bond is taxed as if it was earned annually. The OID on a municipal bond is exempt from taxation.
OTC market	*See* over-the-counter (OTC) market.
out of the money	The relationship of an option's strike price to the underlying security's price when exercising the option would not make economic sense. A call is out of the money when the security's price is below the option's strike price. A put is out of the money when the security's price is above the option's strike price.
outstanding stock	The total amount of a security that has been sold to the investing public and that remains in the hands of the investing public.
overlapping debt	The portion of another taxing authority's debt that a municipality is responsible for.
overriding royalty interest	A type of sharing arrangement that offers an individual with no risk a portion of the revenue in exchange for something of value, such as the right to drill on the owner's land.
over-the-counter (OTC) market	An interdealer market that consists of a computer and phone network through which broker dealers trade securities.

P

par	The stated principal amount of a security. Par value is of great importance for fixed-income securities such as bonds or preferred stock. Par value for bonds is traditionally $1,000, whereas par for a preferred stock is normally $100. Par value is of little importance when looking at common stock.
parity	A condition that results when the value of an underlying common stock to be received upon conversion equals the value of the convertible security.
partial call	A call of a portion of an issuer's callable securities.
participation	The code set forth in the Employee Retirement Income Security Act of 1974 that states who is eligible to participate in an employer sponsored retirement plan.
passive income	Income received by an individual for which no work was performed, such as rental income received from a rental property.
passive loss	A loss realized on an investment in a limited partnership or rental property that can be used to offset passive income.
pass-through certificate	A security that passes through income and principal payments made to an underlying portfolio of mortgages. Ginnie Mae is one of the biggest issuers of this type of security.
payment date	The day when a dividend will actually be sent to investors. The payment date is set by the corporation's board of directors at the time when they initially declare the dividend.
payout stage	The period during which an annuitant receives payments from an annuity contract.
payroll deduction plan	A nonqualified retirement plan where employees authorize the employer to take regular deductions from their paychecks to invest in a retirement account.
pension plan	A contractual retirement plan between an employee and an employer that is designed to provide regular income for the employee after retirement.
percentage depletion	An accounting method that allows for a tax deduction for the reduction of reserves.
periodic payment plan	A contract to purchase mutual fund shares over an extended period of time, usually in exchange for the fund company waiving its minimum investment requirement.
person	Any individual or entity that can enter into a legally binding contract for the purchase and sale of securities.
personal income	Income earned by an individual from providing services and through investments.
phantom income	(1) A term used to describe the taxable appreciation on a zero-coupon bond. (2) The term used to describe taxable income generated by a limited partnership that is not producing positive cash flow.
PINK OTC	An electronic quote service containing quotes for unlisted securities that is published by the OTC Markets Group.
placement ratio	A ratio that details the percentage of municipal bonds sold, relative to the number of bonds offered in the last week, published by the *Daily Bond Buyer*.
plus tick	A transaction in an exchange-listed security that is higher than the previous transaction.

point	An increment of change in the price of a security: 1 bond point equals 1% of par or 1% of $1,000, or $10.
POP	See public offering price (POP).
portfolio income	Interest and dividends earned through investing in securities.
portfolio manager	An entity that is hired to manage the investment portfolios of a mutual fund. The portfolio manager is paid a fee that is based on the net assets of the fund.
position	The amount of a security in which an investor has an interest by either being long (owning) or short (owing) the security.
power of substitution	See stock power.
preemptive right	The right of a common stockholder to maintain proportional ownership interest in a security. A corporation may not issue additional shares of common stock without first offering those shares to existing stockholders.
preferred stock	An equity security issued with a stated dividend rate. Preferred stockholders have a higher claim on a corporation's dividends and assets than common holders.
preferred stock ratio	A ratio detailing the amount of an issuer's total capitalization that is made up of preferred stock. The ratio is found by dividing the total par value of preferred stock by the issuer's total capitalization.
preliminary prospectus/red herring	A document used to solicit indications of interest during the cooling-off period for a new issue of securities. All of the information in the preliminary prospectus is subject to revision and change. The cover of a preliminary prospectus must have a statement saying that the securities have not yet become registered and that they may not be sold until the registration becomes effective. This statement is written in red ink, and this is where the term *red herring* comes from.
price-earnings ratio (PE)	A measure of value used by analysts. It is calculated by dividing the issuer's stock price by its earnings per share.
price spread	A term used to describe an option spread where the long and short options differ only in their exercise prices.
primary earnings per share	The amount of earnings available per common share prior to the conversion of any outstanding convertible securities.
prime rate	The interest rate that banks charge their best corporate customers on loans.
principal	(1) The face amount of a bond. (2) A broker dealer trading for its own account. (3) An individual who has successfully completed a principal exam and may supervise representatives.
principal transaction	A transaction where a broker dealer participates in a trade by buying or selling securities for its own account.
priority	The acceptance of bids and offers for exchange-listed securities on a first-come, first-served (FCFS) basis.
private placement	The private sale of securities to a limited number of investors. Also known as a Regulation D offering.
profit sharing plan	A plan that allows the employer to distribute a percentage of its profits to its employees at a predetermined rate. The money may be paid directly to the employee or deposited into a retirement account.

progressive tax	A tax structure where the tax rate increases as the income level of the individual or entity increases.
project note	A municipal bond issued as interim financing in anticipation of the issuance of new housing authority bonds.
prospectus	See final prospectus.
proxy	A limited authority given by stockholders to another party to vote their shares in a corporate election. The stockholder may specify how the votes are cast or may give the party discretion.
proxy department	The department in a brokerage firm that is responsible for forwarding proxies and financial information to investors whose stock is held in street name.
prudent man rule	A rule that governs investments made by fiduciaries for the benefit of a third party. The rule states that the investments must be similar to those that a prudent person would make for him- or herself.
public offering	The sale of securities by an issuer to public investors.
public offering price (POP)	The price paid by an investor to purchase open-end mutual fund shares. Also the price set for a security the first time it is sold to the investing public.
put	An option contract that allows the buyer to sell a security at a set price for a specific period of time. The seller of a put is obligated to purchase the security at a set price for a specific period of time, should the buyer exercise the option.
put buyer	A bearish investor who pays a premium for the right to sell a security at a set price for a certain period of time.
put spread	An option position created by the simultaneous purchase and sale of two put options on the same underlying security that differ in strike prices, expiration months, or both.
put writer	A bullish investor who sells a put option in order to receive the option premium. The writer is obligated to purchase the security if the buyer exercises the option.

Q

qualified legal opinion	A legal opinion containing conditions or reservations relating to the issue. A legal opinion is issued by a bond counsel for a municipal issuer.
qualified retirement plan	A retirement plan that qualifies for favorable tax treatment by the IRS for contributions made into the plan.
quick assets	A measure of liquidity that subtracts the value of a corporation's unsold inventory from its current assets.
quick ratio	See acid-test ratio.
quote	A bid and offer broadcast from the exchange or through the Nasdaq system that displays the prices at which a security may be purchased and sold and in what quantities.

R

range	The price difference between the high and low for a security.
rate covenant	A promise in the trust indenture of a municipal revenue bond to keep the user fees high enough to support the debt service.
rating	A judgment of an issuer's ability to meet its credit obligations. The higher the credit quality of the issuer is, the higher the credit rating. The lower the credit quality is, the lower the credit rating, and the higher the risk associated with the securities.
rating service	Major financial organizations that evaluate the credit quality of issuers. Issuers have to request and pay for the service. Standard and Poor's, Moody's, and Fitch are the most widely followed rating services.
raw land program	A type of real estate limited partnership that invests in land for capital appreciation.
real estate investment trust (REIT)	An entity that is organized to invest in or manage real estate. REITs offer investors certain tax advantages and can avoid double taxation if the REIT passes through at least 90% of net investment income.
real estate limited partnership	A type of direct participation program that invests in real estate projects to produce income or capital appreciation.
real estate mortgage investment conduit (REMIC)	An organization that pools investors' capital to purchase portfolios of mortgages.
realized gain	A profit earned on the sale of a security at a price that exceeds its purchase price.
realized loss	A loss recognized by an investor by selling a security at a price that is less than its purchase price.
reallowance	A sales concession available to dealers who sell securities subject to an offering who are not syndicate or selling group members.
recapture	An event that causes a tax liability on a previously taken deduction, such as selling an asset above its depreciated cost base.
recession	A decline in GDP that lasts for at least 6 months but not longer than 18 months.
reclamation	The right of a seller to demand or claim any loss from the buying party due to the buyer's failure to settle the transaction.
record date	A date set by a corporation's board of directors that determines which shareholders will be entitled to receive a declared dividend. Shareholders must be owners of record on this date in order to collect the dividend.
recourse loan	A loan taken out by a limited partnership that allows the lender to seek payment from the limited partners in the case of the partnership's failure to pay.
redeemable security	A security that can be redeemed by the issuer at the investor's request. Open-end mutual funds are an example of redeemable securities.
redemption	The return of an investor's capital by an issuer. Open-end mutual funds must redeem their securities within 7 days of an investor's request.
red herring	See preliminary prospectus.
registered	A term that describes the level of owner information that is recorded by the security's issuer.

registered as to principal only	A type of bond registration that requires the investor to clip coupons to receive the bond's interest payments. The issuer will automatically send the investor the bond's principal amount at maturity.
registered options principal (ROP)	An individual who has passed the Series 4 exam.
registered principal	A supervisor of a member firm who has passed the principal examination.
registered representative	An individual who has successfully completed a qualified examination to represent a broker dealer or issuer in securities transactions.
registrar	An independent organization that accounts for all outstanding stock and bonds of an issuer.
registration statement	The full disclosure statement that nonexempt issuers must file with the SEC prior to offering securities for sale to the public. The Securities Act of 1933 requires that a registration statement be filed.
regressive tax	A tax that is levied on all parties at the same rate, regardless of their income. An example of a regressive tax is a sales tax. A larger percentage of a low-income earner's income is taken away by the tax.
regular-way settlement	The standard number of business days in which a securities transaction is completed and paid for. Regular way settlement is the business day after the trade date.
regulated investment company	An investment company that qualifies as a conduit for net investment income under Internal Revenue Code subchapter M, so long as it distributes at least 90% of its net investment income to shareholders.
Regulation A	A Regulation A offering allows a company to raise up to 75 million dollars in a tier 2 offering and up to 20 million dollars in a tier 1 offering in any 12-month period.
Regulation D	A private placement or sale of securities that allows for an exemption from registration under the Securities Act of 1933. A private placement may be sold to an unlimited number of accredited investors but may only be sold to 35 nonaccredited investors in any 12-month period.
Regulation G	Regulates the extension of credit for securities purchases by other commercial lenders.
Regulation T	Regulates the extension of credit by broker dealers for securities purchases.
Regulation U	Regulates the extension of credit by banks for securities purchases.
Regulation X	Regulates the extension of credit by overseas lenders for securities purchases.
Rehypothecation	The act of a broker dealer repledging a customer's securities as collateral at a bank to obtain a loan for the customer.
REIT	*See* real estate investment trust (REIT).
rejection	The act of a buyer of a security refusing delivery.
reorganization department	The department in a brokerage firm that handles changes in securities that result from a merger or acquisition or calls.
repurchase agreement (REPO)	A fully collateralized loan that results in a sale of securities to the lender, with the borrower agreeing to repurchase them at a higher price in the future. The higher price represents the lender's interest.
reserve maintenance fund	An account set up to provide additional funds to maintain a revenue-producing facility financed by a revenue bond.

reserve requirement	A deposit required to be placed on account with the Federal Reserve Board by banks. The requirement is a percentage of the bank's customers' deposits.
resistance	A price level to which a security appreciates and attracts sellers. The new sellers keep the security's price from rising any higher.
restricted account	(1) A long margin account that has less than 50% equity but more than 25% or a short margin account that has equity of less than 50% but more than 30%. (2) A customer account that has been subject to a sellout.
restricted stock	A nonexempt unregistered security that has been obtained by means other than a public offering.
retail communication	Any communication that may be seen in whole or in part by an individual investor. Retail communication must be approved by a principal prior to first use and maintained by the firm for 3 years.
retained earnings	The amount of a corporation's net income that has not been paid out to shareholders as dividends.
retention	The amount of a new issue that an underwriter allocates to its own clients.
retention requirement	The amount of equity that must be left in a restricted margin account when withdrawing securities.
return on equity	A measure of performance found by dividing after-tax income by common stockholders' equity.
return on investment (ROI)	The profit or loss realized by an investor from holding a security expressed as a percentage of the invested capital.
revenue anticipation note	A short-term municipal issue that is sold to manage an issuer's cash flow in anticipation of other revenue in the future.
reverse repurchase agreement	A fully collateralized loan that results in the purchase of securities with the intention of reselling them to the borrower at a higher price. The higher price represents the buyer's/lender's interest.
reverse split	A stock split that results in fewer shares outstanding, with each share being worth proportionally more.
reversionary working interest	A revenue-sharing arrangement where the general partner shares none of the cost and receives none of the revenue until the limited partners have received their payments back, plus any predetermined amount of return.
right	A short-term security issued in conjunction with a shareholder's preemptive right. The maximum length of a right is 45 days, and it is issued with a subscription price, which allows the holder to purchase the underlying security at a discount from its market price.
rights agent	An independent entity responsible for maintaining the records for rights holders.
rights of accumulation	A right offered to mutual fund investors that allows them to calculate all past contributions and growth to reach a breakpoint to receive a sales charge discount on future purchases.
rights offering	The offering of new shares by a corporation that is preceded by the offering of the new shares to existing shareholders.

riskless simultaneous transaction	The purchase of a security on a principal basis by a brokerage firm for the sole purpose of filling a customer's order that the firm has already received. The markup on riskless principal transactions has to be based on the firm's actual cost for the security.
rollover	The distribution of assets from a qualified account to an investor for the purpose of depositing the assets in another qualified account within 60 days. An investor may only roll over an IRA once every 12 months.
round lot	A standard trading unit for securities. For common and preferred stock, a round lot is 100 shares. For bonds, it is 5 bonds.
Rule 144	SEC rule that regulates the sale of restricted and control securities requiring the seller to file Form 144 at the time the order is entered to sell. Rule 144 also regulates the number of securities that may be sold.
Rule 145	SEC rule that requires a corporation to provide stockholders with full disclosure relating to reorganizations and to solicit proxies.
Rule 147	An intrastate offering that provides an exemption from SEC registration.
Rule 405	The NYSE rule that requires that all customer recommendations must be suitable and that the representative must "know" the customer.

S

sale	*See* sell.
sales charge	*See* commission.
sales literature	Written material distributed by a firm to a controlled audience for the purpose of increasing business. Sales literature includes market letters, research reports, and form letters sent to more than 25 customers.
sales load	The amount of commission charged to investors in open-end mutual funds. The amount of the sales load is added to the net asset value of the fund to determine the public offering price of the fund.
satellite office	An office not identified to the public as an office of the member, such as an agent's home office.
savings bond	A nonnegotiable U.S. government bond that must be purchased from the government and redeemed to the government. These bonds are generally known as Series EE and HH bonds.
scale	A list of maturities and yields for a new serial bond issue.
Schedule 13D	A form that must be filed with the SEC by any individual or group of individuals acquiring 5% or more of a corporation's nonexempt equity securities. Form 13D must be filed within 10 days of the acquisition.
scheduled premium policy	A variable life insurance policy with fixed premium payments.
SEC	*See* Securities and Exchange Commission (SEC).
secondary distribution	A distribution of a large number of securities by a large shareholder or group of large shareholders. The distribution may or may not be done under a prospectus.

secondary offering	An underwriting of a large block of stock being sold by large shareholders. The proceeds of the issue are received by the selling shareholders, not the corporation.
secondary market	A marketplace where securities are exchanged between investors. All transactions that take place on an exchange or on the Nasdaq are secondary market transactions.
sector fund	A mutual fund that invests in companies within a specific business area in an effort to maximize gains. Sector funds have larger risk-reward ratios because of the concentration of investments.
Securities Act of 1933	The first major piece of securities industry legislation. It regulates the primary market and requires that nonexempt issuers file a registration statement with the SEC. The act also requires that investors in new issues be given a prospectus.
Securities Act Amendments of 1975	Created the Municipal Securities Rulemaking Board (MSRB).
Securities Exchange Act of 1934	Regulates the secondary market and all broker dealers and industry participants. It created the Securities and Exchange Commission, the industry's ultimate authority. The act gave the authority to the Federal Reserve Board to regulate the extension of credit for securities purchases through Regulation T.
Securities and Exchange Commission	The ultimate securities industry authority. The SEC is a direct government body, not a self-regulatory organization. The commissioners are appointed by the U.S. President and must be approved by Congress.
Securities Investor Protection Corporation (SIPC)	The industry's nonprofit insurance company that provides protection for investors in case of broker dealer failure. All member firms must pay dues to SIPC based upon their revenue. SIPC provides coverage for each separate customer for up to $500,000, of which a maximum of $250,000 may be cash. The Securities Investor Protection Act of 1970 created SIPC.
security	Any investment that can be exchanged for value between two parties that contains risk. Securities include stocks, bonds, mutual funds, notes, rights, warrants, and options, among others.
segregation	The physical separation of customer and firm assets.
self-regulatory organization (SRO)	An industry authority that regulates its own members. FINRA, the NYSE, and the CBOE are all self-regulatory organizations that regulate their own members.
sell	The act of conveying the ownership of a security for value to another party. A sale includes any security that is attached to another security, as well as any security which the security may be converted or exchanged into.
seller's option	A type of settlement option that allows the seller to determine when delivery of the securities and final settlement of the trade will occur.
selling away	Any recommendation to a customer that involves an investment product that is not offered through the employing firm without the firm's knowledge and consent. This is a violation of industry regulations and may result in action being taken against the representative.
selling concession	See concession.
selling dividends	The act of using a pending dividend to create urgency for the customer to purchase a security. This is a violation and could result in action being taken against the representative.

selling group	A group of broker dealers who may sell a new issue of securities but who are not members of the syndicate and who have no liability to the issuer.
sell out	A transaction executed by a broker dealer when a customer fails to pay for the securities.
sell-stop order	An order placed beneath the current market for a security to protect a profit, to guard against a loss, or to establish a short position.
separate account	The account established by an insurance company to invest the pooled funds of variable contract holders in the securities markets. The separate account must register as either an open-end investment company or as a unit investment trust.
separate trading of registered interest and principal securities (STRIPS)	A zero-coupon bond issued by the U.S. government. The principal payment due in the future is sold to investors at a discount and appreciates to par at maturity. The interest payment component is sold to other investors who want some current income.
serial bonds	A bond issue that has an increasing amount of principal maturing in successive years.
Series EE bond	A nonmarketable U.S. government zero-coupon bond that is issued at a discount and matures at its face value. Investors must purchase the bonds from the U.S. government and redeem them to the government at maturity.
Series HH bond	A nonmarketable U.S. government interest-bearing bond that can only be purchased by trading in matured Series EE bonds. Series HH bonds may not be purchased with cash and are issued with a $500 minimum denomination.
settlement	The completion of a securities transaction. A transaction settles and is completed when the security is delivered to the buyer and the cash is delivered to the seller.
settlement date	The date when a securities ownership changes. Settlement dates are set by FINRA's Uniform Practice Code.
75-5-10 diversification	The diversification test that must be met by mutual funds under the Investment Company Act of 1940 in order to market themselves as a diversified mutual fund: 75% of the fund's assets must be invested in other issuer's securities, no more than 5% of the fund's assets may be invested in any one company, and the fund may own no more than 10% of an issuer's outstanding securities.
shareholder's equity	See net worth.
share identification	The process of identifying which shares are being sold at the time the sale order is entered in order to minimize an investor's tax liability.
shelf offering	A type of securities registration that allows the issuer to sell the securities over a 2-year period. Well-known, seasoned issuers may sell securities over a 3-year period.
short	A position established by a bearish investor that is created by borrowing the security and selling in the hopes that the price of the security will fall. The investor hopes to be able to repurchase the security at a lower price, thus replacing it cheaply. If the security's price rises, the investor will suffer a loss.
short against the box	A short position established against an equal long position in the security to roll tax liabilities forward. Most of the benefits of establishing a short against the box position have been eliminated.

short straddle	The simultaneous sale of a call and a put on the same underlying security with the same strike price and expiration. A short straddle would be established by an investor who believes that the security price will move sideways.
simplified arbitration	A method of resolving disputes of $50,000 or less. There is no hearing; one arbitrator reads the submissions and renders a final decision.
Simplified Employee Pension (SEP)	A qualified retirement plan created for small employers with 25 or fewer employees that allows the employees' money to grow tax-deferred until retirement.
single account	An account operated for one individual. The individual has control of the account, and the assets go to the individual's estate in the case of his or her death.
sinking fund	An account established by an issuer of debt to place money for the exclusive purpose of paying bond principal.
special assessment bond	A municipal bond backed by assessments from the property that benefits from the improvements.
specialist	Member of an exchange responsible for maintaining a fair and orderly market in the securities that he or she specializes in and for executing orders left with him or her.
specialist book	A book of limit orders left with the specialist for execution.
special situation fund	A fund that seeks to take advantage of unusual corporate developments, such as takeovers, mergers, and restructuring.
special tax bond	A type of municipal revenue bond that is supported only by revenue from certain taxes.
speculation	An investment objective where the investor is willing to accept a high degree of risk in exchange for the opportunity to realize a high return.
split offering	An offering where a portion of the proceeds from the underwriting goes to the issuer and a portion goes to the selling shareholders.
spousal account	An IRA opened for a nonworking spouse that allows a full contribution to be made for the nonworking spouse.
spread	(1) The difference between the bid and ask for a security. (2) The simultaneous purchase and sale of two calls or two puts on the same underlying security.
spread load plan	A contractual plan that seeks to spread the sales charge over a longer period of time, as detailed in the Spread Load Plan Act of 1970. The maximum sales charge over the life of the plan is 9%, while the maximum sales charge in any one year is 20%.
stabilizing	The only form of price manipulation allowed by the SEC. The managing underwriter enters a bid at or below the offering price to ensure even distribution of shares.
standby underwriting	An underwriting used in connection with a preemptive rights offering. The standby underwriter must purchase any shares not subscribed to by existing shareholders.
statutory disqualification	A set of rules that prohibit an individual who has been barred or suspended or convicted of a securities-related crime from becoming registered.
statutory voting	A method of voting that requires investors to cast their votes evenly for the directors they wish to elect.

stock ahead	A condition that causes an investor's order not to be executed, even though the stock is trading at a price that would satisfy the customer's limit order, because other limit orders have been entered prior to the customer's order.
stock certificate	Evidence of equity ownership.
stock or bond power	A form that, when signed by the owner and attached to a security, makes the security negotiable.
stock split	A change in the number of outstanding shares, the par value, and the number of authorized shares that has been approved through a vote of the shareholders. Forward-stock splits increase the number of shares outstanding and reduce the stock price in order to make the security more attractive to individual investors.
stop limit order	An order that becomes a limit order to buy or sell the stock when the stock trades at or through the stop price.
stop order	An order that becomes a market order to buy or sell the stock when the stock trades at or through the stop price.
stopping stock	A courtesy offered by a specialist to public customers, whereby the specialist guarantees a price but tries to obtain a better price for the customer.
straddle	The simultaneous purchase or sale of a call and a put on the same security with the same strike price and expiration.
straight line depreciation	An accounting method that allows an owner to take equal tax deductions over the useful life of the asset.
strangle	The purchase or sale of a call and a put on either side of the current market price. The options have the same expiration months but different strike prices.
stripped bond	A bond that has had its coupons removed by a broker dealer and that is selling at a deep discount to its principal payment in the future.
stripper well	An oil well that is in operation just to recover a very limited amount of reserves.
subchapter S corporation	A business organization that allows the tax consequences of the organization to flow through to the owners.
subscription agreement	An application signed by the purchaser of an interest in a direct participation plan. An investor in a limited partnership does not become an investor until the general partner signs the subscription agreement.
subscription right	*See* right.
suitability	A determination that the characteristics of a security are in line with an investor's objectives, financial profile, and attitudes.
Super Display Book System (SDBK)	The electronic order-routing system used by the NYSE to route orders directly to the trading post.
supervise	The actions of a principal that ensure that the actions of a firm and its representatives are in compliance with industry regulations.
support	The price to which a security will fall and attract new buyers. As the new buyers enter the market, it keeps the price from falling any lower.
surplus fund	An account set up for funds generated by a project financed by a municipal revenue bond to pay a variety of expenses.
syndicate	A group of underwriters responsible for underwriting a new issue.

systematic risk	A risk inherent in any investment in the market. An investor may lose money simply because the market is going down.

T

takedown	The price at which a syndicate purchases a new issue of securities from the issuer.
tax and revenue anticipation note	A short-term note sold by a municipal issuer as interim financing in anticipation of tax and other revenue.
tax anticipation note (TAN)	A short-term note sold by a municipal issuer as interim financing in anticipation of tax revenue.
tax-deferred annuity	A nonqualified retirement account that allows an investor's money to grow tax deferred. A tax-deferred annuity is a contract between an insurance company and an investor.
tax equivalent yield	The interest rate that must be offered by a taxable bond of similar quality in order to be equal to the rate that is offered by a municipal bond.
tax-exempt bond fund	A bond fund that seeks to produce investment income that is free from federal tax by investing in a portfolio of municipal bonds.
tax liability	The amount of money that is owed by an investor after realizing a gain on the sale of an investment or after receiving investment income.
tax preference item	An item that receives preferential tax treatment and must be added back into income when calculating an investor's alternative minimum tax.
tax-sheltered annuity (TSA)	A qualified retirement plan offered to employees of governments, school systems, or nonprofit organizations. Contributions to TSAs are made with pre-tax dollars.
technical analysis	A method of security analysis that uses past price performance to predict the future performance of a security.
Telephone Consumer Protection Act of 1991	Legislation that regulates how potential customers are contacted by phone at home.
tenants in common	*See* joint tenants in common.
tender offer	An offer to buy all or part of a company's outstanding securities for cash or cash and securities.
term bond	A bond issue that has its entire principal due on one date.
term maturity	A type of bond maturity that has all principal due on one date.
testimonial	The use of a recognized expert or leader to endorse the services of a firm.
third market	A transaction in an exchange-listed security executed over the Nasdaq workstation.
third-party account	An account that is managed for the benefit of a customer by another party, such as an investment adviser, a trustee, or an attorney.
30-day visible supply	The total par value of all new issue municipal bonds coming to market in the next 30 days.

time deposit	An account that is established by a bank customer where the customer agrees to leave the funds on deposit for an agreed upon amount of time.
time value	The value of an option that exceeds its intrinsic value or its in-the-money amount.
tombstone ad	An announcement published in financial papers advertising the offering of securities by a group of underwriters. Only basic information may be contained in the tombstone ad, and all offers must be made through the prospectus only.
top heavy rule	The rule that states the maximum salary for which a Keogh contribution may be based. This is in effect to limit the disparity between high- and low-salary employees.
trade confirmation	The printed notification of a securities transaction. A confirmation must be sent to a customer on or before the completion of a transaction. The completion of a transaction is considered to be the settlement date.
trade date	The day when an investor's order is executed.
tranche	A class of collateralized mortgage obligation (CMO) that has a predicted maturity and interest rate.
transfer agent	An independent entity that handles name changes, records the names of security holders of record, and ensures that all certificates are properly endorsed.
transfer and hold in safekeeping	A request by customers for the brokerage firm to transfer their securities into the firm's name and to hold them in safekeeping at the firm. A brokerage may charge a fee for holding a customer's securities that have been registered in its name.
transfer and ship	A request by customers for the brokerage firm to transfer their securities into their name and to ship them to their address of record.
Treasury bill	A U.S. government security that is issued at a discount and matures at par in 4, 13, 26, and 52 weeks.
Treasury bond	A long-term U.S. government security that pays semiannual interest and matures in 10 to 30 years.
Treasury note	An intermediate-term U.S. government security that pays semiannual interest and matures in 1 to 10 years.
Treasury receipt	A zero-coupon bond created by a brokerage firm that is backed by U.S. government securities. It is issued at a discount and matures at par.
treasury stock	Stock that has been issued by a corporation and that has subsequently been repurchased by the corporation. Treasury stock does not vote or receive dividends. It is not used in the calculation of earnings per share.
trendline	A line used to predict the future price movement for a security. Drawing a line under the successive lows or successive highs creates a trendline.
trough	The bottoming out of the business cycle just prior to an new upward movement in activity.
true interest cost (TIC)	A calculation for the cost of a municipal issuer's interest expense that includes the time value of money.
Trust Indenture Act of 1940	Regulates the issuance of corporate debt in excess of $10 million and with a term exceeding 1 year. It requires an indenture between the issuer and the trustee.
trustee	A person who legally acts for the benefit of another party.
12B-1 fee	An asset-based distribution fee that is assessed annually and paid out quarterly to cover advertising and distribution costs. All 12B-1 fees must be reasonable.

two-dollar broker	An independent exchange member who executes orders for commission house brokers and other customers for a fee.
type	A classification method for an option as either a call or a put.

U

uncovered	*See* naked.
underlying security	A security for which an investor has an option to buy or sell.
underwriting	The process of marketing a new issue of securities to the investing public. A broker dealer forwards the proceeds of the sale to the issuer minus its fee for selling the securities.
unearned income	Any income received by an individual from an investment, such as dividends and interest income.
uniform delivery ticket	A document that must be attached to every security delivered by the seller, making the security "good delivery."
Uniform Gifts to Minors Act (UGMA)	Sets forth guidelines for the gifting of cash and securities to minors and for the operation of accounts managed for the benefit of minors. Once a gift is given to a minor, it is irrevocable.
Uniform Practice Code	The FINRA bylaw that sets guidelines for how industry members transact business with other members. The Uniform Practice Code establishes such things as settlement dates, rules of good delivery, and ex-dividend dates.
Uniform Securities Act (USA)	The framework for state-based securities legislation. The act is a model that can be adapted to each state's particular needs.
Uniform Transfer to Minors Act (UTMA)	Legislation that has been adopted in certain states, in lieu of the Uniform Gifts to Minors Act. UTMA allows the custodian to determine the age at which the assets become the property of the minor. The maximum age for transfer of ownership is 25.
unit investment trust (UIT)	A type of investment company organized as a trust to invest in a portfolio of securities. The UIT sells redeemable securities to investors in the form of shares or units of beneficial interest.
unit of beneficial interest	The redeemable share issued to investors in a unit investment trust.
unit refund annuity	An annuity payout option that will make payments to the annuitant for life. If the annuitant dies prior to receiving an amount that is equal to his or her account value, the balance of the account will be paid to the annuitant's beneficiaries.
unqualified legal opinion	A legal opinion issued by a bond attorney for the issue where there are no reservations relating to the issue.
unrealized	A paper profit or loss on a security that is still owned.

V

variable annuity	A contract issued by an insurance company that is both a security and an insurance product. The annuitant's contributions are invested through the separate account into a portfolio of securities. The annuitant's payments depend largely on the investment results of the separate account.
variable death benefit	The amount of a death benefit paid to a beneficiary that is based on the investment results of the insurance company's separate account. This amount is over the contract's minimum guaranteed death benefit.
variable life insurance	A life insurance policy that provides for a minimum guaranteed death benefit, as well as an additional death benefit, based on the investment results of the separate account.
variable rate municipal security	Interim municipal financing issued with a variable rate.
vertical spread	The simultaneous purchase and sale of two calls or two puts on the same underlying security that differ only in strike price.
vesting	The process by which an employer's contributions to an employee's retirement account become the property of the employee.
visible supply	*See* 30-day visible supply.
voluntary accumulation plan	A method, such as dollar-cost averaging, by which an investor regularly makes contributions to acquire mutual fund shares.
voting right	The right of a corporation's stockholders to cast their votes for the election of the corporation's board of directors as well as for certain major corporate issues.

W

warrant	A long-term security that gives the holder the right to purchase the common shares of a corporation for up to 10 years. The warrant's subscription price is always higher than the price of the underlying common shares when the warrant is initially issued.
wash sale	The sale of a security at a loss and the subsequent repurchase of that security or of a security that is substantially the same within 30 days of the sale. The repurchase disallows the claim of the loss for tax purposes.
western account	A type of municipal security syndicate account where only the member with unsold bonds is responsible for the unsold bonds.
when-issued security	A security that has been sold prior to the certificates being available for delivery.
wildcatting	An exploratory oil- and gas-drilling program.
wire room	*See* order department.
withdrawal plan	The systematic removal of funds from a mutual fund account over time. Withdrawal plans vary in type and availability among fund companies.
workable indication	An indication of the prices and yields that a municipal securities dealer may be willing to buy or sell bonds.

working capital	A measure of a corporation's liquidity that is found by subtracting current liabilities from current assets.
working interest	An interest that requires the holder to bear the proportional expenses and allows the holder to share in the revenue produced by an oil or gas project in relation to the interest.
workout quote	A nonfirm quote that requires handling and settlement conditions to be worked out between the parties prior to the trade.
writer	An investor who sells an option to receive the premium income.
writing the scale	The procedure of assigning prospective yields to a new issuer of serial municipal bonds.

Y

yield	The annual amount of income generated by a security relative to its price; expressed as a percentage.
yield-based option	An interest rate option that allows the holder to receive the in-the-money amount in cash upon exercise or expiration.
yield curve	The rate at which interest rates vary among investments of similar quality with different maturities. Longer-term securities generally offer higher yields.
yield to call	An investor's overall return for owning a bond should it be called in prior to maturity by the issuer.
yield to maturity	An investor's overall return for owning a bond if the bond is held until maturity.

Z

zero-coupon bond	A bond that is issued at a discount from its par value and makes no regular interest payments. An investor's interest is reflected by the security's appreciation toward par at maturity. The appreciation is taxable each year even though it is not actually received by the investor (phantom income).
zero-minus tick	A trade in an exchange-listed security that occurs at the same price as the previous transaction, but at a price that is lower than the last transaction that was different.
zero-plus tick	A trade in an exchange-listed security that occurs at the same price as the previous transaction, but at a price that is higher than the last transaction that was different.

Made in the USA
Columbia, SC
06 February 2025